The author

Vittorio Vandelli is a teacher of English Language and Literature, a translator, an essayist and a writer of fiction.
He was born and raised in the country in which he still lives, Italy, the cradle of the best and the worst.
He went to grammar school in the early seventies, a time of high ideals of change that taught him to see behind closed doors and to love folk and rock protest music, becoming a musician himself. His latest performance is a live tribute to American folk protest music, titled *The Sound of the Greenwich Village*.
He has written articles and essays on education and a series of satirical novels and short-stories on the Italian school system: *Il professor Bingo* (2000), *Il professor Bingo e il nuovo che avanza* (2001), *Questa scuola non è un'azienda* (2006), *Il professor Bingo e le Idi di Marzo* (2008), *Le Pillole del prof. Bingo* 2000-2010. He has also published noir novels: *Scrivere o Uccidere* (1989), *Runaway - fuga a Venezia* (2003), *Dark City* (2013). The author's personal site is
http://www.vittorio-vandelli.com

Vittorio Vandelli

Silvio Berlusconi's Italy

a portrait of the country and its godfather

from today's erosion of democracy
to a near-future new kind of
non-violent totalitarianism

First published in 2014 by Narcissus with the title
1994-2014 – Berlusconi's new ventennio

This revised edition published in 2016

Copyright © Vittorio Vandelli 2014

ISBN: 1533295344
ISBN-13: 978-1533295347

Vittorio Vandelli is hereby identified as author of this work

All rights reserved. This book is sold subject to the condition that it shall not, by way of trade or otherwise, be lent, re-sold, hired out or otherwise circulated without the publisher's prior consent in any form of binding or cover other than that in which it is published and without a similar condition including this condition being imposed on the subsequent purchaser.

Proof-reader: Jacqueline Gallagher

Cover sketch: Antonino Roccaverde
(antonino.roccaverde@gmail.com)

Back cover picture: Gabriella Ascari
(gabriella.ascari@gmail.com)

Published by: SelfPublishingVincente.it

CONTENTS

Author's biography

Foreword to the 2016 edition
   From il Cavaliere to Demolition Man:
   is Matteo Renzi Berlusconi's royal baby? 7

Introduction 19

PART ONE - The present
   Chapter one
   Tax fraudster and slush funds creator:
   The *pregiudicato*[1] who leads Italian politics 33

   Chapter two
   Bunga-bunga, MPs calciomercato and much more:
   the trials of the Knight 57

PART TWO - Looking back in anger
   Chapter one
   A gangster and mafia story: *The Scent of Money* and *Clean Hands*
   (from the seventies to the fall of the First Republic in the early
   nineties) 81

   Chapter two
   Deal with the devil? the *trattativa Stato-mafia* and Berlusconi's
   discesa in campo (1992-94) 109

   Chapter three
   Erosion of democracy: Big Brother is brainwashing you,
   conflicts of interests. Berlusconi's philosophy 127

---

[1] *Pregiudicato* means *previous offender, convict,* a person definitively sentenced by a criminal court. *Calciomercato* means *football players' transfer market*. *Trattativa Stato - mafia* means *State – mafia negotiations*. *Discesa in campo* means *entering the football pitch*. *Teatrino della politica* means *cheap theatre show of politics*, the everyday vaudeville-like show of Italian politics.

PART THREE - From the present to the future
  Chapter one
    Every line tells a story: dystopian novelists saw it coming 137

  Chapter two
    Never ending story: the would-be conviction of the alleged natural born corrupter, the frantic Italian *teatrino della politica*, Prime Minister Renzi as vicarious Berlusconi: a natural born corrupt society.. 151

  Chapter three
    Corruption, violence, beauty in Italian football: a mirror of society 183

  Chapter four
    Conclusion: what can be done? 203

Italy – country profile.. 209

Foreword to the 2016 edition

From il Cavaliere to Demolition Man:

is Matteo Renzi Berlusconi's royal baby?

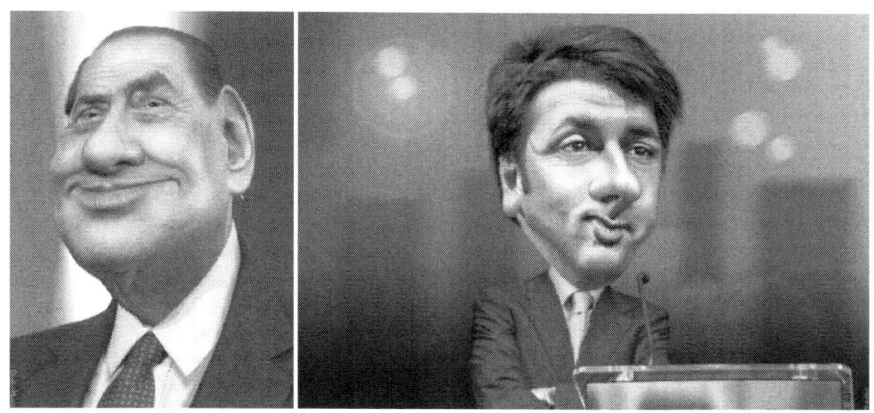

Photos from DonkeyHotey, www.flickr.com, Creative Commons licence

I clearly remember that long bright summer's day, August 1, 2013, the day that is now easy to see as the beginning of the end of the Berlusconi Age, that long dark *ventennio* – twenty years – full of sound and fury, of collective foolishness and of erosion of democratic institutions. Notwithstanding *his beloved folly is now bordering on clinical insanity* and *a delusional side to his character which seems to preclude rational behaviour and which appears to distance him even further from reality* (as Tobias Jones wrote in the revised postscript to his 2007 edition of *The Dark Heart of Italy*), in 2013 Berlusconi was still the master and the godfather of the country, even after he was forced to resign from his last disastrous mandate as Prime Minister in autumn 2011. In those days, Matteo Renzi's bright star was not shining yet in the Roman firmament. Il Cavaliere's fall had been prophesied time and again but it was not visible until that day, a day in which an Italian institution, the Magistracy, did something quite normal for a democracy but very special for Italy: it sentenced *il Cavaliere* to four years in jail for massive tax fraud despite the (in)famous *laws ad personam* Berlusconi had produced since he had become Prime

Minister in 1994. For just one single day, the statute of limitations could not make the trial disappear, like it had done so many times before. Berlusconi did not actually go to jail or serve a credible alternative punishment (let's not ask for too much), but that tiny crack through which the light of justice shone was the spark that lit the fire of decadence that had been burning under the ashes for so long. A few months later, in November, Berlusconi was expelled by the Senate, and I'd say that that was his final exit and the curtains soon fell on il Cavaliere's *ventennio*.

Those were the months in which I wrote the first draft of this book, straight from the beginning to the end, without stopping and looking back. That crack of light had pushed me through an old project that had been in the back of my mind for so long, a story that had to be told, the exposure of a danger which could not be hidden any longer. And, even if in those days the imminent end of the political *Berlusconismo* was not in sight, I unconsciously knew that that would be a definitive account of that shameful period.

Writing this book has meant for me a way to clear my conscience, to fulfil a moral duty to give voice to the astonishing events I was witnessing, while the majority of the people accepted them as normal facts. Once the book was finished, I felt a sense of relief, as if to say: it is all written here, and there is no way to let it all slip into oblivion. Besides, to understand Berlusconi means to understand the dark heart of Italy and, in part, the New Age of Matteo Renzi we have just entered. The book was first published one year later with the title *1994-2014 Berlusconi's new Ventennio* and, as a counterpart to Berlusconi's story, it took an unexpected upturn when it was shortlisted for the final of the *The Write Stuff* competition at the London Book Fair in 2015.

Since that dull 2013 November day, *il Cavaliere*'s visibility and his political influence have dissolved unexpectedly quickly, like in a classical gangster movie after the main climax. While he was running down the stream of forgetfulness, he desperately tried to hold on to some floating trunk to which he could not cling for too long. But, for the more malicious, there is an alternative ending. For the malevolent thinkers, now the image of Berlusconi as an old retired gentleman in political and judiciary ruin, spending his days with his official fiancé Francesca, 50 years younger than him who fell in love with him because of his charm and not because of his wallet – as she declared – and their miniature poodle Dudù, that image is just a façade. The truth lies someplace else and tells a very different story.

The feeling that after his fall Italy was a family without its patriarch, an association without its godfather, that spread out in the weeks that followed his expulsion from the Senate, did not last long. Berlusconi's fall and his disappearance from the political scene, in fact, was symmetrical to the sudden rise of the next *uomo forte*, the strong man and absolute leader the Italians have loved so much since the Mussolini *ventennio*. A month later, Matteo Renzi, former mayor of Florence, all of a sudden took the leadership of the sleepy centre-left *Partito Democratico*, became the youngest Prime Minister ever in February 2014 and then led his party to a stunning victory at the European elections in May 2014. The Italians fell immediately in love with his pervasive energy and his promises for a real change got to the people's belly, an energy similar not only to that of Obama in 2008, but also to Berlusconi's in 1994. Renzi is another strange product of post-modern politics, a factory that produces contradictory and ambiguous goods: after two years in office, in the media and on TV, it is now clear that Renzi is a Tory in left-wing shoes, a self-appointed *demolition man* accused of maintaining the status quo, a revolutionary politician who seems to come out from the highly corrupt mafia-linked old-fashioned centrist *Democrazia Cristiana* of the so-called Prima Repubblica (the First Republic, the post WWII period that ended in the early nineties because of a nationwide corruption scandal).

The first clue that Berlusconi's exit and Renzi's entrance was not a coincidence and that il Cavaliere's departure could not be what it seemed was suggested by the so-called Patto del Nazareno. In January 2014, on his way to be appointed Prime Minister by President Napolitano – not by the people -, Renzi made a deal with the convicted Berlusconi, negotiated at Democratic Party headquarters on the Largo del Nazareno – hence the name Nazarene Pact. Renzi asked Berlusconi's support for two key reforms that would form the backbone of his future cabinet: a new electoral law and the amendment of the Constitution. In return, il Cavaliere expected a say in the selection of the country's next President so that he could have his sentence pardoned and could regain his longed for *agibilità politica* – the political practicability he had lost after being banned from public office because of the tax fraud sentence. That would have meant a comeback to the political arena and a swift stop to his downfall. The Nazarene Pact was never published or even, presumably, written down, and no one knows what kind of agreement lay under the public part (in themselves, two very dangerous topical items since they will alter our balance of powers). Il Cavaliere, who had left the Senate from the back door, re-entered the political scene through the front door of the *Partito Democratico* and sat under the giant portrait of Che Guevara to try to decide once again the destiny of Italy.

Since that day, for those of malicious bent, Renzi started to be seen as Berlusconi's royal baby: for them Berlusconi, to a certain extent, was a kind of shadow Prime Minister behind his 'blue-eyed son' Renzi since the Nazarene Pact carried on the basic ideas of constitutional changes Berlusconi had proposed in his *ventennio*. The idea of the royal baby was confirmed by journalist Giuliano Ferrara, the founder of the conservative daily *Il Foglio* and one of Berlusconi's notorious devotees. He said "There's something very psychological between Renzi and Berlusconi. Berlusconi has no political heirs, so Renzi is the royal baby…" (the quotation is from the June 29, 2015 *New Yorker* article *The Demolition Man*).

Of public domain is the fact that the Nazarene Pact, after a while, was a thing of the past. When Renzi became Prime Minister, many of *Forza Italia*'s parliamentary deputies had already defected and formed their own party, the *New Centre Right* - they vote in a coalition with Renzi's party now -, and one of them, Angelino Alfano, is his interior minister: *saltare sul carro del vincitore* – jumping on the winner's cart - is another very practiced sport in my country. Even 'pluri-inquisito' – person under multiple investigations - senator Denis Verdini, one of il Cavaliere's favourites and the man behind the Pact, has now left Berlusconi with some faithful senators and is helping Renzi to have a stable majority (Verdini was sentenced to two years in jail on corruption charges in the first trial in March 2016). So after a while the Nazarene Pact was a thing of the past, but so, it appeared, was Berlusconi. But what we saw may just have been the tip of the iceberg and, possibly, the deal had secret parts, it was a real gentlemen's agreement to govern the country in continuity, the royal baby vicariously acting. This is the theory of Renzi's enemies who think that, despite his speeches – Renzi has learnt Berlusconi's media management really well –, up to now no real privilege has been attacked and the continuity of Italian bad politics is a fact. They think that Renzi has continued Berlusconi's conservative politics disguising it as progressive and that this fact is allowing the Renzi government to pass most of Berlusconi's reactionary reforms il Cavaliere was never able to establish. According to them, Renzi is for sure more presentable as a person and as a leader than the truculent bunga-bunga addicted Cavaliere, but his clean-cut-kid face is politically dangerous and a further proof that ours is the age of 'unique thought'. Or, to remain local, the age of the *inciucio*, a mean secret deal between apparent adversaries for their own mutual benefit, different from an *en plein air* political agreement or coalition.

"I'm the scrapper," he told me. "I'm cleaning up the swamp." He meant the waste, the deadly bureaucracy, the notoriously padded ranks of Italy's public administration, the unemployment now at forty per cent among the country's youth, the outrageously slow pace of the justice system, the culture of cronyism, political perks and payoffs, tax evasion, casual everyday criminality, and open cheating—not to mention the various mafias, from the Cosa Nostra to the Camorra and the 'Ndrangheta, that still hold much of the economy of the South (and not a little of the North) in thrall, The Demolition Man article reports.

For those who think differently, Demolition Man is the guardian angel of the swamp. Berlusconi, after a brilliant career as a liar, has recently told the truth about the new Prime Minister. At *Porta a Porta*, the TG1 political talk-show considered the third House of Parliament and hosted by one of Berlusconi's long term devotees, journalist Bruno Vespa, he declared: "Renzi non è un uomo di sinistra, tant'è vero che gli uomini della sinistra portano verso di lui un sentimento negativo perché pensano che con un gesto di destrezza gli ha sottratto il partito e ora alla guida c'è un vecchio Dc seppur giovane di età – Renzi is not a man of the left, in fact the left-oriented people have negative feelings towards him because they think that he has taken away the party from them with a gesture of dexterity and now its leadership belongs to an old Christian Democrat, even if of young age ".

Looking back at the first two years of the Renzi Age, it is a fact that the reforms he has already approved, the ones that are in progress and the many he has only announced come from a conservative perspective and seem to have fulfilled most of the desires of *Confindustria*, the industrialists' association. Renzi has promised the country too much, too fast and too soon for any politician to deliver. His '100 days' revolution has already shifted to '1,000 days' since realpolitik has stepped in, leaving inexperienced Renzi and his mediocre ministers trapped into the sinister reality of Italy. Time will tell, of course: 1,000 days, three years, means the end of his mandate, and this a more reasonable time to make reforms for good.

Giuseppe Civati, one of the Democrats' left leaders, before leaving the party described the new electoral law called *Italicum* – and nicknamed *Silvium* – as "genetically modified Presidentialism", especially if combined with the amendments to the Constitution which have almost reached their final approval. The *Italicum*, approved in May 2015, is a "majority-assuring system" that boosts the seats of the winner in parliament and consequently shrinks the opposition, forming an artificially created House. As I write in this book *the Prime Minister and the government might have a favourable new non-elected Senate (which will have parliamentary immunity as well), they might indirectly influence the election of the President of the Republic, of the Constitutional Court and of the 'Consiglio Superiore della Magistratura' … It sounds like a sort of dictatorship of the majority, another forthcoming event in the erosion of democracy show.* And the *dictatorship of the majority* was exactly what Berlusconi wanted and the Founding Fathers did not, after the Mussolini *ventennio*. Many 'cries of freedom' have been launched by the best intellectuals and constitutionalists of the country. They all agreed that an update of the Charter had to be done and bicameralism had to be overpassed but the new amendments bring, according to famed professor Stefano Rodotà, *the risk of leaving representative democracy and of altering the constitutional balance*. Professor Rodotà was one of the candidates in the presidential election of 2013, an internationally recognized constitutionalist and intellectual who has held important offices at home and abroad, with a long political experience as MP in the Italian and European Parliaments and very appreciated by the civil society. Consequently, just too good to became President.

Renzi's *Jobs Act*, approved in 2014-15, follows Fiat Chrysler Automobile's CEO Sergio Marchionne's logic in job contracts: it weakens the role of the unions, puts an end to nationwide contracts but gives bonuses to the workers who behave properly, allows the master to fire his employees without good reason, so that every worker is limited in his freedom. It is all very Thatcheresque, I daresay, or maybe even XIX centurish: it brings back a first Industrial Revolution kind of master-worker relationship, an act of contemporary servitude that Berlusconi has always tried to approve in vain.

La Buona Scuola is the name given to the reform of Education approved in 2015. Here again there is a clear line of continuity between this reform and Berlusconi's reform of the school system called Riforma Gelmini. Once again, it is a homage to the ideology of the scuola/azienda – the school/enterprise. This vision of the school system actually shows an idea of society at large that reminds one of pyramidal control and of an educational system subjugated to the world of business. It instantaneously raised the hostility of all the school unions, of almost all of the teachers and of that small portion of decent politics that survives in Italy.

Among his continuous announcements, Renzi promised he would approve a law to solve the most important of the many conflicts of interests that has biased the whole political and social life of the Berlusconi period, the one regarding the ownership of the media. Incredibly, up to now Renzi has 'forgotten' to pass such an urgent law, exactly like all previous centre-left governments in charge during the Berlusconi Age accidentally did. Given the anomaly in the Western world of a politician, and former PM, who owns half of the media and controlled almost all of them when in power, this should have been a priority. Honestly, it is quite difficult to believe it is just another inadvertency. Renzi's cabinet, instead, in late 2015 produced a reform of public television, the RAI, that is the opposite of his declared intentions: "The political parties out of the RAI [Radio Televisione Italiana, the public service]", the PM said in March 2015 but his new reform moves in the opposite direction, consolidating the status quo. In Enrico Mentana's words "Con questa riforma torniamo a prima del 1975, a una RAI che dipende dall'esecutivo … soprattutto, l'amministratore delegato con pieni poteri è Palazzo Chigi. Non si può dire 'fuori i partiti da viale Mazzini' e poi approvare una legge del genere – With this reform we will go back to the years before 1975, to a RAI that depends on the executive power … above all, the chief executive is Palazzo Chigi [home of the government]. One cannot say 'the political parties must leave viale Mazzini [RAI headquarters]' and then approve this kind of law".

Mentana is the director of the *LA7* news department, the only nationwide private TV network not owned by Berlusconi.

As far as a real fight against the various mafias, tax evasion and corruption is concerned, the real spending reviews worth doing in the most fraudulent of the European countries, Renzi has shown his Christian Democratic attitude. On the one hand, one of his first appointments was Raffaele Cantone, a magistrate from Naples who had heroically chased the camorra for twenty years. Renzi created an anti-corruption authority for Cantone called *Autorità Nazionale Anticorruzione (ANAC)*. On the other hand, at local elections he has appointed candidates with criminal records or under investigation, the all Italian way to win the elections and maintain territorial control. The iconic case is that of the new Governor of Campania De Luca, who was suspended from his position soon after the elections because of his criminal record and his alleged links with the local camorra (I am writing 'camorra' and 'mafia' without capital letters intentionally). Roberto Saviano's words set the scene:

> **I'll ask you without beating about the bush: is there Gomorrah in the lists of the Democratic Party and in the coalition that supports De Luca?**
>
> *I answer bluntly: yes, absolutely. In the Democratic Party and in the lists there is the whole Gomorrah system, regardless of whether or not there is the bosses' will. In Southern Italy the Democratic Party has not had any intention to terminate an established tradition. That is, we approach politics to get rights such as: work, a place in the hospital ... The law does not exist. The rights are obtained by mediating: I'll give you my vote, in exchange I'll receive a right. The politician does not give visions, perspectives, paths, but he gives opportunities in exchange for consent. And De Luca, in this, is one that knows his way. Politics should be something else. (...) This Democratic Party does not have a soul that considers anti-mafia as a priority. Obviously I do not feel like saying that we are talking about collusions as happened in Forza Italia, but at this point to consider themselves, in fact, an anti-mafia party ... there is a big gap. Even the story of De Luca proves it.*[2]

---

[2] *Te lo chiedo senza tanti giri di parole: nelle liste del Pd e della coalizione che sostiene De Luca c'è Gomorra?*

(*Huffington Post Italia*, interview published on May 7, 2015)

The *Mafia Capitale* scandal, which exploded in late 2014, is symptomatic and symbolic of the relationship between politics and the crime syndicates that run the cities, the regions and, in the end, the country. As a shocking Christmas gift to the Italian people, in December 2014 the magistrates found out that the Eternal City was controlled and actually run by an up-to-then unknown cupola that was named *Mafia Capitale*. The mafia system of the capital city was a step up from the original *Tangentopoli*, the 'mother of all corruption investigations' which exploded in 1992 and wiped away the politicians who had run the Prima Repubblica so far – beside paving the way for il Cavaliere's discesa in campo, i.e. Berlusconi's entrance in the political arena: *Mafia Capitale* showed that the cupola was in total control and that the corrupt politicians, who had run the show in the original *Tangentopoli*, were just puppets in the criminals' hands. *Mafia Capitale* also reinforced the idea, suggested by the other recent top scandals, that there is no more moral and practical differences between left and right: the two main bosses were a former fascist activist and a 'red' cooperative chief who kept making business both with the right wing and the left wing regional and communal councillors who alternated in power.

Another non-priority of the Renzi government is the contrast to tax evasion, a number one item for a Demolition Man who wants to bring back legality. I wish I could see the same emphasis the Prime Minister put in the Constitutional changes and in the Job Acts in the fight against tax evasion—a national sport that Berlusconi decriminalized in 2002 abolishing the law against false accounting. Renzi recriminalized it in 2015, but the overall effect is that, here

---

Ti rispondo senza giri di parole: assolutamente sì. Nel Pd e nelle liste c'è tutto il sistema di Gomorra, indipendentemente se ci sono o meno le volontà dei boss. Il Pd nel Sud Italia non ha avuto alcuna intenzione di interrompere una tradizione consolidata. E cioè alla politica ci si rivolge per ottenere diritti: il lavoro, un posto in ospedale... Il diritto non esiste. Il diritto si ottiene mediando: io ti do il voto, in cambio ricevo un diritto. Il politico non dà visioni, prospettive, percorsi, ma dà opportunità in cambio di consenso. E De Luca, in questo, è uno che ci sa fare. La politica dovrebbe essere tutt'altro ... Questo Pd non ha un'anima che sente come una priorità l'antimafia. Ovviamente non mi sentirei di dire che stiamo parlando di collusioni come succedeva in Forza Italia, però da qui a considerarsi, appunto, un partito antimafia... ce ne passa. Anche la vicenda De Luca, lo dimostra.

again, a very similar line has been followed so far. Why has Renzi recently set the cash limit to 3,000 euros for payments, instead of the previous 1,000, if not to give a helping hand to tax evasion and black payments? Tax evaders vote, and their party is indeed huge. We all know we would be at least as rich as Germany if the amount of illegal money became legal. But that is just daydreaming in a country of immaculate homes and dirty streets.

Berlusconi è un ex presidente del consiglio, un ex senatore, un ex cavaliere, formalmente un pregiudicato condannato per frode fiscale, in attesa di altri processi, capo di un partito in dissesto, voglioso di correre verso la soglia di sbarramento, di un impero economico che accumula debiti. E non parliamo della moglie: cattiva, ha voluto tutto. E non parliamo dei magistrati. - Berlusconi is a former Prime Minister, a former senator, a former Cavaliere, formally a convict sentenced for tax fraud, waiting for other trials, leader of a party in distress ... of an economic empire accumulating debts. *Not to mention his wife: bad, she wanted everything. Not to mention the judiciary* writes journalist Enrico Deaglio in an article titled *Berlusconi ultimo atto* in the weekly *il Venerdì* on May 22, 2015. Deaglio's portrait of il Cavaliere today is the official ending, but many think that the alternative conclusion is the real one. Comfortably sitting in one of his luxury mansions, Berlusconi is monitoring the appointed Prime Minister doing the things he was not able to do, feeling secure that his shameful laws *ad personam* are going to stay where they are for a long time and the *longa manus* of the judiciary will not be able to grab him once again.

Whatever one may think of the Berlusconi – Renzi bloodline, politically speaking the *Berlusconismo* may be over, but the philosophy that inspired it remains. Berlusconi has boosted the worst instincts and behaviours of the immoral majority, instincts and procedures that were there before il Cavaliere and are going to remain as part of our national psyche in the future. A change in collective mentality, the development of civic consciousness and care for the *res publica* are preconditions to make a real revolution in society and in politics possible. Without it, no government can transform Italy for good and what we will have in the future will be another pantomime of change. And, again, Aldous Huxley's foretelling words will echo in our minds: *by means of ever more effective methods of mind-manipulation, the democracies will change their nature ... The constitutions will not be abrogated and the good laws will remain on the statute book; but these liberal forms will merely serve to mask and adorn a profoundly illiberal substance… a new kind of non-violent totalitarianism.*

February 2016

The original 2014 text of this book has been updated up to today. The new information is in this kind of brackets: [ ].

Introduction

Dear English-speaking reader,

Have you ever heard of a Prime Minister who says that the judiciary, one of the three pillars of the same democracy the PM personifies, is a 'cancer of democracy' and that some judges – except the ones he was not able to, allegedly, bribe – are like the Red Brigades terrorists of the Seventies?

Have you ever met a PM who hired a mafioso killer in one of his private luxury mansions for years as stableman in a house with no horses or a political party whose ideologist is a former senator sentenced to seven years in prison for mafia connections?

Have you ever come across a Prime Minister of a contemporary Western democracy who, while in office in Paris, received an evening phone call from an underworld Brazilian prostitute 'operating' in Milan who had his private mobile number?

Have you ever heard of a PM who successfully forced Parliament to vote what all MPs and the whole country knew was a lie, that is the fact that an underage Moroccan girl, 'Ruby Rubacuori' – 'Heartstealer' –, one of his *bunga-bunga* lovers, was Egyptian ex-president Mubarak's nephew?

Would you believe that 'damsel-in distress' Ruby, according to Berlusconi, was a poor girl in need that he helped for charity, inviting her to his Arcore mansion in Milan, *bunga-bunga* official headquarters, since il Cavaliere is good at heart and a fervent Christian?

Have you ever seen a PM that, probably trying to turn the truth upside down, had the possibility to broadcast on his own media empire a documentary TV film that manipulates the story behind a trial in which he is the defendant the night before the final court verdict?

Have you ever heard of a senator and previous Prime Minister who kept his seat for four months after being definitively sentenced to prison and banned from public offices in a country in which a law, that he himself voted, says that a condemned MP must lose his position immediately?

Have you ever heard of a former PM condemned to four years in jail whose real penalty was spending a few hours once a week for a few months in an asylum for elderly people to help patients socialize?

Have you ever seen a convicted politician, sentenced for massive tax fraud, forced to lose his senatorial seat, banned from public offices, defendant in a trial for corrupting an opposition senator, who officially encounters the President of the Republic as party leader in the Constitutional meetings to form a new government?

Have you ever heard that the same convicted politician, who had lost the right to vote, was allowed to appear regularly on his TV channels, and on public networks as well, to campaign for the 2014 European elections in which he had been banned as candidate?

Would you believe that in early 2014 the just elected 'revolutionary' 'left wing' Prime Minister Matteo Renzi, absolute winner of the 2014 European elections, made a deal with convict Berlusconi, absolute loser of the same elections, in order to change the Constitution and consequently the democratic balance?

If you haven't and if you wouldn't, I hope this paper will help you understand why all this has been possible, so that I won't hear the 'overwhelming question' you have kept asking me for all these years once again.

I actually heard it for the first time in L.A., California, in the summer of 1994, after Berlusconi's first electoral victory. "How is it possible that a media tycoon, one of the richest men in the world, with an obscure past, a lot of trials going on and alleged mafia connections has become Prime Minister?" So plain to see from the other side of the world, where tax fraudsters, for example, just go to jail. Also on the other side of the Channel it has always been evident: *The Economist* wrote on April 26, 2001: *In any self-respecting democracy it would be unthinkable that the man assumed to be on the verge of being elected Prime Minister would recently have come under investigation for, among other things, money-laundering, complicity in murder, connections with the mafia, tax evasion and the bribing of politicians, judges and the tax police. But the country is Italy and the man is Silvio Berlusconi, almost certainly its richest citizen. As our own investigations make plain, Mr. Berlusconi is not fit to lead the government of any country, least of all one of the world's richest democracies.*

In 1994 Italian people were seduced by a short video in which Berlusconi announced his *discesa in campo* – entering the football pitch of politics – and promised everything to everybody. We said, back then, that the Italians who had been lured and deceived were the less cultured ones, running on empty politically because of the void caused by the *Mani Pulite* investigation – *Clean Hands* –, which showed us that all of our country, from politics to business, was based on corruption (implausibly, even former PM Mario Monti, president of the famed Bocconi university in Milan, admitted being fooled by il Cavaliere). *Clean Hands* brought to extinction the major political parties which had run the show since WWII, the Christian Democrats and the Socialist Party mainly, and paved the way to il Cavaliere's new *ventennio* (Il Cavaliere is Berlusconi's nickname. It refers to his former title *Cavaliere del Lavoro*, Knight of Labour. Berlusconi renounced the title in March 2014, before it was confiscated after the guilty verdict of August 2013).

Since I am a teacher of English and I happen to take students abroad at least twice a year, for the last twenty years the overwhelming question has followed me abroad wherever I roamed, becoming more and more oppressive as the Cavaliere's game became more and more obvious. The second last time I heard it I was crossing Kew bridge in London last July (2013): that was too much, I just felt I couldn't take it anymore, I would try to explain it all in writing, once and for all. But I soon realized how difficult it is to give an explanation for such an incomprehensible incident, the twenty years we have spent with il Cavaliere and his Weapons of Mass Deception. The paper that follows is an attempt to find logic where there's none to be found, to suggest motives and causes with a light tone in order to find relief where there's none to be found: I have tried to avoid an aseptic reconstruction of this very grim but also tragicomic historical period in which, alas, what is at stake is democracy itself! Political opinions and ethic views will be hinted and proposed because this is not a court trial which needs evidence beyond doubts, even if the facts and figures in this essay are true and may easily be checked.

Tobias Jones, a British journalist and writer who married a girl from Parma and lived in our country for some time, in his enlightening book *The Dark Side of Italy* said that he inevitably stumbled into Berlusconi as if by accident as soon as he set foot in Italy. Jones too saw the state of our country with a clarity unknown to the native dwellers:

> Thus I began writing about Berlusconi almost by accident. I had wanted to write about the country's recent history, about all those aspects of Italy ignored by tourists. And yet, each time I wrote about the history, contemporary politics imposed itself. I tried writing about other things ... and Berlusconi and his coalition reappeared ... he is, I realized, the 'owner' of Italy. As the words of one famous song comment, he seems to own everything from Padre Nostro (Our Father) to Cosa Nostra (the Mafia). Living in Italy it's impossible to move without, inadvertently, coming up against his influence. If you watch football matches, or television, try to buy a house or a book or a newspaper, rent a video, or else simply shop in a supermarket, the chances are you're somehow filling the coffers of il Cavaliere (last estimated to be worth $14 billion). When you lie on any beach during the summer months, one of his planes is likely to fly overhead with a banner trailing behind: 'Liberty' it reads, or 'Forza Italia!'.
>
> Berlusconi is, without doubt, the most unconventional and controversial political leader on the world stage. The consistent accusation against his government (from both Italy and abroad) is that it's made up of 'black shirts' and 'white collars': that is, of former Fascists and white-collar criminals. Moral indignation is the standard response, because from every angle the government really does seem contrary to normal, democratic discourse.

The Dark Side of Italy was published in 2003; today it still is a very good portrait of the country, that obviously needs to be updated. After that very little has been printed on the Italian dystopia in English, even if Jones has regularly written articles on Italian politics in *the Guardian*. In 2012 the documentary film *Girlfriend in a Coma* was realized, co-written and narrated by Bill Emmott, former editor-in-chief of *The Economist*. According to Berlusconi, it is another example of the worldwide communist plot against him and his universal role of freedom fighter: the physical resemblance of Mr. Emmott with Lenin proves it beyond any doubt. The documentary shows the good Italy and the bad Italy, it is an act of love for a 'girlfriend' now in blackout but it fails to understand the core of the Italian situation. The lack of an essay like mine was another motive for my picking up paper and pen.

Jones' words came back to my mind some time ago. There's a wonderful little bay called Paraggi between Santa Margherita and Portofino, in the Italian Riviera: azure clean warm water, a little sandy beach behind which the Mediterranean greenery covers the mountains sloping down to the sea. It's a VIP area where a small stretch of sand has remained of public domain, allowing a poor peon like me to enter the water without dilapidating a week's salary. Since I'm spending my summer holiday not far from there, a few days ago I went for a cycle&swim outing. It was a gorgeous sunny day and there I was, swimming in that little heaven here on earth with the intention to roundtrip the long fjord-shaped bay. *A poet could not but be gay in such a jocund company!* Then, all of a sudden, I realized that Big Brother was watching me: at the very top of the bay, as it can be seen in the opening picture, there's a huge villa overlooking the sea, one of the many extra luxury residences of il Cavaliere who never leaves you alone: *living in Italy it is impossible to move without, inadvertedly, coming up against his influence*. In my train of thought, while swimming, I fancied that Italy is like Paraggi, a wonderful surface under which lies an Inferno of corruption, inefficiency and *malcostume – common bad habits* –, a paradise for holidaymakers and a nightmare for honest people living there. And it's always been like this: this is exactly the image conveyed by Dante Alighieri in his *Inferno*, the famous first *cantica* of his well-known narrative poem *The Divine Comedy* written in the XIV century. As you all know, at least from Botticelli's *Mappa dell'Inferno*, Dante imagined Hell under the earth surface, a reversed funnel going towards the centre of the earth. The idea came, I suppose, exactly by watching the beauty of the land, its creative artists who shaped in the course of time an open-air-museum nation, behind which sin and corruption were hidden. Many people Dante knew personally in his days are there, together with the bad rulers and the fraudulent high clergy of Florence, of the Vatican and of Italy in general. It would be so easy to substitute the characters the poet set in Hell with today's personae, even basically leaving the sins Dante wanted to punish untouched. At the very heart and at the very bottom of the Inferno lies Lucifer, the devil itself, a three headed scary monster Dante is afraid to meet. Could you imagine who might take its place in the modern version? So if you want to scrape the surface willing to find the rotten interior I can be your Virgil, your guide and docent in the descent, hoping in the end we might as well be able to *behold the stars again*.

Indeed, if we look carefully, a Virgil to tell us what to expect in the future as far as democracy is concerned was already there last century, a new bard in the shape of some Anglo-Saxon authors of fiction who prophesied with astonishing precision the inferno democracy we're living in today. A character like Berlusconi was predicted about seventy years ago, we just forget to remember. In the final part of this essay I want to take you back there to re-read the words of these prophets. My attempt to explain is also a civic duty, a way to get rid of my heavy burden and to leave shame behind. *One of the punishments awaiting you for not having taken part in politics is to be governed by inferior beings* wrote Plato, but Dante went further saying that *the darkest places in hell are reserved for those who maintain their neutrality in times of moral crisis*.

I started writing in the 'big heat' of August 1, 2013, the day B. was given an irreversible guilty verdict and condemned to jail for the first time (B. for Berlusconi, an acronym used by some Italian press, is often used hereafter). He was sentenced for tax fraud and evasion: in the first chapter of part one I discuss the idea, shared by many journalists, magistrates and ordinary people, that tax evasion and the subsequent creation of black money in off-shore accounts, which has characterized B.'s career since the beginning, has been a means to corrupt everyone he needed to in his shortcut climb to business and political success. In the caring people's minds, B. is perceived as a natural born corruptor and I debate if – and possibly how - he has used the slush funds for this purpose in every possible way. I use the world 'corrupter' both in its meaning of 'one who practices or endorses corruption especially in politics', and of 'making someone or something morally depraved' (as the Oxford Dictionary reads). As I wrote in 'real time', I also kept wide-open eyes on the chain reactions the guilty verdict created in the foolish Italian politics and reported it, going back and forward in recent political life. I also decided to end my paper when, or if, B. would be forced to step down, knowing that I would have a fairly long period to write. The law says he must lose his seat as senator 'immediately', but I have lived in this country long enough to know better. At last D Day came on November 27, 2013, a wintry windy day that I took as an omen; and so, as promised, I laid down my pen. But since new political events occur every day, I have updated this paper up to the summer of 2014, the period in which I finished the revision of this text, one year after I started writing (in this 2016 edition, the new updates are in *[ ]* brackets). I was forced to, since in spring Berlusconi, even if he had started to serve his pro-forma penalty in April 2014, was campaigning for the EU elections (May 2014) for the party still bearing his name in the symbol as if nothing had happened, as if he was a free man (like he actually was). When I turned on the TV there he was all the time, his Big Brother made-up face invading every media channel, campaigning for an election he had no legal right to take part in, the final sad evidence that the State has little power against the owner of Italy that, in turn, is further evidence of the process of the erosion of democracy this essay deals with.

In the second chapter of part one I discuss the new court trials awaiting il Cavaliere in the very near future; the coming proceedings gave me the possibility to begin exploring the realms of B.'s public and private life, from his alleged connections with the mafia to *bunga-bunga* practices. In this first part Berlusconi's rotten philosophy and ethics, that we call Berlusconism, springs out naturally and inevitably, just like his Weapons of Mass Deception (his media empire), his conflicts of interests and his *doublethink* strategy.

The second part is a sort of 'crimes and misdemeanors' biography of il Cavaliere, a story that might belong to the 'true crime' genre since it comes across mafiosi and gangsters and, inevitably, it becomes an excursus on the last twenty years of Italian history, with its dark secrets, its forbidden links between State and the mafia, its violence, its fascist nostalgia. The protagonist of this narrative reveals himself as the personification of the worst Italian frame of mind, of our negative attitude towards society, of our lack of civic sense and our overflowing egotistic manners. This selfish attitude may have given birth to the creativeness, the artistry and the genialness of the 'made in Italy', but in general it has spoiled our society. As Niccolò Macchaivelli pointed out, not differently from Dante, in the XV century *we Italians are irreligious and corrupt above others because the Church and her representatives set us the worst examples*. Macchaivelli, who philosophized that in politics *the means justify the goal*, had seen the coming of an Italian *Prince* long before Mussolini's and Berlusconi's Ages. This is the part in which the erosion of democracy and the open road to non-violent techno-totalitarianism are exemplified; it also a further attempt to explain il Cavaliere's 'philosophy', to analyse his conflicts of interests and his brainwashing techniques.

As I was reviewing this work, on February 3, 2014, the European Commission issued its first *Anti-Corruption Report*. It stated that half the corruption of the whole of Europe, 60 billion euros a year, is Italian. In reading it I was both relieved and annoyed at the same time. On the one hand they confirmed all I had written so far with their authoritative voice, reassuring myself I was not a visionary lunatic, but on the other hand I felt they were kind of overlapping my writing and my effort. To further prove that the European Commission and I are not day-dreamers, in May 2014 a new *Tangentopoli*, a huge corruption scandal linked to the Milan 2015 Expo, was discovered. It proved, if need be, that since the original *Tangentopoli* unveiled by the Milan *Clean Hands* investigation in 1992 nothing has really changed.[3] On the same day, the former Home Secretary and Economic Development Minister of the Berlusconi governments Claudio Scajola was arrested for helping a Southern Italian businessman convicted of mafia association to flee Italian justice and escape abroad. Scajola, by the way, is famous all over the country because in 2010 he seriously declared he did not know that his house near the Colosseum in Rome had been partially paid by a corrupt construction firm owner who had just been arrested. In June 2014, another corruption scandal, a *Tangentopoli* bigger than the 2015 Expo's, exploded in Venice, revealing that behind its world famous gondolas and Renaissance palaces the *Serenissima – Most Serene City –* and all its institutions were owned by a criminal construction company which has literally spread their hands over the city during Berlusconi's *ventennio*. Later that year, we discovered that also Rome was not willing to stay behind. The magistrates, in fact, found out that the Eternal City was controlled and actually run by an up-to-then unknown cupola that was named *Mafia Capitale*. The mafia system of the capital city was a step up from the original *Tangentopoli*: like the Venice case, it stated that the cupola was in total control and that the corrupt politicians, who had run the show in the original *Tangentopoli*, were just puppets in the criminals' hands. *Mafia Capitale* also

---

3 *Tangentopoli*, (*Bribe City*, a.k.a. *Bribesville*), was the nickname given to Milan. It is also used to identify the corrupt system *Clean Hands* uncovered.

reinforced the idea, suggested by the other recent top scandals, that there is no more moral and practical differences between left and right: the two main bosses were a former fascist activist and a 'red' cooperative chief who kept making business both with the right wing and the left wing regional and communal councillors who alternated in power. That's evolution, I dare say!

In part III I claim that the Berlusconi phenomenon was anticipated, foreseen and theorized by English and American writers of the XX century, from G. Orwell's *Nineteen eighty-four* to S. Collins's *Hunger Games*. These dystopian writers show a near-future or future society which is a new kind of non-violent but more effective totalitarian regime which is only a few steps ahead of our contemporary reality. They were able to see how the development of technology, of which we are so proud of, is the main weapon in the would-be dictator's hands: they predicted that the concentration of media, economic and political power in fewer and fewer hands would create a new Big Brother. Consequently, Berlusconi's Italy has become a privileged observatory as far as erosion of democracy is concerned. In the eBook format of this essay, an appendix is dedicated to one of the most acute writers of the genre, Aldous Huxley, whose essay *Brave New World Revisited*, published in 1958, is astonishingly precise in describing a Berlusconi-like new type of dictator. I borrowed from Huxley's essay the title of the conclusion, *what can be done?*, in which I share the novelist's scepticism and his idea of the inevitability of the anti-democratic development of society. In this last section I also go back to the contemporary social and political reality of *Il Bel Paese (The Beautiful Country)* to report on the state of the art in our apparently godfatherless country: B.'s shadow, and the foolishness of the 'immoral majority' of the Italian people, are still there, against all odds, darkening our life like a sun that refuses to set, notwithstanding the laws of nature.

This paper of mine has also given me the chance to report personal anecdotes and events or public life incidents linked to the topic I am discussing, examples of the fact that 'every picture tells a story', that a microcosmic episode in time and space can be paradigmatic of the whole. Discussing of which, in April 2014, the period in which I was revising this text, I spent a week in Edinburgh and again, like a malediction which follows me everywhere, the overwhelming question came again, with a little attachment this time.

As I was walking the Princes Street gardens, still blown by the cold wind in this land of permanent winter, the old well-mannered guide who was taking my students to the castle made a theatre aside to ask me the same ole question while the kids were taking pictures. Notwithstanding his age, to back up his query he fished a mobile from his pocket and showed me a Wiki page titled *Trials and allegations involving Silvio Berlusconi* which begins like this: [On February 29, 2016] the page opened with the following sentence: *trials and allegations involving Silvio Berlusconi have been extensive and include abuse of office, defamation, extortion, child sexual abuse, perjury, mafia collusion, false accounting, embezzlement, money laundering, tax fraud, witness tampering, corruption and bribery of police officers, judges and politicians.* For the first time I had the chance to tell him about the imminent publication of my essay and I felt a bit proud of my enterprise, a feeling of relief I got, I suppose, from the sense of civic duty that has pushed me forward in writing.

In this last part I also dedicate a chapter to Italian football, whose craze, corruption and violence, and its (former) beauty as well, make it a mirror of our society.

In order to find hope where there's none to be found once again, let me tell you that in my country there also is a large 'moral minority', ('minoranze virtuose', to use the expression British historian Paul Gisnborg used in his 1998 *L'Italia del Tempo Presente)* which is difficult to be seen from abroad. The Italian *minoranze virtuose* are those *recalcitrant elements obstinately convinced that the official morality of the Republic, its laws and its constitution, could not be simply a fig leaf to cover non-codified practices.* This minority is a colourful collage of different people with different ideological backgrounds that now hold on to our endangered Constitution like a sailor to the main mast during a perilous storm. It has its intellectuals, its artists, a few journalists, a few newspapers and internet sites – asking for a TV network is daring too much – that sing a different tune from the one of the political caste. In my work I have used these independent Italian sources and the foreign press, still out of B.'s reach, for research and quotations. Ironically, one of the moral minority's most outstanding representatives, professor and constitutionalist Stefano Rodotà, might be the President of the Republic today, had the centre-left opposition dared to elect him in 2013. Prof. Rodotà *has always been a defender of rights, of the rights of minorities, of civil rights above all, a man who has defended our lives with privacy policies, with bioethics, with equality, with his intransigence on the Constitution and on conflicts of interest* said independent journalist Marco Travaglio in *Servizio Pubblico*, an independent talk show on contemporary social issues broadcast by the only nationwide (almost) independent TV network, *La7*, on April 11, 2013. But the Democratic Party and the 'immoral majority' were – and are – not ready to let go of the godfather's deadly but reassuring embrace.

A final note: even if the Berlusconi period is almost finished, it is not definitively over yet. Anyway, the writing of this book in 2013-14 has meant 'celebrating' the 1994-2014 *ventennio* in the year of its completion. I do believe that today we have almost all the elements to describe the Berlusconi saga, even if we miss the conclusion which, I presume, will be a slow inevitable fade out. But never say never with Berlusconi, whose 'seven lives' make alternative endings possible. B.'s strategy is clear: the early 2014 deal with the new PM Renzi to write down together amendments to the Constitution and change the structure of the State are B.'s last stance. His aim is to become a Founding Father and, consequently, get the President's pardon and regain a new virginity to start again. B.'s victory in the *Rubygate* appeal and cassation trials in July 2014 and March 2015, possibly obtained thanks to his last law *ad personam*, might be a starting point even if, objectively, his chances are slim. In any case, I promise I'll keep track of the future events and, when the time comes, I will add a last chapter with the conclusion of this incredible story. It's a promise to my patient reader – and to myself. In the meantime, you can follow my blog for real time updates of what is happening in the backstage of the 'country of the pastoral bliss'.

Note: Italy is a Parliamentary Republic similar to many Western states, and so quite easy to understand in its institutional architecture, but Italian politics, like the English weather, is very bizarre and changeable and consequently very difficult to follow for foreign people who are used to having a few traditional parties. The constant changing of names and alliances, the merging, the splitting up and the birth of political parties are a reflection of the Italian confused and inefficient society I describe in this essay. In order to give the reader some basic background, at the end of this essay there is a note titled *Italy – country profile dealing with State organization and government*,

Political parties in Berlusconi's ventennio, Elections and governments in Berlusconi's ventennio, The Judiciary.

PART ONE

The present

The curtain falls on Rome's Buffoon
(*Financial times*, August 2, 2013)

Photos from Aeneastudio, www.flickr.com, Creative Commons licence

Chapter one

Tax fraudster and slush funds creator:

The *pregiudicato* who leads Italian politics

> *The constitutions will not be abrogated and the good laws will remain on the statute book; but these liberal forms will merely serve to mask and adorn a profoundly illiberal substance…*

It's a very hot Mediterranean summer's day here in Italy; the bright sun and the deep blue sea invite me to go down to the beach for a refreshing dive. Instead here I am, sitting in my holiday home in the Riviera Ligure in the late afternoon of August 1, 2013, watching *Rainews 24* with the prophetic words of Aldous Huxley echoing in my mind like the refrain of a summer's hit.

> *…we may expect to see in the democratic countries a reversal of the process which transformed England into a democracy, while retaining all the outward forms of a monarchy…*

Rainews 24, *Skynews* and most of the world networks are scattered around Rome broadcasting live, waiting for what in a Western democracy should be a routine event which, in this case, has turned into a very special incident, in this country that in recent years has become a very privileged observatory as far as democracy is concerned. Also the *Mediaset* channels are all there, its reporters and managers anxious to find a way to manipulate the 'bad news' to come about their boss and employer, in order to save their job positions. *Explain live on air that you are forced to obscure the news to save your jobs. You are the pawns of a dictatorship that does not use bullets* wrote Beppe Grillo, the Italian Lenny Bruce who has carried his former televised political comedy shows to the political arena, forming a brand new 'qualunquistico' (*everymannish*, in the sense of *ordinary-man-in-the-street's attitude*) angry-young-men party which has won a stunning 27% share in the February 2013 elections amid the dry desert of Italian politics.

> *... by means of ever more effective methods of mind-manipulation, the democracies will change their nature; the quaint old forms -- elections, parliaments, Supreme Courts and all the rest -- will remain. The underlying substance will be a new kind of non-violent totalitarianism.*

The Supreme Court now in question is the Court of Cassation, which is about to pronounce a definitive verdict in a case of massive fiscal fraud, a tax evasion plot which went on for many years and whose trial started in 2001. Apparently there's nothing new under the sun – tax evasion being the country's favorite sport together with football, and the snail speed of Italian justice well known. This time however there's something special attached to the case: the man at the bar is Silvio Berlusconi, il Cavaliere, whose laws *ad-personam* have up to now done their job of driving B.'s never ending river of trials to the cul-de-sac of the statute of limitations or to the decriminalization of the crime in question, leaving his criminal record formally clean. Now for the first time, in almost twenty years of B.'s absolute rule, his lawyers have arrived 'a little late'. As for former trials, one of his lawyers in this case is B.'s 'con-man' Niccolò Ghedini, whose viscid and arrogant behaviour makes him a modern plaster copy of Uriah Heep. Avv. Ghedini is also an MP elected by B.s' party *Popolo della Libertà – People of Freedom* – (the most paradoxical name ever for a party invented and led by an untouchable baron), thanks to an electoral law which gives the party leaders, not the people, the possibility to choose MPs (this electoral law, by the way, was introduced by B.'s former allies of the *Lega Nord – Northern League –*, the small town racist guys from the Deep North who send bananas to the first ever colored Minister for Integration, Cécile Kyenge, and say she looks like a chimpanzee). Together with other faithful lawyers who sit in Parliament thanks to B., avv. Ghedini also sits in the various judiciary commissions in charge of proposing laws to Parliament, and there's only one guideline in their mission: to make laws for the convenience of their leader, regardless the devastating effect they may have on justice in general. This time again the flood of attempts to carry this trial to the statute of limitations dead-end through the use of laws *ad-personam* was about to succeed. The trial started in 2006, its first stop was from February to April 2008 because of the general elections, then B.'s defence claimed one of their magic creatures, the 'lodo Alfano', according to which the Prime Minister can't be judged while in office. The lodo was later declared illegitimate by the Supreme Court and the trial started again in 2010 (the trick of making and then taking advantage of an anti-constitutional law before it is cancelled has been an extensively used technique up to now). Then B.'s lawyers claimed another of their creation, the 'legittimo impedimento' – legitimate impediment: when the Prime Minister is institutionally busy, he can't go to his trial's sessions. By chance when a new session was summoned, B. was always busy, being the certification of his engagement issued by himself. In 2011 the 'legittimo impedimento' was again declared anti-constitutional, so the government brought on the 'conflitto di attribuzione' – conflict of attribution. It was an act against the court because it did not accept the premier's 'legittimo impedimento' on March 1, 2010 (in June 2013 however the Constitutional Court rejected the 'conflict of attribution' too). On October 26, 2012 and May 8, 2013 B. was sentenced by the lower court and on appeal to four years' imprisonment, three of which amnestied (a gentle gift from the opposition while in power), and to five year ban from holding public office. The appeal was stopped twice, because of the electoral campaign and of the waiting for the Cassation decision on the 'istanza di rimessione' – rejection claim – presented by B.'s defence (they claimed another more 'neutral' court), issued on March 15 and, naturally, rejected on May 6. Desperate to seek delay, B. also peppered the appeal trial when he was the first patient in the whole wide world to be hospitalized for many days because of conjunctivitis. Overall, the defense lawyers were able to stop the trial for 2 years, 3 months and 5 days, according to the calculation made by the most important Italian newspaper, the *Corriere della Sera*. As a consequence of all this, the third and final verdict was supposed to be in September 2013, the same period as the statute's deadline: had this happened, everything would have been smooth as usual.

Unbelievably, in early July the Court of Cassation decided to examine the case on July 30 and give their verdict straight away, that is two days later – today –, betraying a tradition seldom disregarded before: the holy summer holiday break. Indeed they dared to challenge the 'big heat', which might mislead judgment, and carry their job to an end before August. The regular Court, in fact, is on holiday from July 15 to September 15, to pay homage to the long

Southern European summer, but the case was handed over to the 'sezione feriale', a section in charge during the holidays for important cases close to time ban. The *Popolo della Libertà* erupted like the Etna volcano, crying out loud it was a golpe, a coup not acceptable in modern democracies; consequently they occupied Parliament for one day making the act of governing impossible, with the consent of the Partito Democratico, the mozzarella opposition party every majority would love to have.

> *… all the traditional names, all the hallowed slogans will remain exactly what they were in the good old days. Democracy and freedom will be the theme of every broadcast and editorial -- but democracy and freedom in a strictly Pickwickian sense. Meanwhile the ruling oligarchy and its highly trained elite of soldiers, policemen, thought-manufacturers and mind-manipulators will quietly run the show as they see fit.*

What is the crime we're talking about in the end, and how is it linked to B.'s story and his other crimes and trials in general? *Mr Berlusconi was "the mind behind scientific, systematic tax evasion on an exceptional scale" from which "he secured vast financial resources abroad at the expense of the state…"* writes the authoritative *Corriere della Sera* quoting the motivations of the appeal court (May 9, 2013). In 2001 a survey ordered by the Milan magistrates discovered that since the 80s B. had invented a tax fraud system worth hundreds of million of euros: according to 'Bolshevik' German news agency *Reuters* (June 18, 2012), *Berlusconi and other executives at Mediaset are accused of inflating the price paid for acquiring television rights via offshore companies controlled by Berlusconi, skimming off part of the sum declared to create illegal slush funds… The investigation centered on TV and cinema rights that Berlusconi's holding company Fininvest bought via offshore companies from U.S. groups for 470 million euros in 1994-1999. Public prosecutors believe that the offshore companies sold back the rights to Mediaset at an inflated price in order to avoid paying taxes and create slush funds for Berlusconi [Fininvest S.p.A. – Finanziaria Investimenti –* is a financial holding company controlled by Silvio Berlusconi's family that contains all his properties. It is one of the most important holding companies in the world. The *Fininvest* group is composed of important companies: *Mediolanum* (an insurance and banking company), *Mondadori* (one of Italy's leading publishing companies),

A.C. Milan (a football team) and *Mediaset*, which is currently the biggest private entertainment competitor in Italy, owning three channels (*Canale 5, Italia 1, Rete 4*), two channels in Spain, *Endemol*, the film production company *Medusa Film*, a digital TV broadcasting network and many other companies related to TV broadcasting.] Two journalists, Carlo Porcedda and Paolo Biondani, have recently published a book titled *Il Cavaliere Nero, il tesoro nascosto di Silvio Berlusconi* (*Chiarelettere* publisher, 2013) in which the story of B.'s incredible amount of supposedly illegal money and the making of it is pointed out. The book is based on trial official documents, published in the book: B.'s black property has no more secrets now: *this is the final story of an illegal system that has conditioned an entire country and has enriched just Silvio Berlusconi's family. The conclusion is all in his favour once again: the greatest treasure hunt of the last ventennio has been won by him. The black knight.*

It is believed that the fiscal paradises mentioned by *Reuters* were created by B.'s British lawyer David Mills in the Channel Island, under her Majesty's eyes, in the Virgin Islands and in other exotic faraway locations. While he was Prime Minister, MP and protagonist of the *Bicamerale D'Alema* (a parliamentary commission created in 1997-98 to discuss changes in the Constitution and in the structure of the State that granted him the title of 'Padre della Patria' – Father of the Nation), this black money in secret bank accounts was used by B. for his everyday activities: the corruption of judges and of Guardia di Finanza officers – the tax police –, secret financing of politicians, corruption of investigators and witnesses, and so on and so forth. At this point a flood of links with B.'s past trials and his persistent production of laws *ad personam* step in, difficult to follow like the route of his obscure money, but always ending, before today, with the same judicial paradox: the material executor is condemned and his assumed instigator is set free. All this can be symbolically seen as corruption turning 'legal', representing one of the many Italian dark tendencies.

Cesare Previti, for example, was one of B.'s earliest 'con-man lawyers' and (consequently) MP from the 80s to the mid-2000s, the period in which he was definitively sentenced to prison and perpetual ban from holding public office. Avv. Previti had corrupted judges for B.'s sake, it's been proved, in various big business legal disputes which gave B. millions of euros, the most famous one being the so called

Lodo Mondadori, a row for the ownership of the publishing giant *Mondadori*. Judges say that the Cavaliere was 'completely aware that the sentence came from mercimonio – illicit trade. B. of course was incriminated and then 'prosciolto'– set free – because of his mutual friend the statute of limitations. From his secret Swiss account called All Iberian, B. gave Previti 16 billion lire both for himself, as black payment, and as 'tangenti' – bribes – to be sent over to the judges, as Marco Travaglio writes in his editorial for the independent newspaper *Il Fatto Quotidiano* on August 7, 2013 titled *Vita di B., l'evasore-corruttore – da Craxi a Mills fino alla frode del fisco (B.'s life, the tax evader-corrupter – from Craxi and Mills to fiscal fraud)* whose subtitle reads: *the career of the Cavaliere: he founded his empire on slush funds, then he paid politicians, judges and taxmen. He cancelled 9 trial proceedings chancing the laws. That's why the Cassation verdict is not surprising.*

As previously stated, B. has often been accused of trying to hide his offshore accounts by corrupting officials of the Guardia di Finanza many times. In the beginning he was supposed to bribe them, then they usually left their jobs to be hired by Mediaset. When the game got tough he went straight to the top asking Bettino Craxi, the socialist Prime Minister in the 80s, for help. Craxi would later be condemned for corruption in the 'Mani Pulite' – Clean Hands – investigation of the early 90s and would eventually end his life as a refugee in Tunisia instead of facing imprisonment. One of the many paradoxes which make up B.'s story and the recent Italian history (the two being more or less the same thing) is that B.'s suspected bribe money to Craxi contributed to the wiping out of the traditional parties of the so-called 'Prima Repubblica' (mainly the Christian Democracy and the Socialist party) of which Craxi was one of the most corrupt representatives. They disappeared when the trials in Milan, which followed Mani Pulite, showed that our political system had always been based on corruption. B., already quite expert in the business, backed up the investigation through the media empire he already owned thanks to special laws on media ownership issued by Craxi. But the paradox is apparent because B., in doing so, created a political void which he himself would soon occupy, playing the part of the brand new saviour of the country: actually a corrupt system, 'Prima Repubblica' style, was soon re-established. Becoming Prime Minister meant not to end up like his friend Bettino: B. understood, being a man of some genius, that being at the same time entrepreneur and politician, law enforcer and (allegedly) corrupter, like no one had ever been before, and simultaneously controlling media information made him untouchable. The contacts and the alleged agreement he had had in the past with the mafia, that many people consider the real origin of his wealth, were possibly useful again in the days of his 'discesa in campo' – 'entering the football pitch' of politics. The suspicion, not proved up to now, is that a new deal with the bloodthirsty mafiosi helped him to win the 1994 elections. According to the same hypothesis, B. tried to honour the covenant during his short first government with pro-mafia bills. Here we enter the realm of the so-called 'trattativa Stato-mafia' – State-mafia negotiation – of 1992-93, whose impenetrable wall of silence has finally been torn down by the magistrates in Palermo and now a trial has started: on the same bench top mafia bosses, top state officials and politicians like the Home Secretary of that period Nicola Mancino, of the DC party, and B.'s evergreen mafia liaison and *Forza Italia* ideologue, former senator Marcello Dell'Utri. Incidentally, Dell'Utri was sentenced to 7 years jail by the appeal court for 'concorso esterno in associazione mafiosa' – external participation in mafia association –, but in our politics' moral code he's innocent and completely legitimate before the final verdict. At present B. still acknowledges him as the Founding Father of *Forza Italia* in public rallies (in spring 2014 the guilty verdict would be definitively confirmed by the Cassation court).

Also today's *PDL* MP Salvatore Sciascia was condemned in the mid 90s when he was discovered corrupting 'finanzieri' – tax officers – using money taken from B.'s accounts, being the *Fininvest* accountant-in-chief at the time. The case is as usual long, complex and in a way funny. It's nicknamed the case of the 'Fiamme Sporche' – Dirty Flames – because the 'finanzieri' are also called Fiamme Gialle – Yellow Flames – because of their logo. You have a fair summary of the case in Travaglio's editorial quoted above. The trials went like this: *In the First Instance trial Sciascia and B. were convicted. B.'s younger brother Paolo was acquitted [Paolo Berlusconi has often been used as Silvio's scapegoat: sometimes he has been charged of his brother's crimes by B. himself when Silvio the Untouchable needed a way out]. On Appeal Silvio was granted the statute of limitations, Sciascia was confirmed guilty. On Cassation Sciascia was confirmed guilty again, Silvio was acquitted because of insufficient evidence since Paolo might have been the offender; but Paolo, previously acquitted,* *could not be brought to trial again. Evidence against B. could, or should, have been supplied by Mills who was interrogated as witness in the trial: alas, he had been corrupted with 600.000 $ and told lies to the judges, saving il Cavaliere.*

For the British public, lawyer David Mills is the most famous name linked to B., the smart guy who is supposed to have created B.'s alleged 64 offshore societies we mentioned before in the 80s and 90s. Italian prosecutors accused him of money laundering besides accepting the 600.000 $ 'gift' from B. we have just mentioned in return for *witness evidence favorable to B. in court*, to quote Wikipedia. Mills was married to Tessa Jowell, a cabinet minister in the days of Tony Blair. In the UK it was a scandal that led the couple to divorce. Here in Italy, a country where the word 'dimissioni' – resignation – is definitely banned from the political arena whatever the accusation, we were much more interested in the 'unbelievable' act of Mrs. Jowel than in the actual political scandal, which, from our point of view, was just a grain of sand in our vast beach of corruption. When the couple divorced, B. made another 'gift' to his faithful lawyer 'becoming very fond of Mrs. Jowell', according to Wikileaks revelations: B. never really misses a chance! Sentenced to four-and-a-half years in prison in 2009 for the 600,000$ received from B., Mills was later acquitted because of the statute of limitations by the Court of Cassation in 2010. B. was inevitably inquired and inevitably acquitted because of the same statute.

Travaglio again, from the same editorial in the part titled *Processi aboliti per legge – trials abolished by law: but the bribes were there, and what the Berlusconi group has to hide the Guardia di Finanza is more than evident. This is demonstrated by the myriad of trials established because of those slush funds in the 90s, when corrupt judges and financiers become scarce. Not being able to neutralize them upstream with bribes, B. deletes them downstream with a flurry of laws ad personam: [decriminalization of] false accounting, tax amnesties and 'former Cirielli' bill [a law to reduce the statute of limitations' time span]. Results: two trials killed because the offense is gone, erased by the defendant (All Iberian-2 and SME-2), and eight proceedings eradicated by the statute of limitations.* By now it should be clear that the spectres of the statute of limitations and of the laws *ad personam* are hunting Italy: in this respect, the Cassation's decision to examine the case today should sound a bit more comprehensible.

As suggested by the Craxi-B. relationship, il Cavaliere's imaginary pay book has never been short of politicians, before and after he himself became one. But the 'Craxi foraging' is a turning point in B.'s ascent: Bettino, as a true *socialist* leader was supposed to do, passed a series of laws to let B. build up a media empire unknown in the Western world to these days. B. became the first man to own three nationwide TV channels, in a country which denied the possibility for a private channel to be broadcast in the whole nation and which unbelievably forgot the conflict of interests the fact gave birth to. When, a few years later, B. entered politics his Weapons of Mass Deception were already there to serve his cause and the conflict became a problem, not acceptable in a real democracy, that nobody bothered to fight. The deed was done: B. entered every home every day until, after winning the general elections three months after the birth of *Forza Italia*, he became Prime Minister, getting to control about 100% of the whole of information, since his own *Mediaset* managers became *RAI* executives. It is the case of Augusto Minzolini, now a PDL senator, who from 2009 to 2011 was editor-in-chief of the *telegiornale TG1*, the most watched public news program, that can be compared to *BBC1 news*. TG1 is a bulletin, as manipulated and grotesque as the *telegiornale* of Rete 4. The 1994 elections were biased for this reason, as would be all the following ones, but nobody bothered to denounce it. Even the opposition has 'failed to remember' to pass a law against the conflict of interests when in power since then. Today as well (September 2014), Renzi's 'revolutionary' government has never mentioned it after five months in office: the promise he made in the primary election campaign in autumn 2013 has been completely 'forgotten' because of the deal Renzi signed with Berlusconi in January 2014, just before becoming Prime Minister, called 'Patto del Nazareno'. I know it all sounds incredible, but it happened, and of course we'll need to go back to this later in this paper. B.'s commercial networks, all 'tette, calcio e soldi', were in themselves WMD, lean, mean brainwashing machines which hit hard at the under cultured majority's belly and transformed them in faithful voters. Telenovelas, soap operas, comedy shows have been the real political message, more important than the factious news we all associate with the iconic face of Emilio Fede, the Rete 4 former director, a gambler and womanizer whose factiousness soon became involuntarily comic, a cartoon-like character in a never ending newsreel comedy show. Today Fede, nicknamed Fido, faithful, a name usually given to pets, has been sentenced to seven years imprisonment by the lower court as one of the providers of the *bunga-bunga* prostitutes for his boss [in September 2015 the Court of Cassation cancelled the sentence and ordered a new appeal trial].

> *But more than just painfully partial towards its boss, Mediaset television has achieved something even more disguised. It has seduced a society to the extent that politics and ideas don't seem to exist. (…) In many ways, the real problem with Mediaset isn't that it is political in the purest sense; it's that it's not political at all. The only thing on offer are bosoms, football and money (…) Talk to anyone brought up in the 1950s or 1960s and they will say that all the hallmarks of the country – its intelligence, its beautiful language, the Catholicism, the style, even that simmering, cinematic erotica – have been eroded by television.*

The quote is again from the wonderful *The Dark Heart of Italy* by Tobias Jones, an author who really understood our nation's black heart.

Il Cavaliere's imaginary payroll has remained filled with names of MPs of the opposition parties both when he was Prime Minister and when he was the leader of the opposition. We call this 'compravendita di parlamentari' – MPs trading – , or 'calciomercato', from the football jargon, and it's a very simple matter: B. has always tried to pay cash to MPs willing to change jersey and wear the *PDL* one, so that he either caused the fall of the centre-left government or the reinforcement of his own in perilous times. Last but not least is senator De Gregorio's case, who confessed having received three million euros illegally to cause the fall of the centre-left government led by Romano Prodi in 2008 (the leader of the *PD*, the same party that today rules with B. – the very same party, yes, please, believe me). Today the corruption of De Gregorio is one of the several other trials awaiting il Cavaliere, in Naples this time. Meanwhile, like a typical 'sceneggiata napoletana' (Neapolitan melodrama), De Gregorio has seen the light, admitted his deed, signed a 'patteggiamento' – an agreement – with the magistrates, entrusted his soul to God and he now leads a humble life of repentance, turning into a character who should by right enter Garrone's 'scary' movie

Reality.[4] (In the first trial, Berlusconi would be sentenced to three years in jail on July 8, 2015 but, as usual, the statute of limitations, due to expire in November 2015, would kill the proceeding that would never reach a final verdict. "The imminent expiration date takes all the pathos out of the verdict" said prosecutor H. J. Woodcock after the sentence was delivered. What remains of the trial is its political value and another notch on Berlusconi's criminal record that would give voice to il Cavaliere's usual media mantra of a political plot against him. In the same trial, Valter Lavitola, former editor-in-chief of the socialist (!!) newspaper *L'Avanti*, would get the same sentence. Lavitola was another B. 'con-man', the middle-man who 'unconsciously' - as he declared - gave part of the purported bribe money to De Gregorio. If need be, this is another example of the judicial paradox I mentioned before: the material executor of the crime and the corrupt person are condemned while the assumed corrupter/instigator is set free.)

The 'dominus indiscusso' never misses an opportunity to remind us of his *natural capacity to commit crimes*, according to the words of the Mediaset trial judges. We should not be surprised if even today his pay books, like in the Mills case, were filled with witnesses' names, to be on the safe side when judges are out of reach. As we all know, very recently a lower court verdict in one of B.'s ongoing trial called Rubygate, which followed the worldwide famous *bunga-bunga* sex scandal, condemned B. to seven years in jail and perpetual ban from public office (the appeal court and the Court of Cassation would cancel the sentence in July 2014 and March 2015 possibly thanks to B.'s last, but not least, law *ad personam*, as some papers wrote: paradoxically it was an anti-corrupton law known as 'legge Severino'). Attached to it, the judges opened a file for false testimony against many pro-B. witnesses (and for his lawyers as well). B.'s witnesses were the famous 'Olgettine' – the young *bunga-bunga* prostitutes he frequented (frequents?) –, housed in his own Olgiata condominium in Milan; they are still on his payroll, with a basic salary of over 2500 euro a month, plus expenses and gifts whose value varies according

---

4 *Reality* is a 2012 Italian film directed by Matteo Garrone. The narrative is set in the world of reality television, and it follows a Neapolitan fishmonger who participates in *Grande Fratello*, the Italian version of *Big Brother*. The film won the Grand Prix award at the 2012 Cannes Film Festival.

to the girls' *bunga-bunga* performances. On November 29, 2013, *The Guardian* would report that the false testimony file has now been forwarded to prosecutors – it is going to become another court case – in an article titled *Silvio Berlusconi paid off witnesses, says Italian court: the accusation in the court's ruling could lead to a new legal headache for Berlusconi*. According to the report *the court said Berlusconi gathered the women at his Milan mansion in January 2011 to meet his lawyers after police raided their homes. (…) "All the people who received this amount of money [the 2500 euros 'salary'] gave declarations at trial that were perfectly overlapping, even in the use of language that was incongruent with their cultural background," the judges wrote. "In particular, there was a repetition of names, terms and phrases that the witnesses, when asked, said they did not know the meaning of [!!]"*.

From many a film clip the staring face of Al Capone, who could not believe his eyes when he heard the jury, which he thought he had corrupted, pronounce him guilty for tax evasion, flashes to my memory while I'm still waiting for the jury to appear on TV. Al Capone, poor fellow, was a dilettante, who never thought of taking complete control of the media and of becoming Prime Minister in order to save his business, stay out of jail and hide the mafia connections which had made him rich.

Exhausted by the never ending waiting and by the 'big heat' I decide to take a stroll on the seaside promenade a few steps away from the house I'm staying at in the Riviera. As I walk I look at the late swimmers and enjoy the oblique rays of the setting sun reflected by the sea like in a mirror. This image of astonishing beauty is no use in contrasting a feeling of uneasiness which follows me. I know, even at an unconscious level, that this is the last chance to prove that Huxley's stunning preview was at least partially wrong, that about seventy years ago the Founding Fathers who wrote down our Constitution were able to prevent a future new Mussolini from gaining complete power by balancing the relationships and the independence of the institutional powers with weights and counterweights. And yes, when I come back the news is there, reverberating on the screen in my house and all around the world: Berlusconi is now a '*pregiudicato*', a criminal, definitively sentenced to four year in jail and banned from public offices. Destined to home arrest and to political death. *Berlusconi è morto, viva Berlusconi! – Berlusconi is dead, long live Berlusconi!* – the online voice of Beppe Grillo cries out loud - *His verdict is like the fall of the Berlin wall in 1989 (…) the declared tax evader, the friend of the mafiosi, the P2 member, card no. 1816, has polluted, corrupted, paralyzed the Italian political life for 21 years, since his 1993 'discesa in campo', to avoid business failure and jail* (P2 is the fascist nostalgia filled, illegal Masonic secret lodge *Propaganda*).

He has entered politics just to escape justice says iconic Mani Pulite former investigative magistrate Antonio Di Pietro (who B., following his protocol, tried to 'buy' offering him the Home Ministry as soon as he became Prime Minister in 1994). *It would be an offence to honest well-meaning citizens and to the international reputation of Italy if this very party led the country one more second* adds Antonio Ingroia, former iconic investigative magistrate in the 'State–mafia negotiation' case. *It is not the first time judges have ruled against the man who has dominated Italian politics for the past two decades. But never before had Berlusconi been convicted. Many of the cases brought against him had elapsed, thanks to the snail-paced nature of Italy's judicial system and the tycoon's shameless tendency to change the law to slow down his trials* writes the *Financial Times*, on August 3, in the article titled *The Curtain Falls on Rome's Buffoon*. In B.'s black and white world, in which there's good on one side (his own) and evil on the other (whatever is against him), the *FT* is of course another instrument of propaganda of the planet-wide communist plot against his holy mission, as magistrates Di Pietro and Ingroia are a two-headed Satanic disguise of his Goldenstein-like archfiend. The fact that communism in the traditional forms doesn't exist anymore is insubstantial for B.'s followers, the majority of whom don't understand the content of a newspaper article and that, to skip the problem, don't read anymore, counting on director Emilio 'Fido' Fede to keep them updated.

So, is this the end of the line? Political death? Does the curtain fall on Rome's buffoon? Just after dinner, as all the networks are broadcasting special edition news programs on the unprecedented event, B. invades the screen with his grotesque Fellinian mask of an aesthetic surgery's addict. It's a freshly recorded nine-minute video – no live whatsoever, just in case an untamed journalist asks him a real question – in which il Cavaliere sits in the studio of Palazzo Grazioli, his Roman extra luxury mansion and official headquarter of the *PDL*, an Italian flag and a European one behind him, and delivers a monologue in self-defense, the usual pathetic pantomime to repeat what he's been saying for the last twenty years: he's the victim of a political persecution orchestrated by the magistrates, *toghe rosse comuniste – communist red robes –*, the most dangerous sect of the 'Goldstein Brotherhood', who he defined *cancri della democrazia – cancers of democracy* – while he was Prime Minister. If you just change B.'s misshapen mask with Terry Gillian's face, here's a pure Monty Python sketch. *Berlusconi swiftly used his TV channels to protest his innocence. He accused the magistrates of political bias. But he failed to produce any evidence to support his claims. Italians have heard this litany many times* before reports the Leninist *FT*. *He who controls the past, controls the future*, Winston keeps repeating in *Nineteen Eighty-four*. The video is broadcast by B.'s *Mediaset* channels and immediately afterwards by *Porta a Porta*, the TG1 political talk-show considered the third House of Parliament and hosted by one of B.'s long term devotees, journalist Bruno Vespa. In this program, an extension of the tycoon's media empire in the public domain, one of the very few in which he sometimes appears, B. signed live his famous 'contract with the Italians' before the 2001 general election he was going to win. *If I fail to reach these goals, I won't be a candidate in the next elections* he said. Of the contract's ten issues, none was fulfilled by his government, but nobody remembered when the next campaign came because B. kept repeating through his TV channels that his objectives were reached. *He who controls the past, controls the future.*

Today's sentence confirms the opinion that part of the Judiciary in our country has become an irresponsible subject; since 92-93 the course of political life has been literally conditioned by the misleading action of a part of the Judiciary, a real judicial harassment which has no equal in the civilized world (…) No-one can understand the veritable violence which has been reserved for me through a series of charges and trials that had no basis in reality (…) I have never invented any system of fiscal fraud (…) there is no hidden funds abroad concerning myself and my family (…) In exchange for the commitments I have made over almost 20 years in favour of my country, I have been rewarded with accusations and a verdict that is founded on absolutely nothing, that takes away my personal freedom and my political rights. That's the way Italy awards the sacrifices and the engagements of its best citizens (…) We are going to put back on the pitch Forza Italia and ask the Italians to grant us that majority which is fundamental to modernize the country, to make reforms, beginning with the most urgent of them all, the Justice reformation [strange coincidence], in order not to be a country under the arbitrary yoke of the most terrible of powers, that of depriving a citizen of his freedom…

The reversal of the logic is quite simple, childlike: the blame is not to be put on the thief arrested in the act of stealing, but on the cop who discovers his crimes. It's pure *doublethink*, and some people – too many – silently still agree by saying nothing or by wishing they could do the same, envious: today's verdict is a victory in a battle, but the war seems doomed. The logic is also very pinteresque: if the magistrates have *the arbitrary yoke of the most terrible of powers, that of depriving a citizen of his freedom and if that's the way Italy awards the sacrifices and the engagements of its best citizens*, then all the mafiosi should be granted the title of Cavaliere, as B. himself. But the ominous part is the one in which he hints at a series of laws to reform justice. It's always been a must of his, an obvious attempt to bend justice to his purposes tout-court, without having to invent a new law *ad personam* every once in a while. Luckily, the weights and counterweights of our Constitution have stopped his attempt up to now. But this is the time for a last desperate attempt, with a new transaction proposal to the *PD* and to King Giorgio.

King Giorgio is the press nickname of the President of the Republic Giorgio Napolitano, 88 years old, former *PD* leader, who was re-elected for a second mandate last April, for the first time in our history, because of the political quicksand the country was into. Since 1994, whether you see him or not, whether he's Prime Minister or leader of the opposition, B. has been the commander-in-chief of Italian politics. After the ruinous fall of his last government in autumn 2011, with the 'spread' value at its highest level, the country on the brink of default and complete international scorn, B. camouflaged like a Vietcong throughout all the insane period of the so called prof. Monti bipartisan technicians' government which followed, a king Giorgio creature to 'save' the country, (*see Italy – country profile*). Polls saw B. at his lower level, so he decided to disappear from TV but he kept dictating the government agenda that he publicly despised. Trying to put on some new makeup of virginity, he became the leader of the protest against the government he was backing. Of course the people, the voters, need long term training to accept all this: twenty years of *berlusconismo* in its philosophical sense and in its everyday practices has trained the less intellectually protected population to accept 'double dealing' and 'double acting': it's the application to reality of the form of mind control Orwell called *doublethink*, sixty-five years after its invention; it's a kind of lobotomy, of brainwashing we all accept as almost natural. Towards the end of 2012 B. re-emerged from his jungle cubiculum, sent Monti home, showing off again as the one who put an end to Monti's anti-popular economic politics and as the personification of novelty and progressive reforms for the government to come. In other words, he himself was the solution to his own last government's disasters: in our brainwashing process memory has slowly been erased, making this possible. The *PD* had victory in its own hands, all it had to do was to plug and play. Instead, their chlorophyll campaign with less than zero ideas let B.'s volcanic eruption of unbelievable promises take over, fuelled by his media empire. Consequently elections were a tie, also because the electoral law, passed by B. for his own political sake, became a boomerang. Its creator, *Northern League* senator Calderoli, defined his own creature 'una porcata' – bullshit –, hence the name 'porcellum' as it is now called. The *PD*, *PDL* and the protest *M5S* party led by comedian Grillo, whose aim is to destroy politics from within, roughly speaking reached a 30% share each: no government was possible and the President was about to end his seven year office. Monti was forced to remain on duty for some time, until the election of a new president who would have the legal and political possibility to deal with the crisis. And here, amid stagnation, a break came through, a road map for a new president, a new type of government and the political fall of the tycoon. A mini revolution to put an end to the new *ventennio*. The spark would have been the election to Presidency of the famed constitutionalist and former *PD* member professor Rodotà, or of former Prime Minister and *PD* leader professor Romano Prodi, the only left wing political leader to defeat B. twice. Both of them, in fact, were possible candidates for the *M5S* and he *PD*.

Had this happened, a new kind of government might have been possible, a new different coalition government deeply focused on the reformation of political morality, on the fight to politicians' privileges and on a series of bills to help average people in this period of economic disaster, after years of B.'s politics of stealing from the poor and giving to the rich like himself. '*If prof. Rodotà or prof. Prodi is elected, a motorway for a new government will open up*' declared Grillo. The *PD* agreed on Prodi in the morning; in the afternoon 101 parliamentary snipers, 'franchi tiratori', 'fired' at him, making this new political course fail before its birth. Why, why on earth, the Pd militants asked, bewildered, burning their affiliation cards like youngsters who didn't mean to go to Vietnam in the 60s. *'Everything must change so that nothing really changes'* says duke Manfredi in Tommasi da Lampedusa's literary masterpiece *Il Gattopardo*. That was the Sicily of the old days which was facing Garibaldi's expedition to free the country and unite Italy under one crown: the period is different but the moral of the story still stands today. Anyway, this is another cup of tea, that we will drink a little later.

At this point we were stuck in quicksand again. In the dramatic days that followed, president Napolitano accepted to be re-elected under bipartisan pressure. *PD* and *PDL* knew that his re-election would mean the imposition of a 'fake wrestlers" coalition government and the complete betrayal of the basic Pd promise: *'mai al governo col PDL e Berlusconi'* – *we will never make a coalition government with the PDL and Berlusconi*. Monti's technicians' government, already bipartisanly backed, had been called 'the President's government'. Now, in charge again, Napolitano invented the present first real bipartisan Letta government, the grand coalition – derogatively called 'inciucio', ignoble agreement –, the epitome of the twenty-year-old status quo, even symbolically: Enrico Letta, the *PD* Prime Minister, is the nephew of Gianni Letta, *PDL* leader and B.'s favorite counselor. B. still directs the show as he sees fit, the *PD* is allied with the one who corrupted Pd senators to make Prodi's government fall, now also a *pregiudicato*. Napolitano has long been a fan of 'larghe intese' – broad agreement, another expression for grand coalition – and his presence on the 'Colle' (the 'Hill' upon which the President's residence called *Quirinale* is built) is trademark of this coalition government. Napolitano was so nicknamed Re Giorgio as he has actually influenced, and keeps doing so, the country's political life like never before, as if Italy was a Presidential Republic like our 'cousin' France. His return was in the end another lifebelt for Berlusconi. But why? Was the President is involved in the 'trattativa Stato–mafia', in which B. is suspected of being a background presence? Can this be considered as a kind of 'voto di scambio' – votes in exchange of favours, a well-known mafia procedure – at top level? Napolitano will be auditioned as 'persona aggiornata sui fatti' – person with useful knowledge – at the trial in Palermo, the most relevant one in recent mafia history. As First Republic's *lider maximo* Giulio Andreotti used to say, 'a pensar male si fa peccato, ma spesso ci si indovina' – 'if we think badly we commit a sin, but we often guess right'. That's another teacup still to be drunk.

On September 14, 2013, I'm sitting in my hometown's main square, Piazza Grande. The piazza is packed with people listening to the orator talking of civil rights, liberties and privacy. In the background the Romanic Cathedral and its bell tower Ghirlandina shine in the blue sky and offer the crowd much needed shelter from the sun. It's a setting of beauty which is a proper frame to the event that is taking place, the annual Festival of Philosophy in which the best minds of the country discuss philosophical and contemporary topics. The town is invaded by the 'moral minority' and, as you stroll the city centre streets, the images and the voices of the orators follow you in your ordinary activities, a counter version of B.'s big brotherish use of the media. The orator now speaking is professor Rodotà. I stop listening to his words as my mind is attracted by this vision of beauty and truth, making John Keats' famous lines come to life under my eyes. My imagination now takes me back to Berlin as, some years ago, I am walking in the Bode Museum. Next to me is our guide and interpreter, a young man who studied Italian in Perugia and that, as soon as we have established a connection, has asked me the overwhelming question again. After repeating my explanation one more time, to confirm what I'm saying he tells me that he has recently been one of the official interpreters for the Italian delegation at the Berlin Film Festival and that he has discovered that there still is 'another Italy that we don't see from here', a different Italy he met when he was a student in Perugia that he thought had disappeared in the Berlusconi age. The cold windy Berlin vanishes and the bright hot Italian summer reappears as the crowd interrupts professor Rodotà's words with roaring hand clapping. The idea that the orator might have been our President seems so unreal, it would have meant a change in life, politics and public behaviour the *PD* and the majority of the people are not ready, preferring, as I said in the introduction, the godfather's deadly but reassuring embrace.

An alternative version of the idea of 'culture' is the one epitomized by a recent piece of news about *PDL* 'assessore alla cultura' – regional culture secretary – of the region Abruzzo Luigi De Fanis, whom we may take as expression of the immoral majority's attitude. In November 2013 he was arrested for asking an entrepreneur bribes in exchange for public funding. Even his thirty-four year old secretary was arrested. De Fanis, married with one daughter, had hired her personally and had her timecard punched by somebody inside the regional offices so she did not have to show up. In the waste bin the police found a torn contract between the two protagonists: 36,000 euros a year (of public money), in addition to her salary, in exchange of four sex encounters a month, champagne included, obviously paid with the region's credit card.

Now, with B. in the criminal record, it is time for the Cavaliere's last desperate attempt, with a new transaction proposal to the *PD* and King Giorgio: the survival of the 'President's government' in exchange for the reformation of justice. Or, better, the counterreformation of justice. Italian snail Magistracy needs money, personnel, technology, structures and know-how, of course, but B.'s indecent proposal goes in the opposite direction. The aim is to limit the possibilities of the judges as far as investigations are concerned (for example limiting wiretapping, which has caused B. so much trouble), to make judges over-responsible for their acts, to make it impossible for them to appeal if the lower court pronounces a not guilty verdict, to have the magistrates subjected to political power and so on. Attached to this gentlemen's supposed agreement, there might be the President's pardon which would cancel the sentence, not the verdict, so that B. would have again that 'agibilità politica' – possibility to act politically – that a Founding Father must have. After almost a fortnight meditation – please remember the heat and the holidays – King Giorgio didn't say no: in an official note Napolitano said that if B. behaves himself (that's for sure, don't you think?), if he keeps Letta's coalition government alive and well, the President would consider a Pardon's request, if he received one, and is in favour of a reformation of justice which is shared by the two coalition parties. Of course an 88-year-old person with a lot of pressure and no break in the last seven years can be excused, but this seems pushing the country's luck really too far. *If the PD leaders belong neither to the former [B.'s blackmailed people] nor to the latter [his accomplishers] – a IF to be written in capital letters – they must stop wasting time, hurry up, as asked by M5S, so that Berlusconi will remain only a disgusting recollection in the political field* writes Paolo Flores D'Arcais, one of Italy's most esteemed intellectuals, in *Il Fatto Quotidiano* on August 14, 2013, in an article titled *La grazia a Berlusconi? Un golpe bianco – Pardon to Berlusconi? A white golpe*. By the way, *M5S* said they would ask the President's impeachment if the pardon was granted, a formal act *M5S* would later put forward in early 2014. *If the PD leaders belong neither to the former (B.'s blackmailed people) nor to the latter (his accomplicers) – a IF to be written in capital letters* – is a sentence that haunts me. Do the Democratic Party, which is supposed to be the heir of the most noble left wing traditions and ideas and of the first ever European Communist Party to denounce Stalin's USSR, really hide a secret, an original sin so that they are in B.'s hand? They have some party members in trouble with the law as well, they have been part of the corruptive system that has always ruled Italy, from the mafia connection to the bribing system, as Mani Pulite showed us, but are they really so deep in the quicksand to need the *pregiudicato*'s helping hand? In the last twenty years, during Berlusconi's reign, they have been in power at least twice for a long period but never a law against il Cavaliere has been issued, not even a law against the conflict of interests that exists in every Western country. They kept saying that talking about B. too much would favour him, he had to be defeated politically, a theory that even a child could label as suicidal. B. kept controlling information, so every ballot vote was a fraud, like in the fake elections of those developing countries ruled by a local dictator.

Through a free association of thoughts, all the mysteries which have ruled Italian politics and spoiled our democracy, at least since War World II, come to my mind. How many episodes of a History Channel series on Italian recent history would there need to report these incidents? There's a common ground in this storyline, and it is the coexistence of a State and an anti-state, of a legal power and an illegal one that superficially are fighting to erase each other, but deep down they have always found a compromise to assure the survival of them both and of their respective political and social counterparts. Mafia and State coexistence, of course, is what we all think about, being mafia one of our national most successful export manufactures, at least up to their dramatic clash in 1992, the period in which the State representatives were almost washed away by the Mani Pulite investigation. The breaking of this historical deal brought an escalation of mafia terrorism and then led to the 'trattativa Stato-mafia', whose story is being written nowadays. In this context B. grasped his great chance to fill in the vacuum entering politics, seizing power, and, as many people suppose from the available clues, making an alleged new deal with the mafia: in this case, State and anti-state would join in one person, a sort of paradise regained. But the assumed – and never officially proved - State-mafia-Berlusconi liaison would be just a part of the movie: the story is filled with fascist terrorism on the one hand and the violence of the Red Brigades on the other in the 70s, the 'lead years'; it is filled also with faithful and unfaithful ('deviati') secret services, a state organization which operated to lead State investigations to dead end tracks or to wrong directions to hide a truth which could not be revealed, basically the fact that part of the State was collided with fascist terror. The vilest terror acts of the 70s, like the iconic Piazza Fontana manslaughters, came to be called 'stragi di stato' – 'state terrorism'. On an international scale, this period also had another aim: to keep the biggest communist party in Western Europe out the government in a West-East borderline nation in the period of the Cold War, whatever the price. Massimo Ciancimino, son of the DC Sicilian leader and mayor of Palermo in the 70s and 80s 'Don' Vito Ciancimino, who was the 'official' liaison between the State and the mafia, wrote a book titled *Don Vito* describing the perfect symbiosis between these two powers, in Sicily and in Rome, a balancing of powers which went on untouched for many many years under the supervision of Giulio Andreotti. Andreotti, *Il Divo*[5] in Sorrentino's film, was the dues-ex-machina of Italian politics before B.'s age. Dc absolute leader, either Prime Minister or cabinet minister, Andreotti epitomizes the gilded age of the Democrazia Cristiana to keep power on the conservative side and the Communists outside government. When it was too late politically, Andreotti would be trialed and condemned for mafia. Retrospectively, it occurs to me as I write that B. can be seen as the element that sprung from this context, delivered by this Inferno; in this sense B. represents an element of continuity and of refinement of the way politics operate, his power of propaganda unknown in those days.

---

5 *Il Divo (The Divine)* is a 2008 Italian biographical drama film directed by Paolo Sorrentino. It is based on the figure of former Italian Prime Minister Giulio Andreotti.

> *The quaint old forms -- elections, parliaments, Supreme Courts and all the rest -- will remain. The underlying substance will be a new kind of non-violent totalitarianism (…) the ruling oligarchy and its highly trained elite of soldiers, policemen, thought-manufacturers and mind-manipulators will quietly run the show as they see fit.*

I don't even happen to smile when, later in the night, I read online the declaration of prof. Coppi, one of B.'s lawyer in the case: *Al massimo possiamo dire che questa è una gigantesca evasione fiscale ma qui non c'è in alcun modo un profilo penale – all we can say is that this is giant fiscal evasion but there no legal profile of any kind.* Deep down in the miasma of the tragicomic 'teatrino della politica' – cheap theatre show of politics –, even a prince of the forum has lost track of everyday logic, another aspect of the devastating *doublethink* mental process as recommended by the Thought Police, whose function in Orwell's fable is the same as B.'s WMD in contemporary society.

But one thing made me laugh in my avant sleep reverie: in the video B. made reference to the 50 court cases he has faced. Other times, in other contexts, he said they were 31, 46, 60, 106, the number varying inevitably every time he speaks. B. is actually proud of having been extensively prosecuted: the more trials he has had, the more he feels justified in considering himself a victim and not a criminal. It's a reversal of logic which brought me to the Ministry of Plenty in which poor Winston is thinking about the use of figures in B.B.'s society while he's doing his job of altering the past:

> *But actually, he thought as he re-adjusted the Ministry of Plenty's figures, it was not even forgery. It was merely the substitution of one piece of nonsense for another. Most of the material that you were dealing with had no connexion with anything in the real world, not even the kind of connexion that is contained in a direct lie. Statistics were just as much a fantasy in their original version as in their rectified version. A great deal of the time you were expected to make them up out of your head. For example, the Ministry of Plenty's forecast had estimated the output of boots for the quarter at 145 million pairs. The actual output was given as sixty-two millions. Winston, however, in rewriting the forecast, marked the figure down to fifty-seven millions, so as to*

allow for the usual claim that the quota had been overfulfilled. In any case, sixty-two millions was no nearer the truth than fifty-seven millions, or than 145 millions. Very likely no boots had been produced at all. Likelier still, nobody knew how many had been produced, much less cared. All one knew was that every quarter astronomical numbers of boots were produced on paper, while perhaps half the population of Oceania went barefoot. And so it was with every class of recorded fact, great or small. Everything faded away into a shadow-world in which, finally, even the date of the year had become uncertain.

Today a few of us know that a disturbing character like B. and its modern pseudo techno dictatorship was predicted, anticipated, forecast; we just forgot to read on: *from the age of uniformity, from the age of solitude, from the age of Big Brother, from the age of doublethink -- greetings!*

As a break after the first chapter of my paper, I ask British readers to picture this: imagine for a second that the leader of the Liberal Democrats, which form the first post WWII coalition government with Prime Minister Cameron's Conservative Party, was condemned for extensive and persistent fiscal fraud. What would the Prime Minister do? Obviously kick him out, and if the Liberal Democrats defended its leader, the Prime Minister would no doubt get rid of that embarrassing partner in government as well. That's normality, and it should be the more so in a country where tax evasion is one of the main reasons for the country's zero economic growth and whose governments keep repeating – without taking any serious action – that fight against tax evasion is one of their main goals. But nothing of the kind happens around here: on the contrary, Prime Minister Enrico Letta and President Napolitano beg B. not to complain too much and too loudly in order not to embarrass them, which means: if your reaction is too noisy we might disavow you, but the suspicion that throughout his career he has evaded hundreds of millions in taxes doesn't really matter because they have already known this for years. Another paradox that is crystal clear but that we cannot see from within.

Chapter two

Bunga-bunga, MPs calciomercato and much more:

the trials of the Knight

Let us picture this made-up scenario: it's late in the evening in Paris on May 27, 2010 when Prime Minister Berlusconi receives a phone call from a Brazilian prostitute 'operating' in Milan who hosts a young underage girl from Morocco, El Mahroug, illegally immigrated to Italy (have you ever heard of a PM who receives calls from underworld prostitutes? Do you think it's normal for a *signorina* of the kind to have the PM's mobile number in her agenda?). The prostitute's voice sounds worried. She tells B. that her flat mate has just been arrested after being accused of a 300 euro theft. She has no ID, and she is now at the local police station for identification and questioning. B.'s expression changes immediately, we might guess, since he foresees the danger of the situation straight away; this time it's not a simple matter to handle like Patrizia D'Addario's case…

Patrizia was 42 when, two years before, she recorded B.'s voice while he was – trying, allegedly – to make love to her in his mansion, Palazzo Grazioli, in Rome. She was a retired actress and an 'escort' from Bari, Puglia, recruited twice to spend the night with attractive good-looking Silvio by Bari young building trade entrepreneur Giampiero 'Jumpy' Tarantini, who was looking for a shortcut for his broken businesses (why do the media use the word 'escort', *scorta*, instead of the much more defining 'whore' or 'prostitute'? This is just misshapen Puritanism). Lady D'Addario himself was in trouble: she was divorced, broke, with an illegal building to be fixed. A visit to the ruling king of illegality and PM might have been useful. Some time later the whole country heard B.'s voice while in bed with blonde, tall, lean Patrizia, his distorted ego maybe pleased to let the world know. Is it not our national male attitude to have extramarital affairs whose pleasure lies more in telling friends afterwards than in the enjoyment of the act? According to B., some extra money and a nomination for the next local elections might well do, being the putting forward as candidate of former show girls from his trash TV shows who had been 'good to him' an accepted strategy of his, even at top level: today's *PDL* top politician and former minister Mara Carfagna or the aging aggressive 'pitonessa' Daniela Santanchè, now turned *PDL* strategy theorist and leader, are two examples. (My third question is merely rhetorical: generally speaking, is the election of brain-seeking empty-shell women acceptable?). To please the Catholics of his coalition, to please the Vatican, whose benediction he wants as a fervent practitioner of the ten commandments, to please Catholic electorate, B. said he didn't know she was a paid escort (is he so dumb or are we, if we believe him? More: is there really, I wonder, anyone who sincerely believes this and his other lies? But then I remember Winston meditations on *doublethink*: *to hold simultaneously two opinions which cancelled out, knowing them to be contradictory and believing in both of them, to use logic against logic…*). Beautiful Patrizia was just one case in the ongoing flow of 'girls' from Bari to Palazzo Grazioli; the desperate Tarantini was looking for easy money, but he pushed his luck a bit too far.

[Tarantini was given a guilty verdict in the so-called 'processo escort' on November 13, 2015: *Hiring of prostitution in more than 20 episodes. With this accusation the Bari tribunal issued a 7 year-10 month imprisonment verdict for G. Tarantini and a 16 month verdict for Sabina Began, the 'queen bee' of the parties organized by former premier S. Berlusconi*, Il Fatto Quotidiano *writes on the same day. The Bari tribunal also transmitted the acts to the 'procura' for possible criminal action versus S. Berlusconi (not a defendant in this trial) … for 'hindrance to justice'.*

Besides, on February 11, 2016, the Lower Chamber of Parliament admitted the use of Berlusconi's wiretaps of the 'escort case' … *against Berlusconi himself and against V. Lavitola*, the daily *Repubblica* points out in the article *Escort, via libera all'utilizzo delle intercettazioni di Silvio Berlusconi nel processo a Bari. … When the facts occurred, Berlusconi was MP and PM. The two of them are accused of induction to give false testimony to the judicial authority. Berlusconi and Lavitola are accused of inducing entrepreneur G. Tarantini to tell magistrates lies saying the il Cavaliere did not know that the 26 girls brought to Palazzo Grazioli, Villa Certosa e Arcore [B.'s mansions] were prostitutes. In exchange for his lies, between summer 2010 and August 2011 Tarantini, the prosecutors say, received about 20,000 euros a month from Berlusconi via Lavitola. According to the prosecutors, 500,000 euros were also transferred to a Uruguayan bank account Tarantini had access to (an amount only partially withdrawn by 'Giampi.]*

A curious 'grapevine' anecdote: the night B. spent with Ms D'Addario was also the night in which Obama became the first black American President, November 4, 2008. According to the rumour, our PM, busy with *bunga-bunga*, simply forgot the event. In the early morning hours there was a knock on his door: a zealous attendant reminded him of the event and handed him a clean suit. Some hours later B. appeared on TV to send Obama his congratulations. A real fact is that some days later, probably still under Patrizia's spell, B. referred to the President of the US as 'tanned', making one of those nasty 'wise remarks' for which he is internationally sadly famous and for which the majority of the Italian population still feels ashamed. We all remember the repeated jokes, gestures and blunder to Chancellor Angela Merkel, his 'cucu' from behind pillars. According to BBC presenter J. Paxman, anchorman of *Newsnight*, B. defined Ms Merkel as 'an unfuckable lard-arse'. All this contributed to bring the 'spread 'between the Italian and the German bonds at its highest level: we are still paying ready money every day because of B.'s repeated kindergarten behaviour on the international scene. Now B. and Patrizia's conversations are on the web, for every peeping tom to enjoy, in the online edition of the magazine *Espresso*.

If you look at the online pictures of Mara Carfagna (former Minister for Equal Opportunity in Berlusconi's fourth cabinet, from 2008 to 2011) before she entered politics, the images themselves are iconic of the feminist attitude of the lady in question, the movement that fought for equality of genders and for the acknowledgment of the intelligence and of the personality of females in contrast with the stereotyped image of women as objects of beauty. On. Carfagna has learnt the lesson from the ladies who fought in the sixties real well. Surprisingly, according to Wikipedia in English *she participated in the Miss Italy contest in 1999 and later she started working in television for the company Mediaset, controlled by the family of Silvio Berlusconi. From 2000 to 2006 she participated as a showgirl in the television program La domenica del villaggio ("Sunday in the Village"). In 2006 she led the program Piazza Grande ("Main Square"). Carfagna has also been part of the television programs I Cervelloni, Vota la Voce and Domenica In* [trash TV shows upon which B. has brainwashed the viewers and then turned them into his voters]. *She later entered politics and was elected to the Chamber of Deputies for Forza Italia party in 2006 (…) Carfagna had been named "the most beautiful minister in the world". Mara Carfagna has in the past posed nude on several occasions, for magazines such as Maxim.* According to Wikipedia in Italian *secondo numerose indiscrezioni, alcune intercettazioni telefoniche effettuate nell'ambito di un'inchiesta per corruzione a carico di Berlusconi avrebbero prodotto materiale non penalmente rilevante riguardante presunti favori sessuali ottenuti dal Presidente del Consiglio dei ministri Berlusconi in cambio dell'incarico da ministro (according to wiretapped conversations in a corruption case against Berlusconi, the PM would have received sexual 'favours' in return for her position as minister).* No doubt Mara Carfagna's contemporary leading position inside in the *PDL* nomenclature is well deserved.

Daniela Santanché is another *PDL* first lady as far as class and elegance are concerned, not to mention her ideas and her political far-sightedness, a refined lady B. would have been proud to bring to a Buckingham Palace party had he ever been invited. Here's a picture that shows her elegant charm. On. Santanché, nicknamed *La Pitonessa* (the female python), is very dangerous, like a python indeed; her aggressive manners and commonplace ideas make it impossible for me to listen to her even for a single moment. She has always been linked to post Fascism, belonging to *Alleanza Nazionale* and then to *La Destra*, the right most party in Italy, always allied with B. at elections. Today she is one of the most credited of B.'s advisers. This leads to a comparison between B. and Mussolini, a parallel only too obvious. First of all, the two of them are physically similar: they look like stubborn dumpy squat men of modest background looking for leadership as revenge. They both served for a *ventennio*, have the dictator's DNA in their spines and are extremely vain. The real difference is that Mussolini's dictatorial *ventennio* needed a physical violence which is unnecessary now because (Huxley again) *the ruling oligarchy and its highly trained elite of soldiers, policemen, thought-manufacturers and mind-manipulators will quietly run the show as they see fit*. Even their sexual habits are quite similar: Mussolini had a different 'girl', the escort of his days, brought to his study almost every day, even if he had a 'regime' fiancé who would be hanged upside down next to him by the Partisans in Milan at the end of the Second World War. Evidently having sex with prostitutes is another way to affirm an all-male leadership and superiority. There's a difference, though, which won't probably enter history books: Mussolini was sexually over efficient, B. is allegedly impotent. That's what is heard through the grapevine. Due to prostate surgery, B. would be sexually ineffective. His erection would be set with a little mechanical pump implanted in his body, hand manoeuvred, like inflating a balloon. Can you imagine B. pumping up his penis during *bunga-bunga*? How can the 'escorts' remain serious? Most likely money and power make it happen. It must be an irresistibly comic sketch, comedians inspiring. If this is true, it means taking away any pleasure in the act, the fake machismo performance underlying the egotistic aspect, the idea of superiority and of greed for power of the performer. Anyway, even if this is just another metropolitan legend, nature takes its toll: B. is 76, so the scrutiny stands.

'La Pitonessa' is engaged to Alessandro Sallusti, director of the newspaper *Il Giornale*, one of the two daily papers directly owned by B.'s family. The Italian slang expression 'ogni badilaccio trova il suo manicazzo' ('every shovel finds its haft') perfectly fits the couple. Sallusti looks like De Niro performing the monster in K. Branagh's movie *Frankenstein*, except for the fact that the journalist is not as kind-hearted as doc. Frankenstein's creature; he is a serpent – a male python – who spits out his poison to everyone B. orders to. Reading *Il Giornale*'s first page headlines is a useful exercise in studying the art of reality control, of *doublethink* and of manipulation of the truth. Besides, headlines, articles and editorials are an insult to logic and intelligence and an incredible homage to vulgarity. On October 24, 2009, for example, the first page headline read 'al *PD* piace il cazzo' ('*PD* like prick'): the popular saying applies here too, between the newspaper and its readers this time. Sallusti is one of B.'s serfs without any dignity left, used by his boss to build up imaginary accusations against his political enemies. This old technique is called 'la macchina del fango' – the mud machine – in our country: it has discredited many adversaries with fake accusations and brought Sallusti to court several times. Sallusti was also sanctioned by the Ordine dei Giornalisti, the Journalists' Association, and in 2012 he was sentenced to jail for one of these mud machine campaigns. President Napolitano granted him pardon, respectful of the 'inciucio' style which keeps dominating our political life. These days the mud machine is in full swing: since B. was definitively condemned on

August 1, *Il Giornale* has published accusations against the head judge of the Court which sentenced B. guilty, 72-year-old Antonio Esposito. It's a series of lies based on past inquiries regarding him: the results were all in favour of Esposito, but B.' newspaper has omitted to refer them systematically. These everyday lies are spread around by B.'s TV channels and we all know well that a lie constantly repeated ends up convincing the reader/listener that it is true:

> *The Party said that Oceania had never been in alliance with Eurasia. He, Winston Smith, knew that Oceania had been in alliance with Eurasia as short a time as four years ago. But where did that knowledge exist? Only in his own consciousness, which in any case must soon be annihilated. And if all others accepted the lie which the Party imposed – if all records told the same tale – then the lie passed into history and became truth. 'Who controls the past,' ran the Party slogan, 'controls the future: who controls the present controls the past.' And yet the past, though of its nature alterable, never had been altered. Whatever was true now was true from everlasting to everlasting. It was quite simple. All that was needed was an unending series of victories over your own memory. 'Reality control', they called it: in Newspeak, 'doublethink'.*

On August 22, 2013 the ANM, National Association of Magistrates, issued an official note that denounced the media lynching to neutralize B.'s guilty verdict: *Once again the ANM publicly again denounces the series of newspaper articles and TV reports containing grave offences against single magistrates and unacceptable attacks against the Judiciary as a whole: the accusations go as far as the creation of magistrates' lists that evokes proscription lists. This journalistic strategy, that spreads again grotesque pieces of news and brings on old topics already repeatedly disclaimed, reveals its arbitrary nature based on the constant use of false highly defamatory arguments of such a gravity and intensity to reach the characteristics of a real media lynching, with the aim of discrediting the Judiciary and the single magistrates' work. This is linked to the conclusion of the Mediaset trial, with the evident goal to diminish the effect of a final verdict and in the obstinate attempt to neutralize its consequences, heavily compromising the main principles upon which the Constitutional State is based.* [6]

---

6   *L'Anm ancora una volta denuncia pubblicamente il susseguirsi di articoli di stampa e di servizi televisivi contenenti gravi offese a singoli magistrati e*

In one case B.'s mud machine became a boomerang: in 2005 *Il Giornale* published protected phone wiretaps, illegally passed over to il Cavaliere by his intelligence network, of an ongoing investigation concerning the bank Unipol, politically close to the *PD*. The aim was clearly to damage his adversaries in the following political elections. On March 17, 2013 the lower court condemned B. to one year in prison and to a fine of 80.000 euros, a nuisance for the multimillionaire in question. The appeal of the Unipol case is the second trial waiting for B. behind the corner (in March 2014 the appeal court would be forced to close down the trial because of the statute of limitations).

Not just an economic annoyance is the third trial waiting for il Cavaliere in the near future: it is not so important politically, but it's for sure the most expensive of them all. It's the divorce civil cause from his second wife Veronica Lario, unexpectedly a former showgirl: in the separation sentence, the judges ordered B. to pay her three million euros a month. 3,000,000 euros a month, I'm writing it in figures too to assure you it's not a printing mistake, it's just an offence to the life and the dignity of normal people. In October 2013 Berlusconi announced that the appeal court had halved the sum he has to pay monthly, lowering it to a mere 1.4 million, but Veronica has proclaimed legal action against the new sentence so that a real 'war' between the two is now raging [in March 2015 the same court confirmed the amount]. The drop which caused the vase to overflow

---

inaccettabili attacchi all'intero ordine giudiziario, giunti fino alla redazione di elenchi di magistrati, che evocano liste di proscrizione. Tale strategia giornalistica, che ricorre anche alla diffusione di notizie grottesche e ripropone argomenti vecchi e già ripetutamente smentiti – prosegue l'Anm – rivela la sua natura di operazione strumentale, fondata sull'uso sistematico di argomenti falsi e gravemente diffamatori, volti a screditare la magistratura e l'operato di singoli magistrati, con una gravità e un'intensità tali da assumere le caratteristiche di un vero e proprio linciaggio mediatico. Ciò avviene in collegamento con la conclusione del processo Mediaset', con l'evidente finalità di sminuire gli effetti di una sentenza definitiva e nel pervicace tentativo di neutralizzare le conseguenze della stessa, con grave compromissione dei principi fondamentali sui quali si basa lo Stato di diritto.

was another awkward B.'s public act due to his irrepressible narcissism which darkens B.'s rational behaviour in many cases. The exploit in question is his public visit to teenager Letizia Noemi: B. showed up at her eighteenth birthday party in her hometown near Naples while he was on duty as PM, with bodyguards and state cars accompanying him, offering the media the event on a silver plate. As I said, probably his old-time macho pleasure in letting the world know his affairs cannot be dimmed and it is most likely associated to a feeling of being untouchable, typical of despots. B. swore he never 'touched' her, had he done it he would resign (the usual assumed set of lies which I am convinced he himself believes in the end, in a kind of *doublethink* process applied to himself). But Noemi's mother confirmed her daughter had spent some days alone with B. in his Sardinian residence Villa Certosa in the period of New Year's Eve 2009. The teenager kept calling B. 'papi' (daddy) publicly and said that papi will take care of her career whether it was in show business or politics, the same thing according to her (and many other Italians). A couple of parenthesis at this point: we don't know whether Noemi's mother approved or regretted her teenage daughter being alone with il Cavaliere, but I suspect the first possibility. Mothers ready to 'sell' their daughters to B. hoping they could enter his majesty's court is a very sad fact we see every day, as if all these *Mediaset*-viewer aging mothers had lost any basic moral standard. Please watch the 2009 docufilm *Videocracy-Basta apparire* by the Italian-Swedish director Erik Gandini on the topic, an investigation on how B.'s rotten values and lifestyle penetrate the national psyche like a pandemic via his commercial television channels. The film was elected by Swedish press as the best 'horror movie' of the year but was hardly noticed in our B.-addicted nation. The second digression is about Villa Certosa in Sardinia, one of B.'s luxury mansions scattered around Italy (and the world) in which maybe B. will have to spend his 'arresti domiciliari'. The mansion is an homage to vulgarity and illegality, two items often linked together in parvenus. Furnished with amenities like fake volcano eruptions, Villa Certosa is illegally built in a natural reservation and no-building area. To solve the problem B. said there was a secret waterway for the PM safety, James Bond style, so a special permission was granted (by himself, I suppose). In May 2008 a local paparazzo shot 500 pictures of B. and his guests on holiday. The Czech Republic PM of the time is seen sun tanning his penis surrounded by topless young girls in what we call a *troiaio* (from the word *troia*, derogative for 'whore'). Back to Noemi, a few days after B.'s visit to her birthday party, his wife asked for divorce and declared in a public letter: "Somebody wrote that all this is for the emperor's pleasure. I agree. What comes out of newspapers is shameless trash. And everything in the name of power. I can't live with a man who frequents underage girls … virgins offering to the drake to run after success, notoriety and economic escalation … for a strange alchemy, the country allows and justifies everything to his emperor. I have tried to help him … I implored the people next to him to do the same, as one would do for a person who is not well. Everything was useless. I thought they understood … I was wrong. Now I say that's enough."

Let's now go back from where we started and let us picture this made-up scenario again: it's late in the evening in Paris on May 27, 2010 when PM B. receives a phone call from a Brazilian prostitute 'operating' in Milan, Michelle Conceicao, who hosts El Mahroug, a young underage girl from Morocco illegally immigrated to Italy, in her flat (sorry for asking again, but have you ever really heard of a PM who receives calls from underworld prostitutes?). The prostitute's voice sounds worried. She tells B. that her flat mate has just been arrested after being accused of a 300 euros theft. She has no ID, and she is now at the local police station for identification and questioning. B.'s expression changes immediately, we might guess, since he foresees the danger of the situation straight away. A little later B., panic stricken, calls the Head of the Police in Milan asking him to hand over the girl, that in no time the world will know as prostitute Ruby Rubacuori (Heartstealer), to *PDL* councillor of the Regional Council of Lombardy Nicole Minetti, that in no time the world will know as a former showgirl and perceive as *bunga-bunga* lady and B.'s personal and trusted pimp. B. puts all the pressure he can put to force the police to break their protocol which said that Ruby has to be consigned to a community for juvenile offenders. Nobody knows what went through B.'s overexposed brain when he invented the story of Ruby being Egyptian president Mubarak's nephew, probably mistaking Morocco with Egypt like a naughty primary school pupil, the same foolish lie our submissive Parliament would later officially ratify. Besides, nobody knows what B. was actually doing when he received his prostitute friend's call, some arguing he was showing his fake virility to a Parisian *belle* who happened to be in his room that night. Whatever the reason, he tells the police that he wants Ruby out because he fears an international diplomatic crisis. B. makes further repeated phone calls to the police authorities and so, using all his power as PM and the Mubarak *balla spaziale* ('space lie', as we call totally unbelievable facts), B. succeeds: on that same night former-showgirl-now-politician Nicole Minetti leaves the police station with Ruby Rubacuori, the two heading to their 'colleague' Michelle's flat. At this point B. has already made one of the worst political mistakes in his career, risking it all because he can't afford the truth to come out: a few weeks later the world will come to know the expression *bunga-bunga* for the first time [The Ruby trial's final verdict cleared Berlusconi of the accusation of 'concussione' – abuse of office - versus the police officers he contacted in Milan on that night].

Since B.'s calls were recorded, an investigation followed. In November 2010, the teenage Moroccan girl told prosecutors in Milan that B.'s 'elegant dinners' in his villas were like orgies where Berlusconi and some young women performed an African-style ritual known as *bunga-bunga* in the nude. Of course there are shades of racism just in the name given to this 'dance'. At the end of the evening, B. chose the lucky one who would spend the night with the boss and had the chance to admire his alleged erection pump, which meant extra money, extra gifts and extra favours in addition to the 'ordinary' token. Various show business girls took part in *bunga-bunga*, among whom Nicole Minetti and Ruby, the latter chosen by the emperor time and again. *The Guardian* reported that, according to a series of media reports in October 2010, Berlusconi had met Ruby, then 17, through Nicole Minetti. Miss Minetti was known for previous associations with Berlusconi, having danced for *Colorado Cafe*, a show on one of Berlusconi's TV channels, and on *Scorie*, an Italian version of Candid Camera. In November 2009 she became a dental hygienist, and shortly afterward treated Berlusconi. We don't know whether for her professional capacity as a hygienist or as a 'escort', she was then, the rumour goes, upgraded to the position of B.'s personal pimp, the person in charge of selecting new entries for *bunga-bunga* nights, together with *puttaniere* – whoremonger, as he is generally considered – Emilio Fede, the director of B.'s *Rete 4* network we have met before and Lele Mora, a sadly famous talent scout for VIPs. Mora was involved in many judiciary cases and in investigations of great media impact. He's taken as example of moral degeneration in the previously mentioned Gandini's film *Videocracy* in which he proudly shows his mobile ringtone, a famous fascist era hymn to Mussolini. Now he's in jail, condemned for drug dealing, fraudulent bankruptcy and abetment of prostitution. As further compensation, in February 2010 Miss Minetti, whose political experience was nil, was selected as one of the candidates representing Berlusconi's *PDL* in Milan and was seated on the Regional Council of Lombardy the following month, earning a salary of about 5000 euros a month we all contribute to pay. Ruby admitted she had received money and jewellery from B. in the beginning but then, when B. was charged with abuse in office, extortion and child prostitution, she changed her mind and insisted that she had not slept with the then 74-year-old Prime Minister. She told Italian newspapers that she merely attended dinner at his Arcore mansion once, that she sat next to Berlusconi, who later took her upstairs and gave her an envelope containing €7,000 and jewels because he is a benefactor. B. backed her, saying that he can't help being generous with people in need. Coincidentally, all the people in need he helps are of the same sex, age and look, like the ladies known as *olgettine* living in his harem-condominium in Milan, all of them on his pay book and all of them called by B.'s lawyers as witnesses to tell the judges what *bunga-bunga* was really like and that it was a shame to take to court such a noble philanthropist. As I said before, today all of them are under trial for false testimony because the wiretaps of the *olgettine* tell a different tale; their voices are online, for anyone to listen. For example, in the trial the prosecution claimed that Berlusconi had paid over 4.5 million euros in total for Ruby's services and silence. In fact we can hear Ruby say, in her bad Italian:

"Silvio mi ha chiamato ieri dicendomi, Ruby ti do quanti soldi vuoi, ti metto tutta in oro, ma l'importante è che nascondi tutto, non dire niente a nessuno.... Silvio mi chiama di continuo... cerca di passare per pazza, cerca di passare per quello che puoi, racconta cazzate, ma io, ti sarò sempre vicino... Avrai da me qualsiasi cosa che tu vuoi, col mio avvocato gli abbiamo chiesto 5 milioni di euro in cambio del fatto che passo per pazza, che ho raccontato solo cazzate, e lui ha accettato" (*Silvio called me yesterday saying, I'll give all the money you want, I'll dress you in gold, but the important thing is that you hide everything, don't say a word to anyone… Silvio keeps calling me… play the fool or whatever, talk bullshit, I will always be by your side… I'll give anything you want, through my lawyer we have asked him 5 million euros in exchange for my pretending to be crazy, for my talking bullshit, and he has accepted*').

Even if the whole wide world can hear these words with just a click, B. keeps portraying himself as a charitable fellow; alas, the more time goes by, the more we get used to it, the more we get closer to the brink of indifference. It means exactly *an unending series of victories over your own memory. 'Reality control', they called it: in Newspeak, 'doublethink'.*

On June 24, 2013, Berlusconi was sentenced to seven years imprisonment and perpetual ban from public life for abuse of office, extortion and child prostitution in the first trial, one year more than the period requested by the public prosecutors. His lawyers are now under investigation for unlawful behaviour together with the *olgettine* [in June 2015 the lawyers were cleared of the accusation]. Recently, in a separate court case for the same facts, *il puttaniere* anchorman Emilio Fede, 'talent' scout Lele Mora and pretty councillor Nicole Minetti have been condemned to imprisonment for abetment of prostitution [in September 2015 the Court of Cassation cancelled the sentences and ordered a new appeal trial for Fede and Minetti]. It's the first judiciary leg and, legally speaking, the accused have all the right to be considered innocent until finally sentenced in the third leg, but… but our moral and political judgment as voters should be firm for the evidence produced. The appeal trial of the Rubygate is B.'s most feared one of the seven cases awaiting him. The funniest thing, which shows that the circus has overcome any line of decency, is that *PDL* MP Gaetano Pecorella, one of B.'s lawyers sitting in Parliament, proposed to lower the age of majority in Italy to solve the case. Then again, in 2010 some unidentified emissaries showed up in Ruby's hometown in Morocco and tried to corrupt local officers to set the *bunga-bunga* dancer's birth date two years back, just the right thing to make her an adult when she met her benefactor. The sender could not be found, can we try a guess? On November 21, 2013, the Milan Magistrates made the verdict motivations of the Ruby trial against B. of public domain, officially confirming both the facts I have just reported and the opening of a new trial for corruption of witnesses against B., his lawyers and the *bunga-bunga* witnesses themselves.

On July 18, 2014, Berlusconi was acquitted in the appeal trial. At first glance the piece of news is astonishing. On that day the principal of the school I was working with in Brighton stepped into the office I was in, came towards me with staring eyes as if I had strangled one of the students. 'He has won the appeal' he said as if he had seen a ghost. I thought it was a joke but soon I realised it was not. However, it did not take long to find out that most likely B. had used another law *ad personam* to win the second leg of the *Rubygate* trial, the 2012 anti-corruption law approved by the Monti government, known as 'legge Severino'. More than a law *ad personam* it is a decree *ad castam*. It was approved bipartisanly by the *PD* and *PDL* for their political leaders under trial, and it has worked out fine: thanks to this decree, the 'Red Coop Tangentopoli' (a huge corruption case which involved co-operative companies linked to the Democratic Party in Lombardy) was cancelled by the statute of limitations and today it has served il Cavaliere well. As Peter Gomez writes in *Ruby, cambiare la legge con il Pd e farsi assolvere. Il delitto perfetto di Berlusconi – Ruby, changing the law with the PD and be declared innocent. Berlusconi's 'perfect murder' –, the splitting up of the offence of concussion, establishing different penalties and cases in point for constraint and induction while the Ruby trial was taking place, has meant paving the road that led to the Forza Italia leader's second degree verdict* (the article, published in *Il Fatto Quotidiano* on July 18, 2014 explains the technicalities). The court could not prove that Berlusconi knew that Ruby was underage and B.'s pressure on the police to unduly release Ruby without offering a reward is not a crime anymore according to the new law. The sentence motivations, published in October 2014, confirmed all the facts, politically and ethically laden with shame, previously checked by the magistrates in the first trial. The president of the Appeal Court resigned the day after the publications of the motivation, an ostentatious gesture to underline his dissatisfaction with the trial results. At this point, in order to stage the final act of his 'perfect murder', B.'s aim is to become a Founding Father of the country thanks to the 'Patto del Nazareno', the early 2014 PM Renzi – Berlusconi agreement to change the Constitution and alter the State structure, a counter reformation menacing some democratic institutions. In this respect, B. seems to act vicariously via Renzi, a picture of Dorian Gray that shows il Cavaliere when the present young Prime Minister looks at his portrait, as I discuss in part three, chapter two. It is not too adventurous to foresee the President of the Republic granting a Father of the Country pardon, giving him back a new virginity and maybe the gut to propose himself once again as the solution to the problems he has caused so far [The Court of Cassation confirmed the appeal verdict in March 2015].

Anyway, as far as this case is concerned, the best has yet to come: on the night before the trial Canale 5 broadcast the documentary film *Ruby Ultimo Atto. La Guerra dei Venti Anni* which unwillingly pointed out what conflict of interests, propaganda, rewriting history and reality control can do when working together for one single man, rich, powerful, corrupt… and shameless.

Ruby case, the greatest swindle of Canale 5: the disappearance of the facts not liked by Berlusconi is the title of a Fatto Quotidiano article published on May 13, 2013. The subtitle reads*: … it tells the defender's version only, in a Soviet propaganda style. No images of the involved girls, censorship of the most explicit wiretapping of what was really happening during the Arcore nights.* Hereafter are some extracts of the article: *… pictures of the bunga-bunga girls would have been enough to let the audience understand what we are talking about. Nothing of the kind, just a ponderous heavy misinformation machine. The ones who spoke were the defense witnesses, introduced as reliable, those who say that only 'elegant dinner parties' took place in Arcore. They were the girls paid by Berlusconi, maintained for years and today still receiving a 2,500 euro salary plus lodging and cars. They were the waiters, the singers, the piano players that owe Silvio all they have… No reference to the conversations in the wiretapping even if they were 'hard', for example 'the more we'll act like whores, the more he'll like us'. They all talked about money, the real obsession in the Arcore nights. Some told they had done the HIV test… No reference to the testimony of the girls who revealed that at the parties there were strip teases, erotic dances, touching of the genitals, simulation of sexual acts. Then, the chosen ones for the bunga-bunga 'X Factor' could spend the night with the president, gaining a higher reward. Nothing of the kind is in the program presented by Andrea Campana, who was a journalist once. The words we hear belong to his lawyer Ghedini, to Ruby and obviously to Berlusconi… Ruby 'moved everyone to tears telling her story'… no sex involved, 'the feeling she gave birth to was just commiseration'… No voice to contradict, to rectify, to re-establish some truth in a before-Breznev-Soviet-regime programme … The show tells that Berlusconi put no pressure on the Milan Police on that night, May 27, 2010 … it tells Berluscoini did not know the girl's age, that he really believed she* was Mubarak's nephew and that the frantic Rome-Paris calls were made only to avoid an international incident ... The magistrate in charge for the child offenders witnessed in court that her disposition was clear: the girl had to be kept at the police station until room was found in a community for under age delinquents. Instead, the show tells the police officers could decide what to do on their own and it doesn't say to whom Ruby was handed over on that night ....

> As soon as all the corrections which happened to be necessary in any particular number of The Times had been assembled and collated, that number would be reprinted, the original copy destroyed, and the corrected copy placed on the files in its stead. This process of continuous alteration was applied not only to newspapers, but to books, periodicals, pamphlets, posters, leaflets, films, sound-tracks, cartoons, photographs -- to every kind of literature or documentation which might conceivably hold any political or ideological significance. Day by day and almost minute by minute the past was brought up to date. In this way every prediction made by the Party could be shown by documentary evidence to have been correct, nor was any item of news, or any expression of opinion, which conflicted with the needs of the moment, ever allowed to remain on record. All history was a palimpsest, scraped clean and re-inscribed exactly as often as was necessary. In no case would it have been possible, once the deed was done, to prove that any falsification had taken place. The largest section of the Records Department, far larger than the one on which Winston worked, consisted simply of persons whose duty it was to track down and collect all copies of books, newspapers, and other documents which had been superseded and were due for destruction. A number of The Times which might, because of changes in political alignment, or mistaken prophecies uttered by Big Brother, have been rewritten a dozen times still stood on the files bearing its original date, and no other copy existed to contradict it. Books, also, were recalled and rewritten again and again, and were invariably reissued without any admission that any alteration had been made.
>
> (...)
>
> Beyond, above, below, were other swarms of workers engaged in an unimaginable multitude of jobs. There were the huge printingshops with their sub-editors, their typography experts, and

their elaborately equipped studios for the faking of photographs. There was the tele-programmes section with its engineers, its producers, and its teams of actors specially chosen for their skill in imitating voices. There were the armies of reference clerks whose job was simply to draw up lists of books and periodicals which were due for recall. There were the vast repositories where the corrected documents were stored, and the hidden furnaces where the original copies were destroyed. And somewhere or other, quite anonymous, there were the directing brains who co-ordinated the whole effort and laid down the lines of policy which made it necessary that this fragment of the past should be preserved, that one falsified, and the other rubbed out of existence (Nineteen Eighty-Four, part 1, chapter 4).

Today B. has a girlfriend; an official one, outside *bunga-bunga*, a real fair lady: her name is Francesca Pasquale, 27 years old, which means a 50-year generation gap. B. says she is 'bella fuori e bella dentro' (beautiful outside and inside) and I wonder if she can say the same! This is another deeply sad but hilarious story like the previous ones: Francesca was a showgirl in one of the most rubbish TV channels ever, whose name is explanatory in itself: *telecafone*, which means *boor television*. You can watch her in the YouTube video from that show: she is 'eating' a *caliph*, a phallus shaped ice cream, in a very sad fellatio miming of the lowest quality. Francesca is another example of B.'s obsession with young trash television low quality starlets. She later became a *PDL* activist and then met il Cavaliere: in order to be B.'s official girlfriend, we could guess she had to take intensive lesson in diction, behaviour, manners and style, a modern version of the transformation from flower seller to duchess in G.B. Shaw's *Pygmalion*. Alas, her manners haven't changed much and, when interviewed, the calippo eater's attitude comes out inevitably. Anyway, she must have worked really hard to conquer Arcore's throne, so longed for by all the *olgettine*. Francesca is just another example of the beautiful surface and the different interior which is typical of our country and of some of its people. To make the whole story real trash, a book about the couple has just been published under the title of *Francesca e il Cavaliere*.

On October 17, 2013 another *bunga-bunga* starlet, the actress and TV drama director Michelle Bonev, appeared in *Servizio Pubblico*, a programme broadcast by LA7, the only surviving independent TV network existing outside the *RAI-Mediaset* duopoly. The show is hosted by the RAI banned anchorman Michele Santoro and by 'media terrorist' Marco Travaglio (see the last paragraph of this chapter); since it is one of the few programmes that guarantees independent information on political and social contemporary issues, a couple of years ago it was closed down by RAI even if it was one of the most successful shows also from an economic point of view. Ms Bonev said that all her TV 'fictions' (both those made for *Mediaset* and for its 'rival' corporation RAI) were obtained by selling her body to il Cavaliere. The spectators were yawing in hearing again another version of the same old story. A little curiosity was aroused when she said that the special prize at the Venice Film Festival in 2010 was fake: forced by B., four ministers of the Italian Republic and some Bulgarian authorities, invited for the occasion, gathered in Venice to take part in a ceremony which was as made up as TV dramas themselves, like in a 'commedia all'italiana' of our cinema golden age, the cup of the non-existing prize made last minute in a shop next to the Italian parliament. And all this at the taxpayers' expenses, as usual. It may well seem just a hilarious matter but again it reveals the 'system' behind it: what happens in B.'s bedroom has direct reflections on society, let alone the criminal part of the matter. The argument that what happens in the Cavaliere's alcove is a private business of his is nonsense, despite the fact that even our Constitution reminds us that a public character has to behave accordingly (article 54). But everybody woke up, despite the late evening hour, when Michelle said that she was the one who introduced Francesca to B.. According to the starlet, Francesca, ruthless in seeking success, is a notorious lesbian who had a relationship with Michelle. The *caliph* licker, she went on, was accepted in Arcore's household because B. had one of his brilliant ideas: she was perfect as public fiancée to try and win back the five million Catholic voters that *bunga-bunga* had alienated by re-establishing a fake public image of a new 'family'. The problem, Michelle carried on, is that B. is continuing his *bunga-bunga* lifestyle as before, notwithstanding the troubles it has created him, also because ladies-attracted Francesca cannot bother him in the matter. But Francesca has gone over the line and now Michelle thinks she is blackmailing il Cavaliere, like so many others now, trying to get as much advantage as possible from the old boss running on empty to his end.

Francesca e il Cavaliere reminds me of one of B.'s first exploits in the beginning of his political career. In March 2001, just before the general elections, all Italian families received a magazine titled *Una Storia Italiana* sent by B. at his own expenses. It's a cult booklet I have jealously kept in my library, 130 pages filled with pictures and text describing B. in every aspect of his public and private life, none of which has probably any resemblance with reality, as the Italians would later discover. These lies are so obvious that even a child could see through them at a glance. On page 126-27, next to Silvio's *lettera agli Italiani*, which contains the usual pre-electoral promises, there are four posters with the party's slogans.

Since the early 2000s B. has literary invaded all the country with mega posters of the same kind, a never ending presence in the public space which was the personification of the idea of a Big Brother *watching you*. I remember coming home from France once and, as soon as I crossed the border at Ventimiglia, B.'s unreal smiling face was all over the place; everywhere I looked B. seemed to be watching me, control me and luring me with his populist demagogical promises. In these mega billboards, on the left a wigless B. is smiling an unreal smile and behind him lies his party's flag in which *Forza Italia*, the football slogan, is visible in white letters over the Italian flags. On the right his *doublethink* slogans are in close up against an azure serene sky in the background.

B.'s slogans strictly follow A. Huxley's predictions about the political propaganda of the non-violent dictator to come:

> *But today, in the world's most powerful democracy, the politicians and their propagandists prefer to make nonsense of democratic procedures by appealing almost exclusively to the ignorance and irrationality of the electors. "Both parties," we were told in 1956 by the editor of a leading business journal, "will merchandize their candidates and issues by the same methods that business has developed to sell goods. These include scientific selection of appeals and planned repetition. . . . Radio spot announcements and ads will repeat phrases with a planned intensity. Billboards will push slogans of proven power. . . . Candidates need, in addition to rich voices and good diction, to be able to look 'sincerely'*

at the TV camera."… *The methods now being used to merchandise the political candidate as though he were a deodorant positively guarantee the electorate against ever hearing the truth about anything.*

His never missing mantra is *Less taxes for everyone without cutting the welfare state*. It is a paradox in itself, the more so during B.'s *ventennio* in which taxation has constantly increased but the welfare state has progressively vanished. Another mantra of his is *Have a good job: 5 million new regular job opportunities* in a society in which permanent jobs have almost disappeared. *More decorous retirement salaries: higher wages to the poorest pensioners* is another contradiction in our country which has taken the retirement age to its limits in the last few years. A whole lot of unreal slogans can be quoted from B.'s demagogical billboards; just a few examples: *A school that prepares for the future: English and Internet at primary school for everybody* is a populist promise never maintained since B.'s last government cut 8 billion euros to education. *Safer towns: less burglaries; -21% street accidents* states that even figures are not objective, a fact confirmed by *-50% illegal immigrants*, a percentage that keeps decreasing but never gets down to zero. The same is true for *Great public works activated with 93.000 billion euros*, among which was the greatest gift to the mafia B. ever thought of: the bridge over the Straits of Messina to connect Calabria and Sicily, a Golden Gate style cathedral in the desert that will most likely never be built. The only true phrase which should be among these ones is *Nineteen-Eighty Four's* slogan *Ignorance is Strength*.

As Huxley wrote, the slogan *Un presidente operaio per cambiare l'Italia - A president-worker to change Italy*, in itself unconsciously comic, is not truer than the fake *Bananas for everybody*: both of them *guarantee the electorate against ever hearing the truth*. Besides, these billboards are always displayed in public spaces among mobile phones and female lingerie, the evident proof that the parties *will merchandize their candidates and issues by the same methods that business has developed to sell goods*.

These examples take me to another main feature of mind control: language, the new language media and politics have recently brought on. The new expressions created by modern politics, the cancellation of 'dangerous' words and the changing in meaning of other phrases have carried on a change in idiom which is also an alteration in thought: the destruction of words and ideas is a means to narrow the range of thought in order to take it towards political orthodoxy in a one way trip. Today's easy language, utilized by the media, by commercial propaganda and by politics, conveys simple thought and dominant ideas. It also makes dissent difficult because people don't think anymore, just use pre-packed ideas:

> *And this was exactly what was aimed at. The intention was to make speech, and especially speech on any subject not ideologically neutral, as nearly as possible independent of consciousness. For the purposes of everyday life it was no doubt necessary, or sometimes necessary, to reflect before speaking, but a Party member called upon to make a political or ethical judgment should be able to spray forth the correct opinions as automatically as a machine gun spraying forth bullets. His training fitted him to do this, the language gave him an almost fool-proof instrument, and the texture of the words, with their harsh sound and a certain willful ugliness which was in accord with the spirit of Ingsoc, assisted the process still further.*

In re-reading these words from *Nineteen Eighty-Four's* appendix *The Principles of Newspeak* the never ending line of contemporary television talk-shows flashes to my mind, with its trained politicians who *spray forth the correct opinions as automatically as a machine gun spraying forth bullets*, an empty language based on a very small vocabulary that in itself narrows thought:

> *So did the fact of having very few words to choose from. Relative to our own, the Newspeak vocabulary was tiny, and new ways of reducing it were constantly being devised. Newspeak, indeed, differed from most all other languages in that its vocabulary grew smaller instead of larger every year. Each reduction was a gain, since the smaller the area of choice, the smaller the temptation to take thought. Ultimately it was hoped to make articulate speech issue from the larynx without involving the higher brain centres at all.*

Back to B.'s trials, his fair ladies have brought him pleasure but a lot of trouble too, as we have seen in the Ruby – Lario – 'Bari escort' – *Ruby Ter* court cases, the third and the fourth ones still awaiting the brand new *pregiudicato* [*Ruby Ter* is the name given to the case of the corruption of witnesses in the Ruby trial which is now in the preliminary phase]. The Unipol - Mondadori – De Gregorio cases (the senator still deep in prayer after his repentance) have already made il Cavaliere's day, as reported in chapter one.

The Lodo Mondadori is also quite heavy to digest for B. since in 2011 the appeal court of the civil trial sentenced him to pay about 540,000,000 euros to the rival corporation *Cir*, led by his political and business antagonist engineer Carlo De Benedetti, plus expenses. As you remember, in this latter case B. is heavily suspected of having bribed the Roman judges to win the ownership of the publishing firm *Mondadori* through one of his faithful servants, lawyer Cesare Previti. In September 2013 the Court of Cassation confirmed that the final amount B. has to pay is approximately 500,0000,000 euros, as the *responsibility of the corruptive fact is ascribable to dott. Berlusconi too*. In the previous Lodo Mondadori criminal case B. had been acquitted from this charge thanks to the statute of limitations while the actual executioner, avv. Previdi, had been sentenced to one year and six months in prison.

Wikipedia has a page titled *Trials and allegations involving Silvio Berlusconi* with a summative chart. [On February 29, 2016] the page opened with the following sentence: *trials and allegations involving Silvio Berlusconi have been extensive and include abuse of office, defamation, extortion, child sexual abuse, perjury, mafia collusion, false accounting, embezzlement, money laundering, tax fraud, witness tampering, corruption and bribery of police officers, judges and politicians:* a good business card to hand out to the world.

I would like to finish this second part in a light way. The 'overwhelming question' has given inspiration to comedians at home and abroad, but Italian humorists have been fired from TV shows by B. in person, in what we call *editto bulgaro* – Bulgarian proscription. In April 2002 PM Berlusconi, on an official visit to Bulgaria, announced live on TV that journalists Enzo Biagi, Michele Santoro and comedian Daniele Luttazzi would be banned by RAI programs because "they have made a criminal use of public television". The crime in question was saying things he didn't approve, they sang a different tune from the scripted one hummed by journalists and comedians keen on bowing to his Lordship. The RAI Board of

Directors, appointed by B., promptly obeyed, and the three were gone. Just to be sure to please the Lord, they also fired some extra artists like comedian Sabina Guzzanti, whose fault was to host a satirical political programme, and journalist Marco Travaglio, whose vice of telling the truth on B.'s circus gave him the title of 'terrorista mediatico' (media terrorist), as he was called in Parliament by Fabrizio Cicchitto, B.'s former *portaborse* and head of the *PDL* MPs (today Cicchitto is one of the new virgin faces of the *Nuovo Centro Destra*). Comedian Luttazzi original sin goes back to 2001 when in his program *Satyricon* he interviewed Travaglio who had just published a book B. would never forget, *L'Odore dei Soldi [The Scent of Money]*, a survey on how B. went from rags to riches so quickly thanks to the laundering of the mafia money which paved B.'s road to success. But B.'s *longamanus* was never able to reach England: in the days of the *Rubygate*, comedian Charlie Brooker made a three minute sketch on B. in his Channel 4 show *Ten o'clock Live* which tells us all there is to know about il Cavaliere, a very funny and witty act I invite you to watch on YouTube. Bakunin's famous phrase 'a laughter will bury you' seems to come alive here. Brooker's opening line, "Berlusconi is an ejaculating penis with a Prime Minister attached" would never be allowed in our country, whose limited freedom of press sets Italy in the 57th position in the international annual ranking, far below almost all Western democracies.

PART TWO

Looking back in anger

The man who screwed an entire country
(The Economist, 11-17 June, 2011)

Silvio Berlusconi and Forza Italia ideologue, former senator Marcello Dell'Utri, sentenced to 7 years in jail for external complicity in mafia association. Photo from Simone Ramella, www.flickr.com, Creative Commons licence

Palermo Anti-mafia Pool iconic magistrates Giovanni Falcone (right) and Paolo Borsellino, slain by the mafia in 1992. Photo from Ho Visto Nina Volare, www.flickr.com, Creative Common licence

Chapter one

A gangster and mafia story:

The Scent of Money and *Clean Hands*

(from the seventies to the fall of the First Republic

in the early nineties)

"*La vera storia della vicenda Berlusconi? Mafia, mafia, mafia, soldi, mafia*"
(The true story of Berlusconi? Mafia, mafia, mafia, money, mafia)

Mediaset's Rete 4 former director Emilio Fede in a 2012 conversation recorded by his personal trainer, an audio admitted as evidence at the 'trattativa Stato-mafia' ongoing trial in Palermo
(http://www.ilfattoquotidiano.it/2014/07/22/fede-la-storia-di-berlusconi-mafia-mafia-mafia-sosteneva-famiglia-mangano/1068423/)

"*A noialtri ci dava 250 milioni ogni sei mesi, 250 milioni ogni sei mesi*"
(He [Berlusconi] gave us 250 million lire every six months, 250 million lire every six months)

Totò Riina in a recorded conversation on August 22, 2014, an audio admitted as evidence at the 'trattativa Stato-mafia' ongoing trial in Palermo
(http://www.ilfattoquotidiano.it/2014/08/30/riina-il-racconto-del-pizzo-di-berlusconi-ci-dava-250-milioni-ogni-6-mesi/1103112/)

> In 1931, when Brave New World was being written, I was convinced that there was still plenty of time. The completely organized society, the scientific caste system, the abolition of free will by methodical conditioning, the servitude made acceptable by regular doses of chemically induced happiness, the orthodoxies drummed in by nightly courses of sleep-teaching -- these things were coming all right, but not in my time, not even in the time of my grandchildren ... there would be a long interval, so I imagined, ... The prophecies made in 1931 are coming true much sooner than I

thought they would ... The nightmare of total organization ... is now awaiting us, just around the next corner.

In the first part of my essay I have let my pen run wild, letting all the connections that came to my mind enter the page and, I figure, creating a quite complex picture. The representation is indeed puzzling for us Italians too because, within our public life, there has always been a row of different dark sides. On the other hand, in letting my pen roam freely I hope the general image has become clear in its basic aspects, enabling the foreign reader to get the gist and form a moral judgment. What I'll try to do now is to sum up the story so far from the seeds I have sown, with the aim of showing the different ways in which democracy, as we know it, has been eroded. In part one I discuss the fact that B. is perceived, basically, as a corrupter since it is believed that the black money he concealed through off-shore companies served as a means to corrupt everyone he needed to. This is the way he is supposed to have operated in business and politics, and it represents in itself an obvious first example of erosion of democracy.

To begin with, il Cavaliere's tale looks like a gangster story. In the sequence of Al Capone's trial in *The Untouchables*, the gangster's words against the law are exactly the same as il Cavaliere's ones we keep hearing at regular intervals; B.'s acting in front of his own TV cameras mimics De Niro's superlative performance in front of the movie camera. B.'s rise and fall looks like a gangster movie we have seen so many times but no Scarface has ever entered politics at its higher levels, in a position in which he would have to chase himself, robber and cop in one person. B.'s early public story seems in fact a traditional 'mafia connection' fictional narrative. B. comes from a lower-middle-class family and in his youth he was an entertainer on big ocean liners. B., ambitious and ruthless, wanted money. Allegedly, in the beginning of his business career, money laundry for the mafia was his main economic activity; if this is true – these possibilities have never been legally proved up to now, and probably never will - gave him ready cash to start his trade, mainly in the real estate field, in the 70s. In *L'Odore dei Soldi* (see following pages), Travaglio writes that the Palermo magistrates engaged a Banca d'Italia officer to find out the provenience of 115 billion lire of the period, a sum so great rendering it difficult to compare to today's worth. The investigation covered a period of fifteen years in the 70s and 80s. Travaglio writes that this amount, cash, was received over a seven year period by the 34 *holdings* which Fininvest was composed of. In the end Banca d'Italia was not able to track down the origin of this flow of cash. According to some mafia turncoats, it was boss Stefano Bontade's treasure.

When B. became a rich entrepreneur who lived in his Arcore mansion, supposedly he started to pay *il pizzo* to the mafia regularly, in order to buy its protection, instead of denouncing the extortion to the State. The opening quotations of this chapter suggest this possibility. The second one was recorded on August 22, 2014: in his daily walking hour inside the prison garden, Riina told his fellow prisoner Alberto Lorusso 'his' truth about the relationship between Berlusconi and Cosa Nostra since the eighties: the payment of millions of lire as part of a deal to get mutual future advantages. The recording is now part of the material admitted as evidence at the 'trattativa' trial. As we know, the purported link Berlusconi – mafia was made more visible by the presence of the mafioso Vittorio Mangano at Arcore, a stableman in a house with no horses. Actually, *stalliere* in mafia slang means drug dealer, as magistrate martyr Paolo Borsellino told us. Mangano was not an ordinary 'picciotto' when he entered Arcore in the mid-70s, he was already a boss, the head of the Portanuova family from Palermo. Later he was arrested by Falcone in 1980, stayed in jail for 11 years and in 1995 was imprisoned again and assigned to the '41-bis' protocol (article 41-bis of the Prison Administration Act, also called *regime di carcere duro – hard prison regime* –, is a provision that suspends or limits the liberties of the prisoners. It was established in June 1992, just after the killing of magistrate Falcone and it is typically used for the mafiosi). Mangano died in 2000, just after getting a life sentence because of three murders, drug dealing and extortion: the perfect servant a country gentleman needs in his mansion. In 2008 Dell'Utri said that Mangano was "a hero, in his own way", a judgment shared by B. the following day, mainly because he never said what he knew. *Had he talked, Mangano would have had many things to tell. Black and white recollections of the seventies, when he moved to Arcore with his family, where he took young Marina and Piersilvio [B.'s children] to school every morning and then in the afternoon they played with Mangano's daughter Cinzia, in jail for mafia as well today* (from the article quoted in the beginning of this chapter).

At a higher level, Marcello Dell'Utri was the real link between the mafia and Berlusconi. Dell'Utri is a Palermo businessman who was one of B.'s best collaborators since the seventies and was a *Fininvest* and *Publitalia* manager in the eighties (*Publitalia '80* is the exclusive publicity dealer of the *Mediaset* group founded by B. in 1979). He did such a good job in connecting the mafia and B., many people suppose, that he was awarded the honour of being the ideologue and co-founder of *Forza Italia* in 1993. Dell'Utri has always been B.'s right arm and close friend and he was a senator ever since B.' s entrance in politics, even after his seven year sentence in appeal for mafia external association up to 1992. His pedigree of corruption was indeed an important passport for the Senate, being *Forza Italia*, now *PDL*, a party which highly value hazardous connections and alleged corrupt MPs under trial, a very good means to control votes and maintain dangerous liaisons. Very recently, when the judiciary storm reached B., il Cavaliere decided not to propose him as candidate anymore, a very risky business since Dell'Utri shares his darkest secrets. It was the period of the Monti government that, under the pressure of public opinion and *M5S*, passed a very mild law against corruption in politics: only after the third and final degree of judgment a MP decays and is not eligible in the future. In the Italian Parliament of the period, as usual overcrowded with MPs under trial, only one would have lost his position. B.' s party signed this anti-corruption facade bill that, in a few months' time, would bury il Cavaliere politically.

The words of the judges of the Palermo appeal court that condemned Dell'Utri on March 25, 2013 are unequivocal. As *Repubblica* reports on September 3, 2013 *for twenty years, up to 1992, the year of the slaughters of Capaci and via D'Amelio, Marcello Dell'Utri was the 'mediatore contrattuale' [contract mediator] of a deal between Cosa Nostra and Silvio Berlusconi. 'He always was the middleman who took care of the interests of the protagonists', the mafiosi and the former PM, who 'personally always preferred paying money as a pre-emptive method to solve the problems caused by organized crime. Beyond any reasonable doubt, as far as criminal proceedings are concerned, Dell'Utri is responsible of external complicity in mafia association.' (…) [the judges] affirm that the meeting which took place in 1974 in Milan among the deceased mafia boss Stefano Bontate [B.'s alleged benefactor], the 'papello' man Gaetano Cinà [see following pages] and Silvio Berlusconi was the beginning of the 'protection pact' that guaranteed Berlusconi from the threats of*

Cosa Nostra. It also helped his [B.'s] business in real estate and in the purchase of TV antennae in Sicilly. Vittorio Mangano, the mafioso taken to Arcore by Dell'Utri, was not there as stableman, he was Cosa Nostra 'presidium' and Berlusconi 'never failed to give large amounts of money to the mafia, as a token for protection'. Dell'Utri acted 'in active synergy with the association and dealt with those who were the personification of the anti-State'. To prove that *buon sangue non mente* – 'good blood does not tell lies' – on September 24, 2013 the *Fatto Quotidiano* published an article titled *Milan, Mangano's daughter arrested for Mafia. She helped Zambetti at election.* According to the investigators, Cinzia Mangano is "vertice, promotrice e capo" (head, promoter and chief) of the mafia organization rooted in Lombardy. She helped *PDL* politician Zambetti to be elected in the Regional Council but he was arrested for corruption. Time goes by, but the story is always the same.

In May 2014 the Court of Cassation confirmed the seven year sentence for *external complicity in mafia association* to Marcello Dell'Utri, which meant imprisonment for the former *Forza Italia* ideologue, classifying him as 'dangerous for society'. Dell'Utri escaped to Beirut in early April, a few days before the Palermo judges re-ordered his arrest fearing he could escape before the final verdict. On April 11 he was apprehended in the Lebanese capital on an Interpol warrant but the former senator, after spending a period in a five star hotel, fell sick and was hospitalized in a luxury private clinic. In late May the Lebanese president signed the extradition document but it took one more month before Dell'Utri came back to Italy and to jail. His escape to Lebanon confirms that that country is the favourite destination for mafia sentenced criminals. First all there is no mafia association offence in the country, but that is not enough to justify the choice. In a reportage published by *Repubblica* on May 9 titled *Ex DC, falangisti ed estrema destra – la rete che protegge i latitanti in Libano*, the choice is made clear: according to the article, former Christian Democrats leaders who joined il Cavaliere's party have established a top level network of connections to protect the fugitives from extradition. This 'black' network goes back to the seventies and it *links the Maronite Christian phalanges to the Italian Christian-Democrat lobbies of the past keen to accept a dialogue with the neo-fascist area (…).* In other words there are three main actors: *former Christian-Democrats who joined Forza Italia, Lebanese phalanges and – here is the third ring of the chain – former Italian neo-fascists* (the *Lebanese Phalanges Party* is a right-wing political party. Although it is officially secular, it is mainly supported by Maronite Christians). In June 2014 Dell'Utri was finally extradited to Italy and jailed in the Parma prison hospital, in the same area where Bernardo Provenzano was hosted in the past and that today houses Totò Riina, a character of the good ole days to keep him company. Dell'Utri in jail with Riina and Berlusconi condemned to social service and banned from public life offer a clear picture of the twilight of Berlusconi's new *ventennio*.

A few days before Falcone's killing, in his last filmed interview made by French reporters, Paolo Borsellino was asked: "Are you saying it is normal for Cosa Nostra to be interested in Berlusconi?" He answered, literary translated: "It is normal the fact that those who own huge amounts of money [the mafiosi] look for instruments in order to be able to use this money, both from the point of view of money laundering, and from the point of view of making this money yield". No Italian network accepted to broadcast this interview in prime time.

Even if B. had entered politics seven years before and had been the *burattinaio* – puppeteer – ever since, in 2001 a tombstone silence on his dangerous past was all over the country. As we know, in that year Marco Travaglio published *L'Odore dei Soldi* in which he revealed the truth on B.'s ascent to success; B.'s story was objectively narrated by quoting judges' accusations and court decisions of the different cases in which il Cavaliere was already involved. The book begins asking an overwhelming question to B.: "Where did you take the money?". Travaglio was invited to the RAI 2 night show *Satyricon*, a kind of David Letterman Show hosted by Daniele Luttazzi, a brilliant and witty comedian who reminds me of David Brooker, a fact that in our country isn't allowed. In a very ironic witty mode Luttazzi asks Travaglio about the content of the book and the journalist, not short of humour himself, answers telling B.'s alleged mafia background which, he says, il Cavaliere has the duty to explain. The twenty minute show develops in a crescendo of overwhelming questions and bitter laughs in which Travaglio reveals all the dark sides of B. which he had never explained, and never will, from his 'friendship' to Craxi to his becoming a media tycoon, to the conflicts of interests caused by B.'s media ownership and by his position as PM and entrepreneur. The show today is cult, easily available on YouTube, but B. didn't like it that much. Travaglio, the 'media terrorist', entered B.'s black list and quickly escalated it up to the top while Luttazzi was one of the victim of the 'Editto Bulgaro' of the following year and has never set foot in public TV programs ever since. B. sued Travaglio for libel eight times in eight separate civil causes asking 70 billion lire for 'damages'. The journalist has won all the causes in the first leg but il Cavaliere stubbornly appealed the verdicts. The appeal court confirmed the verdict of the first case on December 26, 2013, a little Christmas gift to truth. The motivation reads that *L'Odore dei Soldi* contains exact pieces of news and legitimate political criticism.

In the years in which B. got billions of lire of 'unknown provenience', the late seventies and early eighties, Bettino Craxi and Licio Gelli were climbing the ladder of power. Craxi became PSI secretary in 1976 and Gelli intruded his illegal Masonic secret lodge *Propaganda (P2)*, fascist nostalgia filled, into institutions and the publishing sector. In 1981 the police discovered the lodge, whose main aim was to establish a new authoritarian regime in Italy, another example of the underground plots and the corruption that characterize our inner Inferno in which State and anti-State forces co-exist, fight and too often reach an agreement. It is also an example of the so-called Italian *trasformismo – political transformism*: the power elite and the Italians in general easily adjust to new situations in order to stay where they are: we have seen officers of the foreign ruling nations turning patriots after the Risorgimento, fascists becoming anti-fascist after WWII, DC and PSI politicians converting to *Forza Italia* in 1994 and now on the verge of leaving falling B. alone. We recycle politicians and officials in great quantity instead of litter, as the world knows from the shaming pictures of the Naples rubbish which have been in every international newspaper. And when something lurks in the dark, B. is always nearby: his P2 membership card was found, not surprisingly, in the organization's documents. Whenever there's a chance of getting personal advantage from an obscure situation B. is present, ready to seize momentum. As we already know, the eighties are the years in which B. became the greatest media tycoon in the world thanks to his godfather-style friendship with Bettino Craxi, the very symbol of the intermingled corruption between politics and business, as the Mani Pulite (Clean Hands) investigations and trials would show us. As we have said, these same dangerous liaisons may be hard to follow in its entirety but are crystal clear in their all-Italian philosophy. They also point out other aspects of the erosion of democracy foretold by Huxley's essay in mid XX century.

Now B., secure and untouchable under the assumed protective wings of mafia and politics, was getting richer and richer, more and more ambitious, more and more ruthless, and was making explicit that sense of pathological omnipotence that has always characterized his personality. B. became more and more omnivorous, entering every field of business and every recess of society you can think of: newspapers, insurances, publicity, football, technology, food industry, publishing, supermarkets and so on and so forth. A popular joke says it all:

> *Hi, my name's Mario Rossi and I live in Milan in a building built by the Prime Minister. I work in a company whose main share-holder is the Prime Minister. My car insurance is provided by the Prime Minister. I stop off every day to buy a newspaper owned by the Prime Minister. In the afternoon I go shopping in a supermarket owned by the Prime Minister. In the evening I watch the Prime Minister's TV, where the films (often produced by the Prime Minister) are continuously interrupted by the adverts made by advertising company of the Prime Minister. Then I get bored and go surfing on the internet using the Prime Minister's service provider. Often I look at football results, because I'm a fan of the Prime Minister's football team. On Sunday I stay at home and read a book from the Prime Minister's publishing house… obviously, he's governing exclusively in my interests, not his own…*

The first indirect crack in B.'s untouchable position came with the establishment of the anti-mafia pool in Palermo. Like in every gangster story, good cops exist, in our case they were the best expression of that 'moral minority' our country can boast: for the first time in mafia history the investigators didn't stop when they came across the powerful and the politicians. And, like in many modern hard-boiled stories, they paid with their lives the challenge to the status quo.

I met Massimo Ciancimino in one of those Italian locations whose beauty may deceive the ingenuous stranger. In May 2010 he came to Modena, my hometown, to launch his book *Don Vito*. The event took place at sunset in the Renaissance gardens of the Estense household, the aristocratic family who ruled the powerful Ducato di Modena. The gardens are shaded by the huge Palazzo Ducale behind which the steeple of the Romanic cathedral called Ghirlandina peeped out towards the red yellow twilight sky. That was the first time I heard the expression 'trattativa Stato – mafia' and saw the 'papello'. It was also the first and last time I met the man who would open another deep crack in the mafia – State embrace.

Massimo Ciancimino is one of the sons of the DC Sicilian leader 'Don' Vito Ciancimino who was Mayor of Palermo, and the 'official' liaison between the State and the mafia, in the 70s and 80s. Together with Sicilian journalist Massimo Licata, Massimo had just published *Don Vito* in whose first part he describes the perfect symbiosis between these two powers, in Sicily and in Rome, a balancing of supremacy which went on untouched for many years under the supervision of Giulo Andreotti (when the Allies landed in Sicily in 1944, they dealt with the mafiosi for help, not with the authorities). Andreotti, played by Toni Servillo in the movie *Il Divo* directed by Paolo Sorrentino (Servillo/Sorrentino won the 2014 Oscar with the movie *The Great Beauty*), was the *dues-ex-machina* of Italian politics before B.'s age. As I said in the previous part, Andreotti, DC absolute leader, is the very symbol of that period. He kept power on the conservative side and the biggest communist party in Western Europe out of the government. He was condemned for mafia many years after his exit from politics. Massimo had been chosen by *Don Vito* as his private secretary, so he knows all his father's secrets and has all his documents to back up his revelations. The publication of the book followed Massimo's decision in the first decade of the twenty-first century to denounce what he knew to the authorities, becoming one of the main witnesses of the Procura di Palermo directed by magistrate Antonio Ingroia.

Tough times for the *pax mafiosa* described by Ciancimino junior came when magistrates Giovanni Falcone and Paolo Borsellino reached Palermo. They formed the famed pool of investigators who for the first time worked as a team, building a database, sharing information and secrets that would not disappear if a single magistrate was gunned down by the mafia, invented the 'pentiti' – turncoats – system to get to know the mafia secrets, and, most of all, as just stated, didn't stop when they came to face politics. In the course of their period they discovered, arrested, trialed and condemned many mafia bosses like never before, putting an end to the Andreotti age. The corrupt politicians *could no longer count on confidence magistrates. They felt guaranteed no more. They started to be afraid, together with the bosses, because a very dangerous enemy had settled down in the rooms of the Palazzo di Giustizia* – Marco Travaglio and Saverio Lodato write *in Intoccabili – perché la mafia è al potere* (BUR, 2004). *All this lead to the 'Maxiprocesso' – Maxi trial – against the mafia, which started on February 20, 1986, that saw at the bar 475 representatives of Sicilian families that dealt with drug dealing, murders, slaughters (…) History has shown that the trial, because of the serious investigations that had preceded it, was a real masterpiece (…) It took seven years to show what that trial had been: on January 30, 1992 the first section of the Court of Cassation confirmed the sentences.* Falcone and Borsellino, today national heroes for the 'moral minority', were both slaughtered in the summer of 1992 in the two most ferocious mafia murders ever seen, a whole piece of a motorway and a street in Palermo destroyed by an amount of dynamite that wanted to tell the nation that a mafia war against the State had started. The killing of MP Salvo Lima, DC Sicilian leader and Andreotti's emissary, in March 1992 had already announced that the war was also against 'traitor' politicians. The list of dead-man-walking politicians was long and panic spread in the palaces of power in Palermo and Rome. Something had to be done to stop it: the alleged 'trattativa' was about to begin, the shadow of il Cavaliere in the background of the political scene ready to take the chance that the 'trattativa' and the Mani Pulite scandal, just begun, were offering him… an offer difficult to refuse!

Meeting Ciancimino in that Renaissance sunset made me feel strange, as if I was physically facing the existence of the mafia for the first time. We all know that the mafia is there when you don't see it and nobody talks about it, so I was pleased when he dedicated my copy of his book to my children, saying that it's them that have to know and 'remember' in a country in which all the protagonists of the events he describes have all entered a state of complete amnesia, a mafia typical attitude that goes under the name of 'omertà'. *This office is aware of the fact that that state of dangerous collective amnesia of the majority of the political-institutional representatives of the time has not been removed at all (an amnesia that has lasted twenty years)* the magistrates of Palermo write in their *Memoria a sostegno di rinvio a giudizio (memory in favour of the prosecution)* of the twelve accused in the trattativa trial. Ciancimino junior has recently been arrested again for external concourse in Cosa Nostra and slander, but the magistrates in their Memoria state that on the one hand he has been a *source of evidence of disputed reliability (he is accused of slander in this case), but on the other hand we acknowledge that his giving news and information, when and because checked, were precious.*

The killing of Falcone and Borsellino, the murder of Salvo Lima, a series of mafia terror attacks to the heart of the country about to take place show that 1992 and the two years that followed were a key period, a phase that saw the death of the First and the birth of the Second Republic, a time saluted as an Italian New Deal that metaphorically brought corruption and the mafia straight to Palazzo Chigi, Palazzo Madama and Montecitorio. 1992 is also the year of the Mani Pulite – Clean Hands – investigation, established by another famous pool of magistrates. Mani Pulite shocked the country showing that the criminal attitudes in Palermo and Milan were two branches of the same tree, two intermingled aspects of the illegality and corruption that has permeated Italy to the core since its birth, national sports that would soon most likely find their champion.

This other pool of investigative magistrates was as tough as their Palermo colleagues. They too built a big database, used strong methods in interrogations, had no shame in using pre-emptive imprisonment as permitted by the law and, most of all, they didn't stop when they reached the top of the political ladder: all the famous untouchable politicians of the First Republic we saw every day on TV were now at the bar, their eyes staring, bewildered, even incredulous that all this was really happening. The entrepreneurs caught in the trap confessed and some of them committed suicide. Paradoxically, the pool showed us what we have always known, the fact that corrupt business had to deal with corrupt politics to carry on its trade. To win public contracts, permits and licenses, to cover an illegal deed, the only itinerary was a 'mazzetta', a bribe, to the right local bunch of politicians in power. Consequently, for example, a kilometer of the underground in Milan or of an Italian motorway was twice as much compared to French prices. The mechanism is simple: a firm takes part in a public contest, offers an inflated price for the work, the politician makes that firm win the contest and receives its bribe in return; we, the people, or, better, the taxpayers, pay the price for all this. In his 'civil theatre' play *Promemoria – 15 anni di storia d'Italia ai confini della realtà* (later published as a DVD/book by Promo Music Books in 2009), Marco Travaglio gives us a paradigmatic example that shows the difference between some inevitable corruption in an healthy system and *Tangentopoli*, based on endemic and pathological corruption:

> *"The matter is about a canned tuna firm named Nostromo",* Bruno Falconieri [a socialist councillor in Milan arrested for corruption] *says. "When that firm won a competition for the school canteens regularly, Claudio Martelli, vice-secretary of PSI, came to me personally. In order to show the firm's gratitude, which belonged to his father-in-law, Martelli gave me a sum of money of about 8 – 10 million lire. The bribe grew up to 50 million a year in the following years."* Martelli does not take it (a unique case for a Socialist leader), but he pays it (with his father-in-law's money, we suppose). Moral of the story: the system of corruption does not admit exceptions. Never let a regular contract exist in the city of the bribes: a dangerous example would be established. If it was heard that in Milan there's an entrepreneur who wins contracts on a regular basis, others would pretend the same and the Tangentopoli system would tumble down. So, once a hole is discovered, Martelli rushes to close it with a nice 'mazzetta'.

I met Marco Travaglio for the first time when he came to my hometown to launch the book on Tangentopoli called *Mani Pulite. La vera storia. Da Mario Chiesa a Silvio Berlusconi* in 2002, the year after *L'Odore dei Soldi*. Travaglio was one of the three authors, the others were G. Barbacetto and P. Gomez. Travaglio had been invited by the very symbol of the Mani Pulite investigation, former magistrate Antonio Di Pietro, who had left the Judiciary after Clean Hands to form a party called *Italia dei Valori – Italy of Values –* in 1998 which meant to give political representation to the 'moral minority' and to be the real parliamentary opposition to B.'s *Forza Italia/PDL*. *Italy of Values* represented about 10% of the voters up to last year, then it almost disappeared since most of its electorate voted for the newly formed *5 Star Movement*. Back to the episode, I thought I knew all there was to know about Mani Pulite but, when I listened to Travaglio, I was deeply upset: I had never heard such a precision in the reconstruction of a contemporary historical period. He had collected data, the witnesses' declarations and the magistrates and the judges' official sentences: in putting them together a clear picture had come out, facts and not fiction, so that the real story of Mani Pulite, its system of endemic corruption became clear to me in its entirety as never before. This is 'Travaglio's way', a journalistic attitude that he has carried on to these days, which is based on the assembling of precise historical facts 'dressed' with the author's personal comments and witty humour. Travaglio has kept informing us on the issues that are regularly hidden in the average press: up to now he has written an impressive number of books, articles, editorials, has appeared in many TV shows, has made DVDs and theatre shows and takes part on a regular basis in the independent programme *Servizio Pubblico* broadcast by TV network *La7*. Even if he has become very famous, he still remains one of the spokesmen of the 'moral minority', a reliable source of information, as this essay proves. That's why I usually quote articles from the independent newspaper *Il Fatto Quotidiano*, of which he is the editor-in-chief, a voice of truth, far away from the political parties' influence.

> *Take the art works of Botticelli, Leonardo da Vinci, Michelangelo, Tintoretto and Caravaggio, the operas of Verdi and Puccini, the cinema of Federico Fellini, add the architecture of Venice, Florence and Rome and you have just a fraction of Italy's treasures from over the centuries.*
>
> *While the country is renowned for these and other delights, it is also notorious for its precarious political life and has had several dozen governments since the end of World War II.*
>
> *There were high hopes at the time that the "mani pulite" scandal would give rise to a radical reform of Italian political culture, but these hopes were dashed when the old structures were replaced by a new political landscape dominated by the multi-millionaire businessman Silvio Berlusconi, who himself became increasingly mired in scandals and corruption affairs* (BBC Italy profile)

We, the Italians, the majority of the Italians with the exceptions of the 'moral minority', have always been at least suspicious about the State. We had centuries of foreign dominations before the

Risorgimento in the XIX century in which state officials were 'enemies'. We have never developed a civic awareness, a sense of community, of belonging to some common ground. We are a nation of immaculate homes and dirty streets. We have always seen taxpaying as acts of 'coglioneria' [crap, a load of balls] and tax evasion as actions of heroic resistance to public unfair burdens. We are a country in which politicians themselves advocate tax evasion in order to get consent, headed by B. who has practiced this national sport in such a brilliant way. Recommendations have always been an everyday form of survival. We have endless metaphorical expression on these attitudes: *fatta la legge trovato l'inganno* [the law is made, the con is found], '*cca nisciuno è fesso* [nobody is dumb around here], a Neapolitan motto used by the great movie comedian Totò. Our national mentality is in those old movies, in every classic 'commedia all'italiana', with its characters portraying the meanness of the average Italian played by iconic actor Alberto Sordi, the con-man tough to the weak and humble to the powerful. In recent years, actor director Nanni Moretti has revised the 'commedia' with his witty hilarious films about our Berlusconian society. B.'s nickname *il Caimano* comes from his 2006 movie, a surrealistic portrait of il Cavaliere. We are a nation of great artists and inventors, the land of Raffaello and Leonardo, the cradle of Renaissance, we are the land of the 'made in Italy' and of the best cuisines in the world: we are so creative also, alas, because we are a country of individualists, a country who created the Roman Empire and that today let the archaeological site of Pompei fall to pieces for public 'sinecura' [carelessness]. We are a land of contradictions: Italy is an open air museum filled with breathtaking landscapes in which living could be easy if below it the Inferno of inefficiency and dishonesty didn't spoil it all.

What's strange reading the story [of Mani Pulite] *with a foreigner's eyes is that everyone had always known that corruption was rife in Italy, many even had the evidence, but until the early 90s nothing was done. It was politically or legally impossible. For years commentators had derisively talked about 'petrodollari' (the money they salted away in offshore accounts thanks to deals cut with the energy industry). Elio Vetri and Gianni Barbacetto had already published* Milano degli scandali, *Giampaolo Pansa had written* Il Malloppo (The Swag). *The scandal of 92-94, then, wasn't shocking because of the discovery of corruption; the real shock came in the fact that it was finally possible for the millions of long-*

suffering, law-abiding Italians to do something about it writes Jones in his exhaustive chapter on Clean Hands in the book aforementioned.

As we have seen in the first part of this paper, Clean Hands razed to the ground Tangentopoli. Politicians and the traditional political parties tumbled down, as if falling in the dark depths of Martin's 'sublime' picture *The Last Days of his Wrath*, the rage of the Lord for the corruption of mankind the rage of magistrate Antonio Di Pietro, the iconic investigator, the Perry Mason of the righteous in the public mind of those days.

The Clean Hands pool enjoyed an enormous groundswell of support writes Jones. *People began wearing T-Shirts saying* 'Milano ladrona, Di Pietro non perdona' *('Thieving Milan, Di Pietro is not forgiving'). Finally it seemed as if those words written in every Italian courtroom,* 'La legge è uguale per tutti, *'the law's equal for all'*, were coming true. Endless graffiti appeared across Italy: 'Grazie Di Pietro', *or* 'Forza Colombo' [another investigative magistrate of the pool] (...) Bettino Craxi was showered with coins outside the Hotel Raphael in Rome: 'Do you want these as well?' chanted the mob*. Seen from today's point of view, this meant that in those days people cared. *The country plunged into the enthusiasm prompted by Clean Hands as if in a rite of collective liberation. With widespread indignation against the corrupt and the corrupters, largely fed by the press, an entire population deluded itself that it could in some way redeem itself of its own vices in the arena of civil ethics*.... Of course those were the days before *Mediaset*, before B.'s WMD, before B.'s occupation of every public space, before its propaganda, before the truth was made to disappear, all instruments that has led to today's indifference. At present the mob throwing coins at Craxi in 1992 is just a vanishing recollection, even if, occasionally, the 'moral minority' still gather to demonstrate against il Cavaliere. As we know from part one of this paper, 'B. backed up the investigation through his media empire he already owned and, in doing so, helped to create a political vacuum which he himself would soon occupy, playing the part of the brand new saviour of the country: actually a corrupt system, 'Prima Repubblica' style, was soon re-established. Becoming Prime Minister meant not to end up like his friend Bettino: B. understood, being a man of some genius, that being at the same time entrepreneur and politician, law enforcer and (allegedly) corrupter, like no one had ever been before, and simultaneously controlling media information made him untouchable'.

In March 2011, during B.'s last cabinet, il Cavaliere announced what he called 'an epochal reformation of the Judiciary', an old obsession of his since the beginning of his public life: the submission of the Judiciary to political power was to be Berlusconi's final legacy. A 'plurinquisito' – multi-prosecuted person – planning a reform of the justice system is bizarre in itself, to say the least; in this particular case the reform was planned as a punishment for the magistrates and inevitably it would have ended up as a favour for the criminals. On march 10, during the press conference to present this epochal 'revolution' just approved by his government, Prime Minister Berlusconi said that if this reformation had been approved twenty years before, the Judiciary would not have invaded politics and Mani Pulite would not have existed, giving this statement a positive meaning without realizing the inner sense of the sentence.

The Judiciary reformation was also linked to the so called 'processo breve' – short trial - "Misure per la tutela del cittadino contro la durata indeterminata dei processi" – "measures to protect the citizen against the undetermined duration of trials", a bill which was allegedly invented in 2009 by avv. Ghedini, B's lawyer and *PDL* MP, and it was approved by the Senate in January 2010. The 'processo breve' is another example of inverted logic and its public acceptance another victory of the *doublethink* process over free will. Since the Italian judiciary system is a snail, as I said in the very beginning, instead of fuelling money, means and intelligence into it, the solution to the problem is to cut down the length of the proceedings. If a trial is not finished by the time established by the law, it dies, and the accused person is set free… and the deadlines are always too short to bring them to conclusion. It's an expansion of the 'power' of the statute of limitations, B.'s best legal friend. The 'processo breve', in association with the 'legittimo impedimento', aimed at killing the Mills and the *Mediaset* cases in which B. was involved, and in general to save the *cricca* – slang word for *dirt* meaning the corrupt –, whose major representatives sat in Parliament (as we already know, the Mills trial was killed but the *Mediaset* trial came to the final verdict on August 1, 2013, just a few days before its deadline). On 12 November, 2009, former B.'s lawyer Carlo Taormina defined it as "vergognoso, criminale, criminogeno e ridicolo" – "shameful, criminal, crime inducing and ridiculous". According to the Palermo president of the *Associazione Nazionale Magistrati* Nino Di

Matteo "only minor trials against poor fellows will reach their conclusion before the statute of limitations. All the other trials, even the most important ones dealing with mafia-linked crimes, will vanish in the air". In September 2010 the bill was abandoned because of the public opinion's negative judgments, but in March 2011 B. picked it up again to match it with his epic reformation.

So, as far as Mani Pulite is concerned, in 1994 B. backed it up and took advantage of it in his first victory at the political elections while in 2011 he said that if this reformation had been approved twenty years before, Mani Pulite would not have existed, and that it would have been a general advantage. The reversal of B.'s opinion is clear: today he is in the same position as the accused Prima Repubblica politicians; consequently the understatement is that the blame is not to be put on corrupt politics, but on the magistrates that fight political corruption and crime, implying the politicians' right to commit offenses and to annihilate the Judiciary. This planned destruction of legality, that in the future will make organized crime less punishable, is taking place in a mafia-infested country. Even if physically B. won't be there, this is really going to be his ultimate legacy, one of the nastiest aspects of Berlusconi's philosophy that is not going to disappear with its inventor, who, politically speaking, has not been completely defeated jet.

Everybody knows that the Tangentopoli system has never died in Italy and that the Mani Pulite investigation and trials put an end to the Prima Repubblica and its ruling parties but not to endemic corruption. On the contrary, Berlusconi's rule helped to create a mood in the country that facilitated the spreading of crooked business since il Cavaliere as Prime Minister was felt as actual and philosophical guarantee of non-punishment for illegality. Everyone who can see behind standard regime information knows it. But just to prove it beyond reasonable doubt in February 2014 the European Commission issued its first *Anti-Corruption Report* that stated that half the amount of corruption in the EU – 60 billion euros – is Italian, as I discuss in part three, chapter one. To give further undisputable evidence of the commission's report, two maxi corruption scandals, precise updated blueprints of the original Tangentopoli, exploded in May and June 2014. The first is linked to the 2015 Milan Expo, setting the crime scene in the same city and with the same protagonists since, almost unbelievably, some of the people that were arrested are the very same who had ended up in jail in 1992, a paradox which is only apparent. The second is the *Mose* scandal in Venice, a corruption case in the rich hard-labouring God-fearing North-East, an area that, socially speaking, is still deeply Victorian, with its façade *perbenismo*, its fake respectability and its hypocrisy. All these 'virtues' are personified in the three leading actors of the scandal: *PDL* former governor of Veneto and today's *Forza Italia* senator Giancarlo Galan – a modern male version of Lady Bracknell –, *PD* mayor of Venice Giorgio Orsoni – who had no problem in accepting illegal funding for his political campaigns – and the great corrupter, engineer Giovanni Mazzacurati, an old-fashioned hyper-catholic construction magnate. Venice too, like all the other landmarks of the beauty of Italy we are discussing, is now showing its hidden dark side. It is not worth saying that the breath of il Cavaliere can be felt just below the surface: the Expo cupola kept sending him pizzini to keep him updated and seek approval, as *Repubblica* writes on May 14 in *Expo, i verbali: così la cupola portava i pizzini ad Arcore e a Maroni* quoting official documents of the 'procura'. Moreover, B. himself and Dell'Utri were the real godfathers at the Great-Gatsby-style wedding of Galan in 2009.

Italian commentators said the scandal surrounding the Universal Exposition, which has been in the planning and construction stages for more than six years and is expected to draw millions of visitors next year, was another example of Italy's inability to keep corruption out of major events writes Reuters in the article *Arrests, corruption probe cast cloud over Italy's Expo 2015*. In Lombardy there existed a full-scale 'contract cupola' of string-pullers that acted like middle-men between construction companies and politicians, public officers and Expo managers. The oldie-but-goldie bribe system was used exactly like in the old days: the builder gives black money to the cupola in order to win a public contract, the cupola keep a percentage and corrupts the politicians and the public officials; so the builder, who submitted an inflated tender, wins it, gets the public money, builds the infrastructures he was paid for – which inevitably will cost many times as much and will be finished much later than planned – and keeps the 'change', much more than the bribe money he spent in advance for the politicians and the 'middle-men'.

Seven people were arrested in the Expo operation. The cupola boss was former DC regional secretary in the eighties Gian Stefano Frigerio, nicknamed 'il professore' and 'l'infame'– 'the infamous'. His special secretary was former DC member Sergio Cattozzo. The 'organizers in charge of connection activities with the political world', as the investigators write in their arrest request, were Primo Greganti, a former senior official in the Communist party; Luigi Grillo, a *PDL* MP until 2013, former DC leader. The main character in charge to manipulate contracts was the Expo's director general of the contracts office Angelo Paris, a former secretary of the *Union of the Christian Democrats* party in Liguria (a small party of ex DC politicians). Since he was hired in September 2013 he 'immediately demonstrated a surprising willingness to work for the criminal organization'. *According to investigators,* writes Corriere della Sera in the article *Seven arrests in Milan Expo Scandal, Angelo Paris was "totally in thrall to the will of the [criminal] association". "I'll give you all the contracts you want if you give me a hand with my career", Mr. Paris says in one transcript in which he is speaking to members of the group. The criminal association was thus able to gain advance knowledge of decisions about Expo 2015, such as plans for the pavilions of a number of countries or problem-solving interventions for the Vie d'Acqua [Waterways] project. The group, which has been operating for "one and a half or two years", is thought since mid-2013 to have influenced, or attempted to influence, a number of Expo contracts, including the tender for service architectures, which was steered towards Vicenza-based businessman, Enrico Maltauro, now in jail. Prosecutors allege that Mr. Maltauro paid out "€30-40,000 a month" in cash or consultancy payments to the "contract cupola".* The last to be arrested was Antonio Rognoni, a former manager of an infrastructure company owned by the Lombardy regional government, *Infrastrutture Lombarde*. The papers published pictures and videos, handed out by the magistrates, which show Maltauro giving a 15.000 euro bribe to Cattozzo.

In the editorial titled *Ora e Sempre Tangentopoli – Tangentopoli forever* – published by *Repubblica* on May 9, 2014 – there is a part dedicated to the role of politics in the matter:

> *The 'reference politicians'? For sure, but they are not as useful as they were once, when they counted more. Now there is a personal system, politicians are in the background. Please do not say it is the new Tangentopoli. It is worse, much worse. It is a different system,*

upon which the Manuale Cencelli of the electoral strength, which was used to share the bribes according to percentage, does not count anymore. Of course politics will be able to favour careers and public office appointments, as Gianni Letta and his right arm Luigi Bisignani have been doing for decades ... For example Enrico Maltauro, chief of the greatest construction company in Veneto, has permeated every space and is always in the judicial chronicles without anybody asking whether it may be the case to leave him out of the biggest public contracts. Arrested in 1992, when the public works cupola governed by Christian Democrats and Socialists reigned, Maltauro has re-entered the lobby in grand style, like Greganti and Frigerio. Worse, like one of the masters of the men of Expo 2015. Should not the Milan epochal event have been the epitome of crystal clear transparency? No 'ndrangheta, no corrupt contracts, no Comunione e Liberazione and Compagnia Delle Opere, no Lupi, no Formigoni ...

As we have said, Greganti and Frigerio were convicted of illicit financing of political parties in 1993 during the Clean Hands operation and their comeback is only apparently a paradox. Actually they have not returned, they have never gone away, like the criminal system they represent, dark Italy's economic backbone. In the investigation hearings it was declared that 'il Gatto e la Volpe' (Greganti e Frigerio) were allowed to enter public offices because the personnel was too young and did not recognize them; in reality, they were allowed to enter just because they were identified, since they hold secrets that would ruin many politicians and officials. Greganti was nicknamed 'the tomb' since he never talked in the period he spent in jail in the days of Tangentopoli, and has always kept his mouth shut up to now, but the Roman palaces and the Milan institutions are still trembling for fear of his revelations. "There is nothing new under the sun," Antonio Di Pietro told *La Repubblica*. "Corruption continues to exist, today like back then, and nothing has been done to introduce transparency in the public administration," he said. The Expo scandal is another piece of evidence that the corruption system has always been bipartisan, a grand coalition – or *inciucio* –, like the Italian governments since the fall of the last Berlusconi cabinet in 2011. The secret deal between *Forza Italia* and the *PD* that has characterized the Berlusconi age in order to leave all the dirty stones unturned – which is a basic idea of this book – is today personified in the so called 'Patto del Nazareno'[7], the 2014 Renzi-Berlusconi deal, of which we discuss in part three, chapter two, which casts a huge shadow over the 'revolution' in public morality so strongly advertised by the new Prime Minister, *demolition man* Matteo Renzi. The presence of B. in the Expo scandal is tangible, discreet but probably fundamental, like his existence in today's political scene. Il Cavaliere is a founding father to whom approval must be asked. The 'infamous' Frigerio, the 74 year old 'contract cupola' boss, an old-fashioned character, felt safe 'because I never speak on the mobile', but sent *pizzini* – mafia word for written notes – instead. For example, Frigerio says – according to prosecutors – that after Rognoni (in charge to manipulate contracts) had gone to jail some months before, he sent a note to B. that read: *the best solution for the direction [of Infrastrutture] is called Paris*. Paris also went to Arcore to meet Berlusconi and his close circle to be sponsored by il Cavaliere promising – as we have said – that *I'll give you all the contracts you want if you give me a hand with my career*. Unluckily, old-fashioned Frigerio did not realize that the Arcore phone cell tracked down all the trips of his confidence-man. A final curiosity: the headquarters of the criminal association was the Tommaso Moro [Thomas More] club near the Central Station, named after the philosopher whose celebrated *Utopia* describes the "best state".

Much ado about nothing seems to be the most appropriate title after the *sentenza di patteggiamento* – a verdict negotiated with the judges before the actual trial – that the major defendants obtained at the preliminary hearing in Milan on November 27, 2014 (Cattozzo, Grillo, Paris, Greganti, Frigerio). The verdicts, more all less the same, are about 3 years in jail, but only virtually: social services, home arrest, 'semilibertà' and of course a 'discount' of the penalty are the privileges they are granted. Only Antonio Rognoni is now facing a regular trial which started in December 2014. The big names of politics did not enter the investigation, and the impression is that again everything is vanishing in the air, Gattopardo style one more time. Similarly, the *Mose* scandal helped the creation of the *Autorità*

---

7 *Nazareno* is the nickname given to the PD headquarter, situated near Via del Nazareno in Rome.

Nazionale Anticorruzione headed by magistrate R. Cantone, but the general impression is the Cupola is still there, alive and kicking.

On the same day, the former Home Secretary and Economic Development Minister of the Berlusconi governments Claudio Scajola was arrested for helping a Southern Italian businessman convicted of mafia association to flee Italian justice and escape abroad. The criminal is Amedeo Matacena, one of the founders of *Forza Italia* in Calabria, MP from 1994 to 2001, a successful entrepreneur in the business of the ferry-boats linking Calabria to Sicily. He was ruined by the anti-mafia magistrates' investigations and sentenced to five years, four months in jail for external concourse in mafia association. Now he is fugitive with an international arrest warrant over his shoulders; he was discovered in Dubai in August 2013, the city in which he is at present, as he was waiting to flee to Lebanon, to join Marcello Dell'Urti, thanks to Scajola's help and the former minister's connections with the Lebanese 'black lobby' I describe in the initial pages of this chapter. A Home Secretary helping a mafia convict to escape abroad is in itself a paradox that I imagine my foreign readers will find at least astonishing; as usual, not so in our society, so drenched in scandals and so used to it even if, in the long run, episodes like the ones I am discussing now explain the unexpected and sudden success of the populist protest *5 Star Movement*. Scajola is another typical former Christian-Democrat who embraced Berlusconism after the crash of his original party and, like his fellow-politicians, has had trouble with justice since 1983, when he spent two months in San Vittore jail in Milan because of an investigation about public contracts for the Sanremo casino. Sacjola is famous all over the country because in 2010 he seriously declared he did not know that his house near the Colosseum in Rome had been partially paid by a corrupt construction firm owner who had just been arrested. Notwithstanding his Roman house with a view, on May 9, 2014, he was arrested in a luxury hotel, in the *dolce vita* area of via Veneto, in which he had spent the night with a young lady who was supposed to be Matacena's lawyer. From the pictures we saw, the lawyer is pretty similar to a *bunga-bunga* girl: once the fashion is launched by the boss, his confidence-men are entitled to follow.

Going on a gondola on the Grand Canal in Venice is for sure one of the most romantic experience in the world, nevertheless under the water surface most of the city is rotten and an occasional bad smell might disturb the lovers' ride. The rotten underwater city turning into the splendour of the outer Renaissance palaces has now become a tailor-made symbol of the *Serenissima – Most Serene Republic*. The city is menaced by rising waters entering Venice lagoon and that's why the *Mose* flood barrier was planned in the eighties. But on June 4, 2014 the *PD* mayor of Venice Giorgio Orsoni and thirty-three other people were arrested as part of an inquiry into fraud linked to the *Mose* project. Investigators also requested the arrest of *PDL* former governor of Veneto and today's *Forza Italia* senator Giancarlo Galan (his arrest must be approved by the Italian parliament). Three hundred officers carried out raids to seize €40m in assets, after a three-year investigation by magistrates, who allege contractors created a €25m slush fund for kickbacks to politicians overseeing the work. As for the Expo scandal, "Politicians have learned nothing," said prosecutor Carlo Nordio. "We have discovered a system which is very similar to Tangentopoli, involving characters who were involved back then, but much more complex and sophisticated." The standard bipartisan political involvement is guaranteed in this case too.

The Venice scandal is actually bigger than the Expo case but very clear as far as its organization is concerned: The *Consorzio Nuova Venezia*, the unique *Mose* project contractor, had literally bought the city and all its institutions so that no one could bother it both in the way the barriers had to be built and while creating slush funds, part of which were used to bribe the institutions the *Consorzio* controlled. It's Berlusconi's alleged way, the same procedure we have seen in the opening chapter of this book in the *Mediaset* case and in general throughout B.'s suspected career of full-scale corrupter. The scandal immediately reminded me of Francesco Rosi's 1963 movie *Mani sulla Città – Hands over the City* – in which a ruthless Neapolitan land developer and elected city councilman manages to use his political power to make personal profit in a large scale suburban real estate deal. The film is also an example of a pre-Berlusconi conflict of interests. It belongs to the golden age of Italian cinema and is closely link to *neo-realism*; above all it tells us that the Tangentopoli system existed long before the new *ventennio*, in the period of the pax mafiosa between the mafia and the State, in the era of Andreotti and Ciancimino.

Gian Antonio Stella is one of the best Italian investigative journalists and editorialists. He writes for the *Corriere della Sera* about injustices in Italy, from minor but meaningful cases to nationwide scandals. He became famous in 2007 as co-author of the bestseller *La Casta – The Caste. How Italian politicians became untouchable –*, a survey on the privileges and the corruption of the Italian politicians who form a sort of unchangeable caste of their own. The book introduced the word into the vocabulary of Italian politics and daily life. In his article *Mose's quadrupled costs* in the *Corriere della Sera*, Stella points out the way in which the *Consorzio* got the public contract, how the deadline has moved further in time up to today and how the costs quadrupled in the course of time, all pre-condition to let the *Consorzio* become absolute master of the city. Hereafter are some extracts:

Pretend emergencies

The Mose affair is emblematic. It has everything, starting with pretend emergencies of work needing to be done at whatever cost to such dramatically tight deadlines that there is no time to properly draft plans, select contractors, put out tenders or award contracts. Emergency followed emergency for 31 years, nine times as long as it took China to build the eight-lane, 32 kilometre-long Donghai bridge linking Shanghai to the Yangshan islands.

The Mose affair has short cuts to get round – "get round", not "change" – over-complicated regulations by setting up a sole operator, the Consorzio Venezia Nuova (CVN), which after three decades of competition-free activity, and with a thoroughly scandal-compromised top management, today denies any wrongdoing and claims to be as pure as the driven snow.

The 1995 deadline

The Mose affair also exposes the unhealthy relationship between the dark sides of politics and business, a connivance impervious to any meaningful monitoring of costs, materials, people or timetables. Remember the 4 November 1988 pledge by the deputy PM of the day, Gianni De Michelis, when he unveiled the prototype Mose after years of wrangling: "The deadline is still 1995. Of course, it might have to be put back a bit". That deadline whooshed past two decades ago. (...) "Left and Right were in agreement on Mose. No one listened to me", Massimo Cacciari [a famous philosopher and former mayor of Venice] has alleged many times over the years. Yesterday, he repeated his charges: "The procedures made it impossible for me as mayor to intervene". The Most Serene Republic would never have tolerated this top-down arrangement.

Budget €1.3 billion, probable cost €6 billion

This unsavoury affair also features the constantly rising costs that plague Italian public works. Mose should have cost €1.3 billion, at today's prices. But year after year, review after review and tweak after tweak, the total has broken the €5 billion barrier and could well reach €6 billion.

Consorzio Nuova Venezia has had a boss for the last thirty years, 82 year old engineer Giovanni Mazzacurati, mastermind and string-puller of the illegal deal, who is now in jail. The never ending trail of public money that reached Venice from Rome was used to create slush funds: investigators said they followed a complex cash trail between companies and politicians that passed through the tiny state of San Marino as well as overseas banks. Thanks to this black money, Mazzacurati and associates formed the *cupola del malaffare* we have just described which had, literally, their hands over the city by controlling every public authority in the area. The most expansive figure in the bribe pay book was Giancarlo Galan's, who allegedly received 1.000.000 euros a year on a regular basis and had his Gasby-style XIV century country villa refurbished for free. Galan was given a 'life salary', regardless of the single piece of work he had to facilitate, also because he was President of the Region (he held this position for 15 years) and afterwards remained the top authority in Veneto and a sure link with Berlusconi. Then on the pay book came the mayor of Venice (PD), who had his 2010 political campaign illegally sponsored (500.000 euros), the region's town planning councilman, who received 250.000 euros to control the Vigilance Commission, the Water Magistrates, who was paid to avoid controls on the work of the Consorzio, and the regional technicians who did not have to interfere with tests. Then there were the national politicians like Milanese, the right arm of former Minister of Economy and Finances Giulio

Tremonti, to guarantee a constant flood of public money from Rome to Venice. So on and so forth, going down the ladder of local power, Mazzacurati spread his hands over Venice. To close down the circle, on June 6, 2014, *Repubblica* published a reportage titled *Cops and Thieves, the double-dealing of the tax policemen. From Spaziante to Milanese, from the Expo to the Mose to the Unipol case: here is why in all the latest bribe scandals the unfaithful officials of the Fiamme Gialle always come out.*

The magistrates say that the very Catholic president Mazzacurati, a devout man of strong DC roots who felt assured by Berlusconi's power, has personally delivered 22.5 million euros in bribes. He was forced to retire in July 2013 and received, after he had been arrested, the end-of-service bonus of €7 million from the *Consorzio*, the equivalent of 31 years of the president of Italy's salary paid to a man facing criminal charges. *Let me ask you one question, is your money that good, will it buy you forgiveness, do you think it could? I think you'll find, when your death takes its toll, all the money you made will never buy back your soul:* young Bob Dylan's words directed to the masters of war of his days seem to fit pious Mazzacurati like a glove.

The last part of Stella's article is titled *So many scandals, so few in jail:*

> *Expo 2015, the restoration of Pompeii, the G8 meeting on La Maddalena and then at L'Aquila, initial work and reconstruction in Abruzzo, the world swimming championships and Mose. For years, no major event in Italy has escaped the taint of corruption. Every arrest has been followed by howls of complaint. Everyone wonders why nothing has changed, why it happens here and so on and so forth. But when the dust has settled, laws that looked ab-so-lu-tely-ur-gent are put off till tomorrow, or next week, or next month, and then from autumn till the next summer.*

Tobias Jones, in the chapter titled *Penalties and Impunities* of his book *The Dark Side of Italy*, makes it very clear: in Italy nobody pays, *non paga nessuno*, and consequently crime keeps operating. B.'s case docet: a powerful serial law offender that has in reality never been punished is like gasoline poured over the fire of criminality (I will be back on *Penalties and Impunities* in the chapter I dedicate to that other foolish craze which is Italian football). Hereafter are Jones's words:

> *The debate is really about another type of penalty, or the lack of it. It's the fact that, as Italy's moral minority always complains,* non paga nessuno, *which basically means that no one in Italy is ever, ever punished for anything: 'nobody pays'. Ever since I had arrived I had heard one half of the country, that law-abiding half, complain bitterly and incessantly about the furbi who appear to bend and break the law at will, without ever facing the consequences. In Italy there are no penalties other than on the football pitch. Crime is never followed by punishment because, at least for the powers-that-be, there's guaranteed impunity. You can get away with anything (…)*

It is easy to foresee hard times for demolition man Matteo Renzi and his advertised intent to fight corruption for good, as part of his 'revolutionary' new government. The young and too optimistic Prime Minister is surrounded and backed by a parliament of bipartisan corrupt MPs, all potential Pat Garrett ready to hunt down the man who they say is their friend.

[The Mose trial is starting on April 14, 2016. There are eight defendants, among whom the former PD mayor Orsoni and Forza Italia senator Altero Matteoli, two times minister in previous Berlusconi's governments. Many other defendants were granted a 'patteggiamento' – an agreement with the judges – in 2014, among whom Giancarlo Galan, the contemporary male version of Lady Bracknell. Galan was arrested in July 2014 but in October he agreed on a 2 year-10 month sentence and a 2,6m euros sanction, even if the estimated illegal money he received was over 15m euros. As far as I understand from different media, Galan, incredibly, is still a MP with a full salary plus a 'vitalizio' – life salary – of 80,000 euros a year and a TFR – a severance package - of 96,000 euros as a former governor of Veneto. There seems to be no law that forces him to step down; in Italy, even objective facts are difficult to understand, another post-Cavaliere legacy.

Even the other iconic figure of this case is hard to locate: as *Il Fatto Quotidiano* writes on May 31, 2015, Mazzacurati is in his rented villa in La Jolla, California, and has conveniently lost his memory because of his old age. But I am not that sure he has forgotten the last tranche of his 7m euros exit bonus he granted himself that he has not got yet, about 1m euros the *Autorità Nazionale Anticorruzione* tracked down and confiscated.

As I write in the introduction, in December 2014 we discovered that also Rome was not willing to stay behind. The magistrates, in fact, found out that the Eternal City was controlled and actually run by an up-to-then unknown cupola that was named *Mafia Capitale*. I published an extensive article on this topic in my official blog that you may want to read, to complete this chapter, titled *Mafia Capitale: dirty hands over the Eternal City.*].

Let's now go back to 1992 – 94, the times of the original Tangentopoli after this long but due digression on the flourishing state of corruption in today's Italy. It is now self-evident that two main consequences of Mani Pulite are essential for our narrative: the sudden erasing of the leading political elite who had ruled the country since the end of WWII and the political vacuum it created. These two facts took place at the same time in which the mafia was waging its most violent war against the State, a conflict that was fought to force the State to make a new deal with *Cosa Nostra* in order to re-establish the lost equilibrium. But the interlocutors were vanishing under Mani Pulite's mighty blows and there was nobody there to talk to anymore. When B. entered politics, we know it, he was the right guy at the right time: this is the subject of the next chapter.

Chapter two

Deal with the devil?

the *trattativa Stato-mafia*

and

Berlusconi's *discesa in campo*

(1992-94)

"Berlusconi, in order to solve his problems, has to solve ours"
Mafia boss Giuseppe Guttadauro in a wiretapped conversation (quote from Wikipedia).

The troubled negotiation between the State and the mafia finally found a conclusion in the guarantees provided by the couple Dell'Utri – Berlusconi in 1994, write the Palermo magistrates, coordinated by Antonio Ingroia, in the previously mentioned *Memoria* in the trial for the 'trattativa Stato – mafia'. The 1992-1994 'trattativa' is an important event that helps to guess B.'s seizure of absolute political power. It was the missing link in a possible logical chain of events, an unbelievable incident that was only imaginable before the new pool in Palermo set out to try to discover the truth.

In those days a desperate Cavaliere was overwhelmed by the burden of justice and consequently by the precarious situation of his business empire: it is logical to presume that entering politics directly was his ultimate chance to protect himself from jail and his firms from economic downturn. It is a fact that Dell'Utri and B. were planning to give birth to *Forza Italia* for the forthcoming political election in 1994. We know that they had to fill the political vacuum since the old 'friends' from DC and PSI were vanishing.

Meanwhile, bloodthirsty Totò Riina and Bernardo Provenzano were the mafia bosses-in-chief. They had won the so called 'second mafia war', an internal feud for mafia leadership that started in 1981 and that ended with the victory of the 'Corleonesi Clan' of the boss Totò Riina. *Cosa Nostra* was bewildered by what the Palermo pool had done: *In 1989 Giovanni Falcone was an anomaly who had broken the mechanism of the peaceful coexistence between State and the mafia* writes Francesco La Licata in *Don Vito. Falcone realized that that was the right time for the final battle against the mafia. The international situation was uniquely favourable: the fall of communism facilitated, in the West, the end of the red danger and made the anticommunist preliminary question almost useless; on behalf of that question every non confessable alliance with the bosses, that were perceived as a barrier to the advent of the Cossacks, had been justified...* Don Totò was worried as well: *the turncoats had massacred Cosa Nostra, the anti-mafia legislation was finally heading to the fight against illegal wealth and, above all, it was understood that Falcone's 'Maxiprocesso' was stable against all the attacks of the 'politica garantista' ['politics in favour of civil rights', an expression used here in a negative sense]. The lower court verdict had panicked Cosa Nostra members and in the meantime the 'maxibis', the 'maxiter' and the trials to the involved politicians were being established. Falcone had to be stopped...* Because of this context the mafia war was launched: the long list of terror attacks they ordered in 1992-93, inside and outside Sicily and both against people and artistic institutions, was unprecedented. As we have just said, the mafia had the same need Dell'Utri presumably had, to fill in the power vacuum created by Mani Pulite, and, moreover, to reestablish a new *pax mafiosa*. But things never go the way they were planned: the intrusion of magistrate Borsellino, a contrast between the two bosses, the arrest of the first 'trattativa' negotiator and the arrival of a new 'traghettatore' – 'ferryman' – made the story take unforeseen turns.

The story of the 'trattativa', not completely unfolded yet, is very complex both because it involves many interconnected people and institutions (mafiosi, turncoats, state officials, secret services, politicians) and because it is based on revealed truth and deviating lies. It is a spy story which, unfortunately, is real. I'll try to keep the story as simple as possible beginning with the timeline which is evocative and useful to back up our discourse: in January 1992, the Court of Cassation confirmed the *Maxiprocesso* verdict and, in so doing, made the final offence to the mafia. According to the revelations of mafiosi turncoats and of Vito Ciancimino, in March 1992 former Palermo mayor, DC MP Salvatore Lima, closely linked to Andreotti, was killed by the mafia. Lima had become the political referent of the 'Corleonesi' as far as justice and mafia trials were concerned and the tie between Andreotti and the mafia. Lima had tried to change the Court of Cassation final verdict of the Maxiprocesso in vain; his murder was a warning to PM Andreotti. The DC and PSI ministers and MPs panicked, the names of future victims were murmured: the first motive for the 'trattativa' had been established. In May 1992 Falcone, the Palermo pool leader, his wife and his three bodyguards were killed while riding on a motorway near Palermo (the 'strage di Capaci', from the name of the village near which the slaughter occurred). A whole part of the motorway exploded: such violence had never been seen in mafia killing up to that moment. In May-June of the same year, with Mani Pulite raging in Milan, the idea of creating *Forza Italia*, a *Fininvest* political party, was developed by Dell'Utri. In the same months two officials of the Carabinieri, on behalf of the State, met Don Vito, who was Riina and Provenzano's emissary, several times: it was the beginning of the 'trattativa' to put an end to mafia violence. Don Vito Ciancimino gave the Carabinieri the 'papello' written by Riina, which is the political programme of Cosa Nostra, a list of requests to the State in exchange for putting an end to violence. As I said previously, these events were told by turncoats and by Don Vito but they have not been confirmed legally up to now, even if the 'giudice per le indagini preliminary' of Caltanissetta, A. Bonaventura Giunta, wrote that *deve ritenersi un dato acquisito quello secondo cui a partire dai primi giorni del mese di giugno del 1992 fu avviata la cosiddetta 'trattativa' tra appartenenti alle istituzioni e l'organizzazione criminale Cosa nostra – it must be considered an acquired fact that in early June 1992 the so-called 'trattativa' between institutional subjects and the criminal organization Cosa nostra started.* In July Borsellino, the other leader of the Palermo pool, and five bodyguards were killed in Palermo (the 'strage di via D'Ameglio', from the name of the street in which the killing took place); the violence equalled Falcone's murder. Borsellino had probably understood that a 'trattativa' was going on between the highest State representatives and Cosa Nostra, a defeat for the State he could not accept. The killings of the two top Palermo magistrates is linked to the embarrassing presence of traitor officials inside the state representatives, aliens with human shapes, a fact our deranged democracy has had to face since the end of the fascist regime; we call it *'Servizi' deviati*, traitor members inside the Italian Secret Services (SISDE, our MI5), working for fascist surviving organizations like the P2 lodge whose aim is to 'deviate' investigations to protect criminals since, generally speaking, their aim is to overthrow democracy. It would later be proved that these villains played an important part in carrying Falcone and above all Borsellino's murder investigations to dead-end tracks.

The story of the investigation and the trials of the Borsellino slaughter is an almost incredible plot, a story within the story that, like so many Italian mysteries, has not been revealed completely yet, and probably never will. It is so fanciful that no Hollywood script writer could imagine such a narrative. The key figure is false turncoat and double-crosser Vincenzo Scarantino, a low rank mafioso who confessed to his taking part in the slaughter and was the key witness in the three Borsellino trials in the nineties (the first was called 'Borsellino primo', 1994-2000, against four mafiosi, the material executors. One was declared not guilty, another given life-sentence, another sentenced to nine years; Scarantino was sentenced to 18 years. The second trial, 'Borsellino bis', 1996-2003, had many mafiosi 'mandanti' – the senders, the masterminds behind the slaughter – at the bar and ended up with many life-sentences and heavy detention verdicts. There was also a third trial, 'Borsellino ter', that started in 1998 in which 26 bosses were accused: the final Cassation verdicts, issued in different times up to 2008, ordered many life sentences and condemned other defendants to various years in jail. Another trial, 'Borsellino quater', started in 2013). The astonishing fact is that Scarantino's declarations were false and consequently seven innocent people were arrested and condemned, some to life-sentence. The truth came out in 2008 when mafioso Gaspare Spatuzza became turncoat and told the real development of the via D'Ameglio slaughter, a report which was proved true and which is much more logical that the one previously provided by Scarantino (Spatuzza has also given explosive information about B. and Dell'Utri's role in the 1993 mafia slaughters that I'll report later on). According to his account, other different mafia bosses like Giuseppe Graviano and Salvatore Madonia were responsible for the killings. A new trial against the real senders and the material executors started in March 2013, the 'Borsellino quater'; Scarantino and other former turncoats are at the bar again for false testimony. Why did Scarantino lie? Who instructed him? Scarantino admitted his lies for the first time in 1995 in a TV interview but was not believed until in 1999 the appeal court in the 'Borsellino primo' trial declared him unreliable and consequently changed some of the lower court verdicts. During the 'Borsellino bis' trial in 1998 Scarantino withdrew his accusations claiming of having been maltreated in jail and having been forced to become a false turncoat by the authorities in charge of the Borsellino slaughter who were questioning him in prison; they also forced him, he said, to learn by heart what he had to say at the trial. The judges did not believe him and the verdicts they gave were based on his former testimony: Scarantino witnessed both against the mastermind bosses, led by Totò Riina, and against the material executioners. In February 2002, at the 'Borsellino bis' appeal trial Scarantino changed his mind again: he declared: "I withdrew because I was threatened [by the mafia], the truth is what I said in the first instance trial". Anyway, Scarantino's original withdrawal had to wait for Spatuzza to be believed. In July 2009, one year after Spatuzza's statements, at the seventeenth anniversary of the slaughter, Riina told his lawyer to tell journalists: "They killed him. I am tired of being the lightning conductor of Italy". His lawyer explained that "Mr Riina meant that the Borsellino massacre was made by characters tied to the institutions". Moreover, the lawyer declared that Riina said that he was "object and not subject of the 'trattativa'" and that "the 'trattativa' passed above him". Incredibly, Scarantino was the 'guest star' of the January 30, 2014 episode of *Servizio Pubblico* in which he confirmed his accusations of having been forced by the investigators to play the role of false turncoat with maltreatments and menaces but he refused to mention the names of the people who 'taught' him, except for the police superintendent of the investigative squad, 'questore' La Barbera, now deceased. As a final climax, Scarantino, who wore a wool hat and a Guy Faulk type white mask on the TV show, was arrested for sexual abuse as soon as the broadcast ended. As I have said, the investigation which followed Borsellino's murder proved the presence of secret services near the location of the explosion since there was an undercover SISDE base nearby. In 2007 the Caltanissetta magistrates opened a fourth investigative leg on the 'mandanti occulti' – the undisclosed 'senders' – that deals with mafia, politics and business connections and with the role played by personnel from the 'deranged' secret services in the slaughter. On that occasion Borsellino's brother Salvatore wrote an open letter to the *Ministro degli Interni* [Home Secretary] of the time, former Senator

Mancino, now a defendant in the 'trattativa' trial and one of the characters that has completely lost recollection of the events of the period, titled *July 19, 1992: a state slaughter*. It is now a fact that a Carabinieri captain was seen leaving the crime scene carrying Borsellino's briefcase just after the explosion. Most likely, inside there was Borsellino's personal red agenda in which he wrote all his professional notes. This agenda, like so many other things in this country, disappeared and was lost forever. At this point, in this too real John-le-Carrè style spy mystery, the overwhelming questions are many. It seems to be a plausible fact that the leader of the Palermo pool was killed because of his knowledge of the negotiations and his opposition. Many clues suggests that Borsellino met Mancino two days before the massacre at the Home Ministry in Rome and that in that moment he came to know about the negotiations, but Mancino keeps denying the meeting. Were the SISDE's alleged cover-up and side-tracking made to hide the illegal 'trattativa'? Were they the 'servizi segreti deviati' or were they the regular secret services? Was it a kind of direct state killing? Was Riina, the image of the bloodthirsty mafioso godfather in the public mind, used as scapegoat, as 'lightning conductor'? This paragraph of mine is another example, among all the possible ones, of the erosion of democracy I am discussing in this work. The foolish fact is the collective loss of memory of the State's high officials while only the mafia talks, forced by the '41-bis' prison protocol that has given birth to the turncoats' revelations. It is not a coincidence that '41-bis' and the status of the 'pentiti' are the two most important requests in the 'papello.' In my opinion, today the State representatives of the period involved in the mafia-State negotiations should admit it; that would open a frank discussion on the State behaviour in a particular historical situation from our contemporary perspective, as it happened with the 'caso Moro', the 1976 kidnapping and killing of Prime Minister and DC leader Aldo Moro, perpetuated by the Red Brigades in those 'lead years'. The secret services were there as well, 'justified' by the 'cold war' in the international scene.

Politics and the mafia are two powers that live on the control of the same area: either they fight each other or they reach an agreement - Paolo Borsellino

Let us now go back to the evocative timeline of the 'trattativa' after the Falcone and Borsellino's massacres. In December 1992 Don Vito was unexpectedly arrested while he was negotiating, according to his testimony. Immediately afterwards, another unexpected fact happened: in January 1993, Totò Riina was arrested in Palermo, a few days after Giancarlo Caselli had become Public Prosecutor in Palermo (as the State answer to the killings of the two top pool magistrates). The circumstances of his arrest are unclear, but one fact is very clear: the police 'forgot' to search Totò's shelter for some days and 'forgot' to keep it under surveillance. As a result, the mafiosi came, took all the documents, 'papello' included, and went away undisturbed. What is alleged is that Riina had been sold out by Provenzano. Two police officials would later be trialled for not arresting Provenzano when his location was discovered. Provenzano, less violent and more political, is supposed to have done a deal with the State: he was to become the new *Cosa Nostra* big boss and in return he promised to stop the war. It is also alleged that Don Vito was arrested because his position as mediator was taken by a new character, Marcello Dell'Utri. But mafia violence continued: on May 4, Maurizio Costanzo, a *Canale 5* TV anchorman who disapproved of Dell'Utri's project for a new political party, luckily survived a killing attempt in Rome. On May 27, in Florence, the explosion of a bomb inside a car killed five people and wounded forty-eight next to the Uffizi gallery. On July 27 two more mafia bombs exploded: one in Milan, near a modern art museum, killing five people and wounding many others; the other bomb exploded near two basilicas in Rome. If we believe Ciancimino junior's words, in autumn 1993 Dell'Utri and Provenzano allegedly made a deal: the mafia puts an end to the slaughters and helps B. to win the following year's election; in return B. guarantees the realization of the 'papello' requests on justice and police investigations. At the trial of the officials who didn't arrest Provenzano, Ciancimino junior, as a witness, had no doubt in identifying the new 'ferryman'. He declared: "It is dr. Marcello Dell'Utri, the senator… the *onorevole*. (…) my father was convinced of this not because he had deduced it or because of his imagination. No, my father's source was Lo Verde, who had established a connection with Silvio Berlusconi's 'new politics' one way or the other" (Lo Verde is the code surname for Provenzano who has always been personally linked to Don Vito). If this scenario is real, it is not difficult to understand why in November the new *pax mafiosa* began. Inexplicably, or maybe by now explicably, the bloodiest slaughter planned for December 1993 or January 1994, an explosion that would kill many policemen outside the Stadio Olimpico in Rome during a football match, failed.

For those who believe the scenario I have just described, the time was now ripe and, they think, B. won 1994 elections with the mafiosi's help and thanks to his 'illegal' possession of TV channels, newspapers and magazines, another obvious example of erosion of democracy. In this hypothesis, the man who fills in the political vacuum is the assumed mafiosi's protégé himself: if so, State and anti-State met, and melted in one subject, the fulfilment of an old engagement. In 2006 Provenzano was arrested in Corleone and today he is in jail at '41-bis' protocol even if he is very sick. The deal was over or was it time for Provenzano to 'retire' in favour of a younger big boss?

The book *Don Vito* has a very detailed account of the 'trattativa': the negotiations between State and the mafia are in fact the main part of the book. What may seem strange to foreign eyes is the fact that since 2010 the 'trattativa' was made public by one of the real protagonists but only the 'moral minority' noticed; the *qualunquistica* majority, the real burden of this country, just didn't care, as usual: they just accept the abnormal as normal. When the Palermo magistrates committed the actors of the 'trattativa' for trial a couple of years later, there was much – fake – surprise, especially from the people involved, the ones suffering from incurable amnesia who keep saying, against all odds, that the 'tratttativa' never existed. Ciancimino junior, on the other hand, has made a tough choice: in denouncing the facts to the authorities he has thrown a stone into the lake even if that stone was tied to his arm. Today Ciancimino is inevitably accused of external links to the mafia, having been his father's private and trusty secretary for so long. A choice not very different from previous senator De Gregorio who, by confessing to being bribed by B. to change political jersey, has made the magistrates' task simple but his personal position precarious.

It is in Ciancimino junior's book that the 'papello' is actually shown and explained for the first time. 'Papello' is a word used for the first time by Giovanni Brusca, a mafia boss turned 'pentito' known for having melted a kid of a rival family into acid. Originally it is a Sicilian word for a parchment given to a 'fresher' that has to pay a fee to senior university students who organize the first-year students' parties. *In our case*, Francesco La Licata writes, *the State would have to pay the fee to the mafia, in return for a civil communal life without slaughters.* The infamous 'papello' *has been the obscure object of desire for all the fans of Italian spy stories.* It has become part of everyday language, like the word 'pizzini', the messages written by mafia bosses in rough pieces of paper. The 'papello' is simply a 'pizzino' in which Riina wrote down his requests to the State in order to stop the terror attacks and the killing of politicians: it basically asked for the abolition of 41 bis, the end of confiscations of the mafiosi wealth and of the use of turncoats as source of information, the return to the 'garantista' attitude which had left mafiosi unpunished up to then. *For years we wondered if a 'piece of paper' that, one way or another, showed the indecent tie between the State and the mafia really existed. Even investigators and magistrates worked hard on this.* In the context of the 'trattativa', the 'papello' became a kind of Holy Grail, whose existence was uncertain, spoken of but never proved. It had an aura of mysticism even if its healing quality had turned into harsh requests to the authorities. Until one day Massimo Ciancimino opened his safe and produced the document, which was more a blow to the State, that kept denying the deal, than to the mafia. Ciancimino says he got it in June 1992, handed it over to his father who concealed it inside a book in the library of his house in Rome and picked it out again ten years later. *He [Don Vito] took out a sheet of paper and showed it to me,* says Massimo in the book. *Twelve numbered lines, twelve items: I recognized it at once, the same paper I had half seen: here was the notorious 'papello'.* Today it is in the safe of the Palermo Hall of Justice, but a copy can be seen in the book. In the picture, under the 'papello' there is a note written by Don Vito that reads 'delivered to Carabinieri colonel Mario Mori'. Another picture in the book shows Don Vito's notes to the twelve requests of the 'papello' meant for 'Mancino / Rognoni / ministro guardasigilli' (Virginio Rognoni was the minister of defence from 1990 to 1992, 'ministro guardasigilli' means minister of justice), politicians considered fundamental to realize the proposal. The authenticity of the document was confirmed by the Scientific Police.

Today Totò Riina and Bernardo Provenzano sit at the bar next to former senator Marcello Dell'Utri and senator Calogero Mannino (a Sicilian lawyer and DC leader, Minister in 1991-92, previously accused of external mafia association but declared not guilty in 2010) and next to previous officials of the Carabinieri Mario Mori e Antonio Subranni (the 'trattativa' frontsmen). At the same bar, former Home Secretary and DC leader of the times Nicola Mancino is accused of false testimony, Giovanni Conso (former Secretary of Justice in 1993-94), Adalberto Capriotti (director of the penitentiary administration from July 1993 to June 1995) and Giuseppe Gargani (former Dc leader and MP) are accused of giving public prosecutors false information: DC Sicilian leaders, alleged champions of mafia connections and of *trasformismo*, are always there whenever an illegal plot is investigated, just like our *servizi deviati* and the couple Dell'Utri – Berlusconi. Coincidentally, in today's newspaper I read the following headline: *Mafia slaughters. For the magistrates 'monster face', liaison between the State and the mafia, has a name. Giovanni Aiello, former agent now retired. He should be the man with a deformed face who was in Capaci and should have played a part in unresolved former murders* (Il Fatto Quotidiano, October 8, 2013).

The final word on the 'trattativa' belongs to the investigative magistrates in Palermo in the already quoted *Memoria* that goes along with the submission of the twelve accused people to trial: the 'trattativa' *was about a new coexistence deal between the State and the mafia, without which Cosa Nostra would not have been able to survive and to pass from the First to the Second Republic. A coexistence deal that meant looking for new referents in politics on the one hand and, on the other, for the guarantee of a new armed truce after the bloodshed of those years*. It is for this reason that since 1993 the 'trattativa' went on behind the curtain, without clamour. *The long journey of a travailed negotiation was thus completed: an agreement was found thanks to the guarantees assured by the couple Dell'Utri – Berlusconi (as the converging declarations of Spatuzza, Brusca, Giuffré point out)*. In fact, without any doubt the magistrates affirm that the new deal State-mafia was signed in 1994 *not before menacing the newly established Berlusconi cabinet again*. In October 2009, Gaspare Spatuzza, the mafioso turned 'pentito' in 2008, confirmed Giuffrè statements. Spatuzza testified that his boss Giuseppe Graviano had told him in 1994 that Berlusconi was bargaining with the mafia, concerning a political-electoral agreement between *Cosa Nostra* and Berlusconi's *Forza Italia*.

Spatuzza said Graviano disclosed the information to him during a conversation in a bar Graviano owned in the upscale Via Veneto district in Rome. Dell'Utri was the intermediary, according to Spatuzza. By now both Spatuzza and Ciancimino junior, the key witnesses in the case, have been granted armed escort.

B. and Dell'Utri were also investigated for the early nineties mafia slaughters by the Public Prosecutors of Caltanissetta and Florence for many years. The accusations are incredible: contribution in the 1992 slaughters and in the terror attacks of 1993. These were the investigations on the so called 'covered face instigators'. Both proceedings were closed because there was not enough evidence, but the magistrates' words sounds shocking: the Florence magistrates write that there was *an objective convergence of Cosa Nostra political interests and some qualifying programmatic guidelines of the new organization [Forza Italia] (…) Important results have been reached regarding the fact that Cosa Nostra acted from external inputs, as to confirm what already assumed on a strictly logic basis (…) the initial hypothesis [B. and Dell'Utri's contribution] to the slaughters has maintained and maybe increased its plausibility.* The same conclusion was reached by the Caltanissetta magistrates. I truly don't know if this is true, alleged, possible, plausible or just fiction: the idea that B. has gone as far as planning, authorizing or accepting killings and bombings for his personal and political objectives is so dreadful I can't even make up my mind about it. This would mean much more than erosion of democracy, it's pure dictatorship's procedures.

As the 'trattativa' trial goes on, new declarations, revelations and burning hot pieces of news come out from the mouths of turncoats. Once again I repeat that a mafia killer who changed jersey cannot be trusted like a normal witness; nevertheless all their declarations point to one direction, and that cannot be a coincidence. Just two more examples: the first is an extract from an article titled *Trattativa Stato-mafia, Giuffrè: "Garanzie da Dell'Utri, votammo Forza Italia"* from the November 22, 2013, edition of *Il Fatto Quotidiano: "Marcello Dell'Utri guaranteed the mafia which 'engaged in a big effort' to vote Forza Italia." This is turncoat Nino Giuffrè's version that he confirmed yesterday at the ongoing trattativa Stato-mafia trial in Palermo: "Non è che la mafia sale su un carro qualunque [mafia does not jump on every passing cart]. We chose to back up Forza Italia because we had certain guarantees (…) between late 1993 and early 1994 the position which had been held by Vito Ciancimino as far as the relationship with Cosa Nostra was concerned was taken up by Marcello Dell'Utri."*

The second example is from an article in the November 7, 2013 edition titled *Processo Trattativa, il pentito: "L'omicidio Dalla Chiesa fatto da Craxi e Andreotti"* – *"The murder of Dalla Chiesa done by Craxi and Andreotti"*. The turncoat in question is Francesco Onorato, the killer who killed Euro MP Salvo Lima on March 12, 1982, *the first politician that had to be eliminated after the unkept promises made to Cosa Nostra about the Maxiprocesso's final non guilty verdict, which had been confirmed a few weeks earlier instead. Onorato said:"Trattativa? What trattativa? I only saw coexistence among politics, the State and the mafia".* On December 19, 2013, in his weekly editorial for *Servizio Pubblico*, Marco Travaglio said that Riina had recently ordered the killing of magistrate Di Matteo, coordinator of the investigation in the 'trattativa'. Riina was heard giving this command during the daily outdoor walk granted to all prisoners. Neither any politician nor any high officer of the State, like President Napolitano, up to now has given their solidarity to the magistrate in what is an unbelievable institutional silence. Di Matteo investigated and took to the bar former DC Home Secretary Mancino and heard him asking for the President's help in a wiretapped conversation that Napolitano forced to destroy. Di Matteo also summoned the Head of State as 'persona informata sui fatti' (person informed on facts) in the trial. The Italian president's hearing is taking place on October 28, 2014, at his official residence, *il Quirinale*, in Rome. The suspicion that the magistrate's action is disturbing is very legitimate. Di Matteo seems to be 'isolated' and this usually is a preliminary condition for the mafia murders of very dangerous people, as the *Carabinieri* general Carlo Alberto Dalla Chiesa pointed out in 1982 in his last interview to *Repubblica* before being killed by the mafia. Carabinieri general Carlo Alberto Dalla Chiesa was one of the best experts on terrorism in the seventies and on May 1, 1982, he was appointed prefect of Palermo to stop the violence of the so called 'second mafia war'. He was murdered in Palermo on September 3, 1982, on the orders of Salvatore Riina.

As I have repeated time and again, we have to be very careful in considering these statements that, anyway, all paint the same nocturnal picture. Believing that B.&Dell'Utri are the masterminds of the early nineties slaughters and of the killings of Falcone and Borsellino, that Craxi&Andreotti are the brains behind the Dalla

Chiesa murder is like believing in the conspiracy theory about 9/11, according to which President G. W. Bush was the organizer of the attacks in order to please the masters of war, the fire weapons lobbies and the oil companies which had sponsored his campaign. There are many clues about this latter case and suspicion is obvious; as far as the Italian topics I am writing about, many clues and much evidence have been and are being produced making suspicion compulsory, in the hope it is only just another SF story.

[The first hearing of the trial was held in Palermo on May 27, 2013. Wikipedia has a page dedicated to the topic which is constantly updated with quotes from the testimonies of the different people heard at the trial: *Trattativa tra Stato Italiano e Cosa nostra / il processo sulla trattativa*. Unfortunately it is not available in English. The reading of these testimonies, mainly turncoats words, has stunned me once again, a couple of years later. The general trend is the confirmation of the scenario I have outlined in the preceding pages and the cloud of doubt about the involvements of politicians and secret service officers - who appear in constant contact with the mafia bosses – has thickened indeed. I do invite my gentle reader to read that page. In particular, two turncoats' testimonies dealing with the alleged attempt to kill Di Matteo, one of the most important magistrates in charge of the trial, were very shocking; they were made on April 17 and May 7, 2015.

Up to now, the only 'rito abbreviato' verdict is the one regarding former minister Mannino. He was acquitted 'per non aver commesso il fatto' – not to have committed the fact – on November 4, 2015. Marco Travaglio, in his article *Trattativa Stato – mafia, Mannino assolto ma il fatto sussiste – Mannino acquitted, but the fact exists* - written soon after the verdict in *Il Fatto* writes *that Mannino met the mafia very closely, as the Cassation judges wrote in 2014 in the motivations of their refusal to fulfil Mannino's request for compensation because of unfair imprisonment: Mannino "knowingly accepted the electoral support of a notorious exponent of the mafia association [the boss Antonio Vella]..."*

Former President Napolitano answered the magistrates' questions on October 28, 2014 at the Quirinale. From what the press reported, he denied he had knowledge of the negotiation.]

The 1994 political election saw an unprecedented victory of the newly born *Forza Italia*: in Sicily all the electoral boroughs were won by B.'s party, and that suggests one possible thing: voting in southern Italy is not free, another issue in the erosion of democracy. Roberto Saviano told us that there's more than the traditional 'voto di scambio', a vote to a politician that will return the favour once elected. 'Prima una scarpa, poi l'altra' – one shoe first, afterwards the second one – is an old saying which means that the mafia used to give the poor fellow one shoe before the vote and one after it. The mafia imposes the party to vote to its affiliates but the 'advice' is followed by that part of the population which accepts the mafia as a fact, an interlocutor, a business partner, an existing organization which is better than the absentee State in the end. Besides, the majority of the other voters are just scared. Saviano told us that a vote has a price, in general 50 euros. As cheap and as little valued as this! That part of our society that has reached the bottom considers voting just a one-minute act, a sign on paper with no moral strings attached.

Roberto Saviano is another author of 'civil fiction' and a favourite of the 'moral minority'. His 2006 book *Gomorra* became an international best-seller quickly and later was made into a mediocre film by director Matteo Garrone in 2008. *Gomorra* is a reportage, a dark voyage inside the economic empire and the dream of dominion of the *Camorra*, the criminal organization operating in the region Campania and in its capital Naples, one of the most beautiful and most corrupt cities in the world, to stick to the all Italian dichotomy I established in the introduction. *Gomorra* is a shocking book, a picture of the economic, ideological and 'moral' dominance of organized crime, a description of little mean old towns ruled by little mean old men, the powerful *camorristi* who, beside their criminal activities, exploit illegal workers like they were modern slaves, with no possibility of redemption. Around the metropolitan belt of Naples there are little towns or villages like the *Export Processing Zones* described by Naomi Klein in *No Logo*: citadels of exploitation of illegal workers in different areas of production, tailoring and fashion in particular. But this time the *EPZ* are here, behind the corner, and not in distant developing countries. Even top Italian fashion brands have their clothed manufactured in these sanctuaries of abuse: in the chapter *Angelina Jolie* the protagonist, a tailor enslaved in Camorra's homemade sartorial factories, sees the actress wearing his handmade gala dress at the Oscar night in Hollywood while all around him the bosses try to behave like the Hollywood stars of gangster movies, imitating their ferocity. In this reality, young desperate local teenagers are turned into drug couriers, the only job opportunity offered them. Besides, *the camorra clans don't need politicians like the Sicilian mafia, it's the politicians who have the necessity to enter the System (as camorra* is called). Everybody knew and knows what Saviano is talking about, but nothing changes, Gattopardo style again. Not surprisingly, B. rushed to say that books like *Gomorra* spoilt the image of the country and should not be read and exported, even if B.'s *Mondadori* published the book and made big money out of it.

Also the Italian regions Calabria e Puglia are dominated by criminal organizations like camorra and mafia: in the former there is the *'ndrangheta*, an organization which is considered the most dangerous and the most international nowadays, while in the latter the local mafia goes under the name of *sacra corona unita*. These criminal organizations have long since moved to northern Italy, as we are witnessing in this paper, to meet and intrude into big business and to Rome, to encroach national politics. In the new millennium they have globalized like capitalism, of which they represent a side effect but also, I think, a tendency: these four organized-crime societies are local 'enterprises' turned multinationals on a world scale which sell brands beside products, to use Klein's categories. *Anime Nere (Black Souls)*, shown at the 2014 Venice Film Festival, is a very good film noir depicting the traditional local 'ndrangheta turned modern and international. The movie gives a very precise and disturbing picture of this dark aspect of our country unknown to the majority of the Italian people as well.

Let's now go back to 1994: B. is now Prime Minister: *in the years 1996 – 2000, almost all the requests carried forward by Riina in the so called 'papello' entered the political agenda and are brought about with 'Bulgarian' majorities, from extreme right to extreme left (with a few appreciable exceptions). These requests had entered PDL's agenda too in 1994, but they weren't turned into law because there was no time [the first Berlusconi government lasted only a few months]. The list of acts that make life difficult for magistrates, turncoats and witnesses, and make it easy for criminals, mafiosi above all, would be infinite* Travaglio writes in *Intoccabili – Perchè la Mafia è al Potere [Untouchables –*

Why the Mafia is in Power], a book co-written with Saverio Lodato on *the hidden truths about Cosa Nostra's accomplices in politics and in the State* (BUR, 2005, p. 121). *La Mafia abolita per Legge [The Mafia abolished by Law]* is the title of a very tough editorial by Caselli in *Repubblica* in 1997 (magistrate Gian Carlo Caselli is a former Procuratore of Palermo, see following paragraphs). Recently Travaglio has updated the list of the pro-mafia bills bipartisanly issued by the governments from 2000 to today: for example the 2006 pardon extended to some mafia crimes, the 2009 bill about the auctioning of the confiscated mafia wealth (giving mafia figureheads the possibility to buy them back), the 'fiscal shields' that allowed dirty money to return to Italy anonymously. For the complete list just log on to Wikipedia at the entry *Trattativa tra Stato Italiano e Cosa nostra, Altre presunte pressioni della mafia sulla politica*.

In 1993, while Cosa Nostra bombs were exploding throughout the country, more than 300 big mafia bosses were reassigned to ordinary penitentiary protocol, putting an end to their '41- bis' isolation. Even Riina benefited by the act in 2001, offering him the possibility to meet other prisoners in the daily outing, as afore stated (today Riina, nicknamed *La Belva – the Beast –* is still considered the head of Cosa Nostra). Capriotti, head of the penitentiary administration, knew nothing about it. Former Ministry of Justice Conso confirmed the fact but he said the 'trattativa' had never existed. Both of them are at the bar now, as we know, for providing false information. Nevertheless, even if the cancellation of '41 bis' headed the 'papello', Don Vito was not satisfied: *I remember that my father's critiques were not only about the delusion for the modest political initiative in favour of the organization. There was a real rage because of the inadequacy in exploiting the potential obtained with the 1994 elections* Ciancimino junior declares in *Don Vito* on p. 226. A State forced or willing to issue laws openly or subliminally in favour of the anti-state needs no comment as far as the erosion of democracy is concerned.

On the other side of the fence, I'd like to have a final word for the magistrate who picked up the legacy of Falcone and Borsellino's pool in the very hazardous years of the Seconda Repubblica, an example of the presence of the 'moral minority' inside the State, its brave and honest officials too often forgotten behind the front line of corrupt representatives. From 1993-1999 Gian Carlo Caselli was Procuratore della Repubblica in Palermo. This period is considered the real 'antimafia' second phase. It is the time in which the mafia had the greatest number of defeats ever: arrests of fugitives, sentences against mafiosi, seizure of property, mafiosi's surrender to the State, turncoats. Above all, the unveiling of institutional collusions brought the untouchables to the bar: the seven times PM and the symbol itself of the Prima Repubblica, the DC 'lider maximo' Giulio Andreotti, is the most famous case of the Caselli years. Thanks to his investigations, in 2004 Andreotti was definitively condemned for external association with the mafia for the period before 1980 but set free because of the statute of limitations. He was declared not guilty for the following years. The Court of Cassation confirmed the verdict. In the appeal sentence's motivations Andreotti's link with the mafia is defined a 'concreta collaborazione' – a factive collaboration; nevertheless most of the media, B.'s ones above all, even today keep saying he was acquitted, another macroscopic example of reality control. Andreotti is really an edifying example of mafia-politics connections: in those days B.'s WMD were launched against Caselli's office to protect the still powerful senator. Vittorio Sgarbi, a provincial dandy and art critic who sold out to B., shouted and cursed like a madman, in an astonishing crescendo of vulgarity, against the 'Caselli theorems' on a lunchtime Canale 5 TV monologue. The same would happen in recent years with Giuliano Ferrara, a notorious journalist under B.'s wing, who appeared in similar monologues on RAI 1 at dinner time during the Minzolini age.

Antonio Ingroia: *Se la strage di via D'Amelia non è stata pensata, attuata, da uomini dello Stato, di certo lo Stato ne è complice. Questo posso dire di saperlo.*
If the via D'Amelio slaughter was non planned and made by men of the State for sure the State has been an accomplice of it. This I can say I know.

Giancarlo Caselli has recently published a book co-written with another symbol of the fight against the mafia, former Palermo magistrate Antonio Ingroia, who fought to set up the 'trattativa' trial against all odds. As the subtitles suggests, *Vent'anni Contro-Dalla eredità di Falcone e Borsellino alla trattativa – Twenty Years against-From Falcone and Borsellino's Legacy to the 'Negotiation'* –, the book is an excursus on the fight against mafiosi, on the unveiled and the still veiled mafia/politics mysteries, on the changing face of the contemporary mafia, written by two magistrates that lived this war from within. Besides, Marco Travaglio is touring Italy with his latest theatre show *È Stato la mafia*, now a DVD as well, a pun that plays with the word 'Stato', meaning both *State and been*, so that the expression means *It has been the mafia* (it's mafia's fault) but also suggests the link between the two entities. *È Stato la mafia* is a very detailed and shocking account of the 'trattativa' that tries to tell us what the media fight to conceal, as usual. At the Venice Film Festival, in September 2014, the comedian Sabina Guzzanti, one of the victims of the 2002 banning of unfriendly journalists and comedians from television – the so called editto bulgaro (see part 1, chapter 2), received a standing ovation for her film *La Trattativa*, a mix of documentary and fiction that sums up the story of the 'trattativa', a work filled with the author's well-known bitter humour, strong criticism, irresistible gags and dark irony. The film trailer can be seen on YouTube where there are also many videos of Sabina Guzzanti playing Berlusconi, very funny gags Sabina has been playing since Berlusconi entered politics. It is because of these stand-up comedian's performances she was banned by state television.

https://www.youtube.com/watch?v=X2onx6eOBps&feature=youtu.be is the link with one of Guzzanti's piece, subtitled in English, in which she plays a gay *bunga-bunga* Berlusconi, the emperor. The piece was an introduction to her 2008 'Vilipendio Tour'.

I planned to a have a final paragraph on the erosion of democracy, but I think I've said enough. So no more comments on the anti-State inside the State and the turning of illegality into legitimacy, just another quote from *Don Vito* final lines: *When I accompanied my father it often happened I had to wait for him inside the car together with other young men aspiring to success. I was his driver, president Schifani, today the second most important State representative [President of the Senate], drove Peppino La Loggia's car and President [of Sicily] Totò Cuffaro was Calogero Mannino's driver. They really worked their way up, didn't they, pa'?*

(PS: Totò Cuffaro is now in jail for mafia association; Peppino La Loggia was another DC Sicilian leader; former Senate president Schifani, one of B.'s long-term political friends, is under investigation for mafia collusion, Calogero Mannino was at the 'trattativa' bar in Palermo but was acquitted in 2015: what a great bunch of noble characters!)

Chapter three

Erosion of democracy:

Big Brother is brainwashing you, conflicts of interests.

Berlusconi's philosophy

Another main aspect of the corrosion of democracy is the conflict of interests that was born when B. became the media tycoon he is today. What I've been discussing up to now – B.'s alleged anti-State inside the State, which seems to tear apart the Constitution and the laws to favour himself and the lawbreakers – has been made possible by his conflicts of interests. The *ad personam* laws he made to kill his trials are not only other aspects of democracy corrosion, they are also examples of one kind of B.'s conflict of interests. The laws he approved to favour his enterprises represent another type of the same conflict. The monopoly of information is an additional one: we have nicknamed it Weapons of Mass Deception, propaganda tools that bias elections and through which he sanctifies the worst aspects of the average Italian, the 'italiano medio', as we say derogatively. What B.'s televisions have actually done is a complete change in the national psyche, a subliminal implantation of a negative philosophy in people's minds, providing a great contribution to the erosion of the democratic system.

We basically know from the introduction how he came to possess nationwide televisions in the eighties. In 1976 private channels were allowed to broadcast on a local scale only. In the same year B. bought *Telemilano*, known as *Canale 5* since 1980, in 1982 he purchased *Italia 1* and two years later *Rete 4*. It was the beginning of modern commercial – and subliminally political – television: advertising and promoting became integrated with programming so that promotional messages to advertise a product or a candidate were transmitted regularly. In 1980 B. established the advertising company *Publitalia* which looked after the *Mediaset* channels, so that the buyer and the seller incarnated in the same person, like the assumed outlaw and the politician, the trombeur-de-escorts and the Catholic moralist: it was an early example of conflict of interests. By 1984 B. owned three national TV networks and could challenge RAI. Illegally, as his style suggests: he broadcast the same programs simultaneously on regional networks linked to his channels, getting a 'live effect' granted only to RAI channels. As a consequence, three prosecutors withdrew his broadcasting machines. Bettino Craxi, in London for a State visit, left Margaret Thatcher alone, rushed back home and put forward the first and soon after the second 'Berlusconi emergency decree' that legalized B.'s illegality. In 1990 the Andreotti government passed the so called 'Mammì law' (named after the Minister for Telecommunications): it is one of B.'s masterstrokes, an antitrust law that legalized trust. B. could keep his channels, and Mondadori too: it was the creation of RAI – *Mediaset* duopoly. In the same period, Craxi's offshore accounts (which a 'good' politician is never short of) were inflated by 23 billion lire arriving from one of the offshore *Fininvest* accounts called *All Iberian* (which a 'good' businessman is never short of as well). In the trial that followed, called *All Iberian 1*, B. was sentenced to two years and four months for bribing, but on appeal he was acquitted because of the statute of limitations, an old friend that never let him down. Craxi was best man at B.'s second marriage and godfather to one of B.'s daughters's marriage, an interfamily tie recalling the Cosa Nostra customs about the patriarchal 'family' and the importance of 'the Godfather'. His *Emittenza* (a play on words on *eminenza*, eminence, and *emittente*, broadcaster), the Great Seducer, the Mind Controller, the owner of the WMD, was fully operative from then on.

Mediaset channels always broadcast B.'s speeches live in every Italian home without comments or any criticism, since the journalists and anchormen are employees of his; they also provide him with an electronic balcony, to match Mussolini's real one, from which he can harangue the adoring – and often paid – audience. But *Mediaset*'s main function is another one, a purpose very clear to foreign eyes but unbelievably blurred to Italian viewers:

> *But more than just painfully partial towards its boss, Mediaset television has achieved something even more disguised. It has seduced a society to the extent that politics and ideas don't seem to exist. Italy's noble visual culture has been reduced to endless erotica, and the small screen is now a cheaper, bittersweet version of La Dolce Vita: a world obsessed with celebrity and sexuality, to*

the exclusion of all moral values (Fellini, not surprisingly, for years objected to his film being shown on television). In many ways, the real problem with Mediaset isn't that it is political in the purest sense; it's that it's not political at all. The only thing on offer are bosoms, football and money.

Bosoms, football and money – the quotation is from *The Dark Side of Italy* again – are indeed what the 'immoral majority' of the Italians want. The gut feelings they have, la *pancia* as we call it, the ethic values upon which these people's lifestyle rests, are what B.'s networks sanctify. Easy sex, sport obsession, appearance, shortcuts to success, selfish attitude, *menefreghismo* ('I don't carism', 'each-to-his-own mentality'), *trasfomismo*, the breaking of any rules for personal purposes and, above all, obsession for wealth, a mania that matches the British care for class: these moral disvalues have been implanted into the Italian psyche like a pandemic with no antidote. Wealth is a person's worth, the issue people are judged from, boasting about money is as important as showing off sexual conquests, facts everybody has to know. Generally speaking, a very rich, *bunga-bunga-*addicted person, perceived as very corrupt, is inevitably the most seductive politician in the country. What B. has done wrong in his career, according to traditional moral and social standards, is a source of admiration, envy and imitation: he wins consent because he is perceived as a gangster, a womanizer, a corrupt mafia-linked businessman; the more so, the more his success. These types of behaviour are an accepted way to reach success, wealth and power, it's the elevation of these proceedings to a political and governmental philosophy. Not just the manipulated news, but all *Mediaset* TV programs subliminally carry on these values: talk-shows, fiction (in the Italian meaning of TV dramas), entertainment, sport, reality shows, quizzes, comedy shows, American B-movies and so on. As a consequence of this brainwashing, the working classes have voted for him abandoning the left, believing that a multimillionaire could do something for their social condition while he was stealing from the poor and giving to the rich in front of them; many middle-class professionals believed he would help them evade taxation, not without reason; the retired people and housewives, soap-operas watchers, fell in love with him, not to say of the young, the voters of tomorrow, who grew up not knowing of any other form of television, swallowing, enjoying and absorbing his wrong values like a freshly baked Neapolitan pizza. …. *thanks to radio and television, he [tomorrow's dictator] is in the happy position of being able to communicate even with unschooled adults and not yet literate children… to condition a million or ten million children, who will grow up into adults trained to buy your product … dictators and the would-be dictators have been thinking about this sort of thing for years, and that millions, tens of millions, hundreds of millions of children are in process of growing up to buy the local despot's ideological product and … to respond with appropriate behavior to the trigger words implanted in those young minds by the despot's propagandists.*

In order to complete this picture, we must consider again what I have already written down, that we are not the land of milk and honey, but the country of *menefreghismo*, individualism and selfishness mirrored in the motto *fatta la legge trovato l'inganno*. We must keep in mind that the majority of the Italians have always been at least suspicious about the State after centuries of foreign dominations before the Risorgimento in the XIX century, considering those alien state officials 'enemies'. We have never developed a civic awareness, a sense of community, of belonging to some common ground, everyone tries to beat the 'system' instead of upholding it.

As I stated previously, I have never thought, and never will, that these people – the adults I mean – can be justified because of their low cultural level, because of the fact that all they know comes from TV while newspapers and books are not part of their everyday life. They are to blame because even a blind man could see the real Berlusconi behind the mask since the beginning, his repeating the same promises over and over again in every electoral campaign without ever realizing them, could not have been taken seriously even for a single moment. At the top of his fame, B. had almost 40% of electoral consent and today, notwithstanding what we know about him and his criminal acts, he has still half as much. It is my firm belief that only a very small minority of his voters got a real advantage from B. in their life, so having a practical, but not a moral, reason to vote him. The others were either deceived or just wanted to be like him, or both of them simultaneously. A very sad situation, whatever the reasons.

Today *Mediaset* TV spies on you in every corner of Italy; it's like the *telescreen* in *Nineteen Eighy-Four* that transmits 24 hours a day propaganda while spying on your behaviour, a machine that cannot be switched off. Every pizzeria and any public place has *Mediaset* TV on all day through, even state institutions broadcast it live, the inanimate picture of the President hanging on the wall and Big Brother's animate image talking to you. I remember being at a public hospital's emergency room some time ago, waiting to be treated: the bosoms were there, intermingled with B.'s and Fede's talking faces, to entertain and inform suffering people waiting for the doctor.

Since the birth of *Mediaset* TV, the State broadcaster has turned into a commercial network as well. RAI slowly turned into a mock-*Mediaset* network obsessed by the 'share' (the ratings) and forced to air swanky variety shows, the more so when B. seized control of it by placing his managers in its leading positions. It meant the end of television both as means of intelligent entertainment and as a vehicle of culture, and it also meant the end of the Italian Golden Age of cinema. Everything was eroded by television like a flood which left a wasteland of cultural desolation in the cradle of artistry.

I suggest foreign readers to watch a 2011 film titled *Qualunquemente*, a comedy about a minor gangster who enters politics in a small town in the Deep South. The movie is a witty ironic bitter summary of all B.'s negative aspects taken to a microcosm in which the majority of its inhabitants are keen to pick up the local criminal/politician's most depressing gut feelings and mafioso attitude. Even the title and the candidate's motto which appears on the film poster, *I have no dream, ma mi piace u pilu!*, are difficult to explain because they are typically Italian. The title makes up an adverb from the adjective *qualunque* ('ordinary', 'whatever' in their depreciative meaning). We have already classified the collective noun *qualunquismo* (the 'ordinary man in the street' or 'Joe Bloggs' attitude in the sense of political cynicism and indifference) as one of the Italian 'virtues': in fact the protagonist's surname is La Qualunque. *I have no dream, ma mi piace u pilu (but I like hair)* is the logical slogan for a *qualunquistico* candidate. *U pilu* (literally 'the hair') is an invented slang expression meaning women's pubic hair: the mayor-to-be has no dream except conquering females, considered just inferior objects to exploit and submit. *Si comincia con dare la precedenza ad un incrocio e finisce che si diventa ricchione* is one of the movie's revealing wisecracks ('one begins respecting the road signals and ends up becoming a gay'; the sentence refers to the risks one takes following the rules, homosexuality being the greatest shame for an Italian self-appointed macho like Cetto). The film is set in *'ndrangheta* land, Calabria, haunted by the spectre of legality. Against this disturbing nuisance, in the shape of a candidate running to become mayor, the 'smart' part of the citizens finds the providence man: Cetto La Qualunque, just come back from a period in hiding in South America with a new wife, whom he calls 'Thing', and her daughter, whose name he does not even know. Cetto comes back home pretending that his wife and kid accept his other 'family' for social appearance's sake. He is vulgar, dishonest, corrupt, happy to be like this and even worse. Cetto uses mafia intimidations, an unthinkable dose of rotten propaganda, he seizes control of the local media, he uses convicted lawbreakers and then he hires a 'specialist' in manners and behaviour. Machiavelli style, the goal, his victory in the local elections, justifies the means: a public speech in church, the offering of girls in the nude, the imprisonment of his son instead of his own, the falsification of the elections. Cetto has no limits, he is a concentration of all-Italian customs and characteristics: he is scared to death of having to pay taxes, he loves paving beaches and archaeological areas, he does not care about drainpipes going directly to the sea, he does not even care about bigamy and visits another local lover of his regularly. He gives petrol vouchers to voters, biases elections and appoints female councillors according to their appeal: Cetto is not only surreal, he is too real too.

A review of another recent *docufilm* about B., *Silvio Forever*, reads: *his secret is that he personifies a vey Italian mask: he speaks the common language, he loves popular songs, jokes and sex, he likes mixing with people, he is vain and a male chauvinist, he genuinely loathes the State and the institutions, he tells lies with tranquillity, predica bene e razzola male [an Italian proverb meaning, literary, 'he preaches well and acts badly']. Borghese in "Goliath" talked of Fascism not as an historical episode but as a category of the Italian spirit.*[8]

---

8 Giuseppe Antonio Borghese (1882–1952) was an Italian writer, journalist and literary critic. *Goliath, the March of Fascism* is an essay published for The Viking Press, New York, 1937.

Fascism not as an historical episode but as a category of the Italian spirit is a phrase that may well sum up what I have shown so far: if we gather the examples scattered in this paper it's easy to see the meaning of the expression. Besides, B.'s morality, the category of the worst Italian spirit, is a never ending line of paradoxes: his omnipotence delirium, a mix of power, sex and scandals boosted by a possible underlying sense of frustration and impotence, reveals a potential psychiatric pathological aspect. Indeed B. gives the impression of a provincial Duce-like leader and, for this reason, he is a world ridicule. Nevertheless, B. has to be taken dramatically seriously because he is just the iceberg tip of a tendency inside our contemporary global neo-con Western world, a society in which democracy is more and more a façade behind which a modern techno dictator may hide. In Huxley's 1958 foreseeing words: *Under their hideous rule [Hitler and Stalin's] [there was] ... a mixture of violence and propaganda, systematic terror and the systematic manipulation of minds. In the more efficient dictatorships of tomorrow there will probably be much less violence than under Hitler and Stalin. The future dictator's subjects will be painlessly regimented by a corps of highly trained social engineers (...) If the first half of the twentieth century was the era of the technical engineers, the second half may well be the era of the social engineers"* -- and the twenty-first century, I suppose, will be the era of *World Controllers, the scientific caste system and Brave New World (...) The impersonal forces of over-population and over-organization, and the social engineers who are trying to direct these forces, are pushing us in the direction of a new medieval system (...) For the majority of men and women, it will still be a kind of servitude.*

A new medieval system and a kind of servitude is not a great future prospect. In fact, if the use of violence in the XX century dictatorships did not erase rebellion, our present-day society's media brainwashing is indeed more dangerous since, trying to cancel thought, it aims at wiping out dissent. It's a contemporary kind of State *soma*, the official drug used in the still very up-to-date 1932 novel *Brave New World*, a synthetic tranquilizer to make people feel happy when the conditioning is not enough. The episode I reported of the angry crowd throwing coins at Bettino Craxi in 1992 (when it was discovered he was crooked to the core, the symbol of a corrupt category of public elected officials) and the public opinion's support of the Mani Pulite investigation are in sharp contrast with today's indifference. In times in which a new partisan civil spirit is much needed, what we witness nowadays is just the lack of concern, the resignation and the 'I don't carism' of the majority of Italian citizens in their Cetto-La-Qualunquish attitude. Demonstrations and street protests still exist, but the symbol of the times is the desperate attempt of the desperate man who threw a souvenir statuette at B. in Piazza del Duomo in Milan in 2009, hitting him on the face and making him look like a freedom fighter TV martyr. The only consequence of this attack was that B. met for the second time the dental hygienist Nicole Minetti who, the gossip goes, he hired as *bunga-bunga* lady and then as *bunga-bunga* maitre.

PART THREE

From the present to the future

Basta – Time for Italy to sack Berlusconi
(*The Economist*, 8 - 14 April, 2006)

Photo from Fabio Venni, www.flickr.com, Creative Commons licence

Chapter one

Every line tells a story: dystopian novelists saw it coming

> *There will be, in the next generation or so, a pharmacological method of making people love their servitude, and producing dictarship without tears, so to speak, producing a kind of painless concentration camp for entire societies, so that people will in fact have their liberties taken away from them, but will rather enjoy it, because they will be distracted from any desire to rebel by propaganda or brainwashing, or brainwashing enhanced by pharmacologica lmethods. And this seems to be the final revolution* (A. Huxley)

As I was driving to school in the early Monday morning sunshine the idea came to me. B. had given me a little gift the previous Saturday – May 11, 2013 – organizing a protest rally in Brescia, called *Tutti con Silvio – everyone with Silvio –*, to cry out loud the same old Orwellian mantra of his against the Milan magistrates who had confirmed the four-year sentence on appeal in the *Mediaset* trial a few days before. On that day I was supposed to lecture my fifth-year students on the first part of *Nineteen Eighty-Four* in preparation of the final *esame di stato* (our secondary school *A level* exam). Students are usually very lazy in May, tired at the end of the final year's work and with summer already knocking at their classroom door. I decided I would read the *two minute hate* passage from chapter one with particular care, comparing what happens in the novel and what had happened the previous Saturday: I did want to show them that literature helps understand the world we live in and it is not only an academic subject. Actually, B.'s rally was a very subversive event. Not only B. himself, as leader of the opposition, but also vice PM Angelino Alfano and some ministers were there to protest against a part of the State they represented with the intention to undermine its authority, backing up their leader's insults to the *Toghe Rosse – Red Robes*, i.e. the judges and the magistrates.

In Brescia there were two demonstrations at the same time, the 'legal' *Tutti con Silvio* and the 'illegal' one organized by anti-B.'s activists to show their dissent. Verbal insults were launched and some physical violence was shown but the anti-riot armed police were able to limit it to a minimum. They kept the anti-B. demonstrators far away from the stage, so that they could not be seen on TV, while the pro-B. activists (probably the majority of them were the usual paid extras) were granted access under the stage to set the scene properly: it was a *Nineteen Eighty-Four* setting indeed and a good starting point for my lecture. So, when I read the extract about the violence of the manipulated crowd watching their disdainful enemy and waiting for their leader and saviour in the text, it was very easy to establish a connection:

> *A hideous ecstasy of fear and vindictiveness, a desire to kill, to torture, to smash faces in with a sledge-hammer, seemed to flow through the whole group of people like an electric current, turning one even against one's will into a grimacing, screaming lunatic. And yet the rage that one felt was an abstract, undirected emotion which could be switched from one object to another like the flame of a blowlamp ...*

Then B. came to the stage and acted his speech:

> *... the face of Big Brother, black-haired, black-moustachio'd, full of power and mysterious calm, and so vast that it almost filled up the screen. Nobody heard what Big Brother was saying. It was merely a few words of encouragement, the sort of words that are uttered in the din of battle, not distinguishable individually but restoring confidence by the fact of being spoken ...*

Even if B.'s words were not distinguishable by the excited crowd, they could be clearly guessed, the traditional clichés of inverted logic and insults to the judges and magistrates. Alteration of the past, *doublethink* and *Newspeak*, all topics I would later read, were there. As B. had said in one of his 'famous' video message on September 18, *we are a halved democracy, at the mercy of a certain politicized judiciary which, unique among civilized countries, has a total lack of responsibility and has complete immunity (...) the judges turned from officials of the State, made up of not elected civil servants, into a counter power capable of influencing the legislative and the executive powers and their mission is, according to their statement, to realize the judicial way to socialism.*

Fictional archfiend of INGSOC Emanuel Goldenstein's function is exactly the same as the *Toghe Rosse*'s: while I kept reading and comparing the audience nodded and was following my words with unknown attention.

> *He was the primal traitor, the earliest defiler of the Party's purity. All subsequent crimes against the Party, all treacheries, acts of sabotage, heresies, deviations, sprang directly out of his teaching (…) Goldstein was delivering his usual venomous attack upon the doctrines of the Party — an attack so exaggerated and perverse that a child should have been able to see through it, and yet just plausible enough to fill one with an alarmed feeling that other people, less level-headed than oneself, might be taken in by it.*

That is a scary passage. The *alarmed feeling that other people, less level-headed than oneself, might be taken in by it* has always been the real core of the Berlusconi question. The two scenes (the fictional and the real ones) ended in a very predictable similar way:

> *At this moment the entire group of people broke into a deep, slow, rhythmical chant of 'B-B! … B-B!' — over and over again, very slowly, with a long pause between the first 'B' and the second — a heavy, murmurous sound, somehow curiously savage, in the background of which one seemed to hear the stamp of naked feet and the throbbing of tom-toms.*

Winston forced to watch the *telescreen* propaganda all day long was just an inch ahead of B.'s speech in Brescia broadcast over and over again on TV that night and the following day, until a new event or fact eager to be used for media misinformation would step in.

The unusual silence that had accompanied my reading made me feel a sense of relief at the end of the lecture, hoping that the Thought Police would not knock at my door in the afternoon.

> *Since Hitler's day the armory of technical devices at the disposal of the would-be dictator has been considerably enlarged. As well as the radio, the loudspeaker, the moving picture camera and the rotary press, the contemporary propagandist can make use of television … Big Brother can now be almost as omnipresent as*

God ... Since Hitler's day a great deal of work has been carried out in those fields of applied psychology and neurology which are the special province of the propagandist, the indoctrinator and the brainwasher... Today the art of mind-control is in the process of becoming a science... the nightmare that was "all but realized in Hitler's totalitarian system" may soon be completely realizable.
(Brave New World Revisited)

As I have hinted in the previous part over and over again, the so-called 'dystopian novelists' of the twentieth century clearly foresaw what today is happening as far as democracy in Western countries is concerned. Now we are in the thick of it, so it should be easy for anyone to see what is going on, even if, alas, we know it is not true. Back then instead it was not that simple, but evidently the seeds were there waiting for the best minds to grasp them. Books like *Brave New World* by A. Huxley (1932), *Nineteen Eighty-Four* by G. Orwell (1948), *Fahrenheit 451* by R. Bradbury (1953), *A Clockwork Orange* by A. Burgess (1962), *One Flew over the Cuckoo's Nest* by K. Kesey (1962), *Do Androids Dream of Electric Sheep?* by P. K. Dick (1968), *The Giver* by L. Lowry (1993), *The Hunger Games* by S. Collins (2008), to name a few, are anti-utopian novels all set in a future society which has developed the worst tendencies of capitalism. If the reader is willing to excuse a minor conflict of interests of mine, also my latest novel *Dark City* is another example of literary dystopia. These works of art portray a society ruled by Big Business, legal or illegal, which is to say dominated by what in the real world are multinational corporations and by their brand philosophy that impose a standard lifestyle to the planet based on implanted needs and profit. They describe a society that has reached almost perfection in mind manipulation and control through the media; a society whose public representatives, being actually appointed by Big Business and not by citizens, are ready to carry on the policies ordered by the multinationals, a political caste soaked in corruption and privileges whose main aim is to maintain social stability and erase dissent. These writers foresaw that it is the concentration of the political, economic and media powers in the same hands that would allow tomorrow's – today's – only apparently democratic societies to exist, a new form of social order which can be defined as a non violent dictatorship, as the opening quotation explains. The dystopian novelists' forecast has found their mentor in B., the symbol of modern deranged liberal societies, the unique example up to now of the concentration of the above mentioned powers in one single person, a situation a democratic society in its traditional sense should not have allowed. The development of B.'s phenomenon has for sure been helped by unique factors like the fertile terrain of historic illegality, lack of civil consciousness and basic egotistic instincts, but these cannot mask the inadequacy of the democratic institutions in today's Hi-Tech globalized social environment. G.W. Bush is another example of what the dystopian writers predicted: he was a President who represented the interests of oil and weapons corporations so closely to wage wars for their sakes, conflicts which were motivated with lies (i.e. Saddam's Iraq having WMD) repeated over and over again in the media. Nevertheless, Bush, who paradoxically had to thank 9/11 for the 'war opportunities', was never in trouble with justice, never issued *ad personam* laws, never delegitimized the judiciary system and the American democratic institutions in general. Instead Berlusconi is a very dangerous example that is going to be imitated in countries with weak democracy.

Without any doubt the most famous novel of this genre is Orwell's fable. Even if today we often forget where the title of the reality show *Big Brother* comes from, a Big Brother watching us as symbol of dictatorship and social control is what is commonly remembered of Orwell's 1948 novel, whose inversion of the last two figures in the date has it defined as SF fiction. Due to B.'s face surgery, hair implantation and make up, the moustachioed face of ever-present evergreen Big Brother is exactly the same as B.'s ageless visage that is watching us from television screens everyday; the more so in the mega posters filled with *doublethink* populist slogans we have already seen. But in re-reading the book today, in the light of what we have said so far and of what we are witnessing in the Western contemporary world, so many current issues I have randomly tried to point out are there.

Last but not least, the *Wikileak Files Gate* and the more recent *Datagate* revelations that the USA are spying on every single piece of communication and information we share were already foretold in that narrative. Our surprise in finding that out seems quite childish.

NSA [National Security Agency] monitored calls of 35 world leaders according to a classified document provided by whistleblower Edward Snowden is the Guardian's headline of today. Prism is a top-secret $20m-a-year NSA surveillance program, offering the agency access to information on its targets from the servers of some of the USA's biggest technology companies: Google, Apple, Microsoft, Facebook, AOL, PalTalk and Yahoo. The UK's spy agency GCHQ has access to Prism data. From what we are learning from the *Datagate* the US is actually controlling any electronic piece of communication that takes place worldwide. Not only world leaders, friends or foes like German Chancellor Angela Merkel whose mobile has been tapped since 2002, are controlled, but also the average citizen. Orwell's slogan B.B. *is watching* you is at work right now in such an efficient way the Thought Police could not have imagined. The *telescreen*-style constant control on the individual, of whose freedom the system is so scared, is what has become evident in these very days. As Noam Chomsky pointed out, *Government will use whatever technology is available to combat their primary enemy – which is their own population.* Besides, today the majority of young and middle-aged people are so addicted to the modern *telescreens*, their mobiles, that they never switch them off even if they could. Whatever they are doing, wherever they are, they have it in their hands, a totem to worship. When the lights grow dim in cinemas, theatres and concert halls you can see the sparkling glow of the touch-screens. Even when you are talking to someone your interlocutor takes a quick glance at it once in a while, a modern version of Chaplin's neurotic tick the factory work has given him in *Modern Times*. Young lovers in restaurants and bars not talking to each other, but either texting each other or concentrating on their mobiles instead, is a saddening spectacle we watch every day. It's the end of human relationships, the complete victory of the brainwashing system, the up-to-date version of *soma*.

On 9 June 2013, in a video interview with Glenn Greenwald and Laura Poitras, 29-year-old Edward Snowden revealed himself as the source of the NSA revelations published that week in *the Guardian* and *the Washington Post*. In the interview Snowden points out clearly what we have been saying so far:

Greenwald: *"Why should people care about surveillance?"*

> Snowden: *"Because even if you're not doing anything wrong you're being watched and recorded. And the storage capability of these systems increases every year consistently by orders of magnitude to where it's getting to the point where you don't have to have done anything wrong. You simply have to eventually fall under suspicion from somebody even by a wrong call. And then they can use this system to go back in time and scrutinize every decision you've ever made, every friend you've ever discussed something with. And attack you on that basis to sort to derive suspicion from an innocent life and paint anyone in the context of a wrongdoer."*

Snowden then shows to understand clearly what the majority of the people today, especially the young, cannot see:

> *you [he means himself] realize that that's the world you helped create and it's gonna get worse with the next generation and the next generation who extend the capabilities of this sort of architecture of oppression.*

In addition to what we have said in the previous chapter, the telescreen that can't be turned off, which is a means of non-stop propaganda and a candid camera to control the personal behaviour of the individual, has basically the same function as the *Mediaset* networks of today. The social engineers and the thought manufacturers at B.'s service are indeed a modern version of the Thought Police. They are also the producers of the contemporary version of *Newspeak*, obtained with the pauperization of the Italian language made by television and with the death of reading habits. We have also seen many examples of alteration of the past and the present in today's Italy which are a direct development of the same changes made by the Party in order to control the future in the novel. Also the labeling as 'communist' of whatsoever is in contrasts with B.'s interests, like the 'red robes' magistrates, is exactly, I repeat, like B.B.'s made up paranoia for the hated arch-enemy Emanuel Goldenstein and his subversive 'Brotherhood'.

Nineteen Eighty-Four's tyranny still needed a good deal of violence to keep the social structure intact; instead, in *Brave New World* physical violence has disappeared but that society is scarier than Orwell's just for this reason: violence is no more necessary to keep society steady and hold power. In fact, the chemical predestination of unborn children and the constant infant conditioning produce a kind of false happiness which is really discomforting for the reader. And just in case a tablet of *soma* is always there, ready to erase a light social uneasiness when human nature wants to come back from its chemical lethargy. Humanity, desires, instincts, passions, love and hate have been scientifically cancelled in individuals, eradicating the risk of rebellion against the social order, a puppy-like humanity which accepts a hyper-capitalistic society based on forced goods consumption. The outburst of the Christ-like character called the 'Savage', the only creature capable of feelings, in one of the climaxes of the book is still very upsetting. The 'Savage' was raised in a Native Americans' reservation and could read Shakespeare, so he has developed a sensibility unknown to others that will lead him to suicide when he gets to know the hollowness of civilization. In the passage below he is talking to Mustapha Mond, one of the ten World Leaders:

> *"Because our world is not the same as Othello's world. You can't make flivvers without steel – and you can't make tragedies without social instability. The world's stable now. People are happy; they get what they want, and they never want what they can't get. They're well off; they're safe; they're never ill; they're not afraid of death; they're blissfully ignorant of passion and old age; they're plagued with no mothers or fathers; they've got no wives, or children, or lovers to feel strongly about; they're so conditioned that they practically can't help behaving as they ought to behave. And if anything should go wrong, there's soma. Which you go and chuck out of the window in the name of liberty, Mr. Savage. Liberty!" He laughed. "Expecting Deltas [the lowest caste in society] to know what liberty is! And now expecting them to understand Othello! My good boy!"*
>
> *The Savage was silent for a little. "All the same," he insisted obstinately, "Othello's good, Othello's better than those feelies [movies for subhuman minds]."*
>
> *"Of course it is," the Controller agreed. "But that's the price we have to pay for stability. You've got to choose between happiness and what people used to call high art. We've sacrificed the high art. We have the feelies and the scent organ instead."*

> "But I don't want comfort. I want God, I want poetry, I want real danger, I want freedom, I want goodness. I want sin."
>
> "In fact," said Mustapha Mond, "you're claiming the right to be unhappy."
>
> "All right then," said the Savage defiantly, "I'm claiming the right to be unhappy."

One Flew over the Cuckoo's Nest is a modern 'western' set in an psychiatric hospital which is the allegory of a repressive society which disguises tortures as cure for the alien characters: lobotomy for example is used for 'hard cases'. The protagonists, McMurphy and 'Chief' Bromden – a cowboy and a Native American – are two American archetypal rebels who try in vain to challenge the institution. In *A Clockwork Orange* the violence of the oppressive social order against the violent rebellious youth, that society itself has created, is the main theme of the novel. Lobotomy is used here too as a form of brainwashing, scientific mind conditioning is a sort of torture of which the politicians boast. In the dark multinational-controlled society of *Do Androids Dream of Electric Sheep?*, a SF novel set in the near future, androids, robots similar to human-beings created by a leading multinational corporation, are a metaphor for today's 'everyman': they are created and programmed to be like power wants them to be, modern slaves of the post-industrial era. *The Hunger Games* is the most recent example of a dystopian futuristic totalitarian society in which an extreme form of TV reality show is offered to the population as entertainment: death is the ultimate destiny of the teenagers taking part in a show in which only the winner survives. This reality show is also a reminder of the rules of a society which punishes rebels with sudden death. These shows satisfy the voyeuristic instincts and the primeval love for violence of the subjugated population: primordial teenagers' fights for survival and consequent death of the unfit are accepted as natural. My latest novel *Dark City* is another example of literary dystopia. Set in a post 9/11 background, the novel deals with a worldwide permanent conflict between Western and Oriental civilizations drenched with terrorism and violence. This clash is actually a means used by these two superpowers to control the behaviour and the attitude of their people, society's main enemy in Chomsky's phrase. It's only through art that the world has a dim hope of salvation even if the protagonist, a rebellious cop/writer, knows that even if in the end justice is done in a single case, success in a solitary battle against all odds will never lead to the winning of the war.

One of the features recurring in all these novels is that books are the most dangerous enemies of dystopian societies, while other electronic media, television at the head of the bill, are the dictatorships' favourite means of social control. *It was a pleasure to burn* is the famous opening line of *Fahrenheit 451* by A. Bradley, the temperature that sets books on fire. Books are banned and book holders chased and caught like criminals, sometimes burned with the volumes in purifying flames, an act which gives the burner pleasure. Books are dangerous because they wake up sleeping feelings that in turn can awake consciousness of the coma-like state of a population who experience a false happiness, induced by the totalitarian regime, that is quite similar to *Brave New World*'s. This fake gladness is actually a social and emotional vacuum whose main responsible is the state television, transmitting non-stop interactive reality shows, invented by the author's foretelling pen, broadcast in every living room's TV mega screen hanging on the wall: the staging of what is really happening today in 1953 is astonishing. Moreover, in the novel's climax, the deceiving power of television, faking reality for its own propagandistic aim while pretending to report objectively, is a sneak preview of the *Mediaset* era. In *Brave New World* classic literature survives only in one of the World Controller's safe. In the author's own words, *in Brave New World non-stop distractions of the most fascinating nature (the feelies, orgy-porgy, centrifugal bumble-puppy) are deliberately used as instruments of policy, for the purpose of preventing people from paying too much attention to the realities of the social and political situation… in Marx's phrase, [non-stop distractions are] "the opium of the people" and so a threat to freedom… A society, most of whose members spend a great part of their time … in the irrelevant other worlds of sport and soap opera, of mythology and metaphysical fantasy, will find it hard to resist the encroachments of those who would manipulate and control it.* In *Nineteen Eighty-Four* books are not banned, they are either 'rewritten' in *Newspeak* or made anew for the 'proles':

> 'The proles are not human beings,' he said carelessly. 'By 2050, earlier probably, all real knowledge of Oldspeak will have disappeared. The whole literature of the past will have been destroyed. Chaucer, Shakespeare, Milton, Byron — they'll exist

only in Newspeak versions, not merely changed into something different, but actually changed into something contradictory of what they used to be. Even the literature of the Party will change. Even the slogans will change. How could you have a slogan like "freedom is slavery" when the concept of freedom has been abolished? The whole climate of thought will be different. In fact there will be no thought, as we understand it now. Orthodoxy means not thinking — not needing to think. Orthodoxy is unconsciousness.'

And the Records Department, after all, was itself only a single branch of the Ministry of Truth, whose primary job was not to reconstruct the past but to supply the citizens of Oceania with newspapers, films, textbooks, telescreen programmes, plays, novels -- with every conceivable kind of information, instruction, or entertainment, from a statue to a slogan, from a lyric poem to a biological treatise, and from a child's spelling-book to a Newspeak dictionary. And the Ministry had not only to supply the multifarious needs of the party, but also to repeat the whole operation at a lower level for the benefit of the proletariat. There was a whole chain of separate departments dealing with proletarian literature, music, drama, and entertainment generally. Here were produced rubbishy newspapers containing almost nothing except sport, crime and astrology, sensational five-cent novelettes, films oozing with sex, and sentimental songs which were composed entirely by mechanical means on a special kind of kaleidoscope known as a versificator. There was even a whole sub-section – Pornosec, it was called in Newspeak – engaged in producing the lowest kind of pornography, which was sent out in sealed packets and which no Party member, other than those who worked on it, was permitted to look at.

You can't come forward against the world's most powerful intelligence agencies and be completely free from risk because they're such powerful adversaries. No one can meaningfully oppose them. If they want to get you, they'll get you in time says Snowden in his interview. The failure of individual rebellion against the regime is a feature that characterizes all the novels I have mentioned. The Savage commits suicide in a solitary lighthouse, Winston is 're-educated' to love Big Brother, McMurphy is lobotomized and later killed by 'Chief' Bromden, who could not stand to see him in a death-in-life state and who in the end escapes in search of a lost wilderness that exists only in his mind. In some cases the conclusion may seem like happy endings but the reader knows that the system's *longa manus* is still there, an oppressive and impenetrable cloak to darken the world. Guy Montag (*Fahrenheit 451*) survives the 'purifying' atomic war by joining the 'book-lovers' but his city is annihilated by the nuclear weapons. Alex (*A Clockwork Orange*) finds himself ready for another night of ultra-violence with a new gang of 'droogs' even if he begins to contemplate entering society as a productive member. Anyway he is aware that his own children will be at least as destructive as himself. Rick Deckard (*Do Androids Dream of Electric Sheep?*) fulfils his mission killing – 'retiring' – the escaped androids but is overwhelmed by a sense of failure. Katniss Everdeen survives in the Hunger Games arena but she becomes a political target. My own Dick (*Dark City*) revenges his partner's killing and succeeds in stopping the terror attack on his native megalopolis but he knows the superpowers' deadly deal he has discovered will never be unmasked.

After having used it extensively, I have come to understand that Huxley's 1958 long essay *Brave New World Revisited* needs a separate space. Its predictions, as we know, are so unbelievably precise that I have decided to add an appendix to the eBook version of this paper, a miscellanea of quotations from that text with notes, to make the reader understand the extent of Huxley's foresight. The writer predicts that, in the future, power will be concentrated in fewer hands, joining together Big Business, media control and political power, and that most likely the future political leader will be the personification of this Power Elite. Huxley also foresees the development of the Thought Manufacturers, social engineers who will apply the same techniques used for publicity to politics, making thought control a perfect working machine thanks to the development of mass communication. Consequently, the would-be political leader will have the opportunity to become a would-be dictator thanks to a scientific apparatus for propaganda unknown to XX century dictators. Hence, only the formal aspects of democracy will remain, allowing the illiberal societies of the future to get rid of the violence needed in past totalitarian systems to obtain a social stability that will be permanent in the future tyrannies. Astonishingly,

Brave New World Revisited is a forgotten text, but the author would be 'pleased' to know that Berlusconi might be seen as the personification of his dystopian vision, a living proof that his message is not sociopolitical SF merely. It is a mirror reflecting our society's distorted face, a looking-glass that we have turned on the opaque side because we can't stand to look at ourselves: it is Dorian Gray's portrait after it has been stabbed by its sitter.

Brave New World Revisited is divided into twelve chapters. In the first ones the authors discusses and compares the type of dystopian societies portrayed in his own 1932 *Brave New World* and in Orwell's 1948 *Nineteen Eighty-four*, two novels considered the milestones of the genre today. Huxley then describes the future non-violent totalitarian regime that he thinks will inevitably take hold of Western democracies. Next the author notices that this new dictatorship is advancing at a speed he could not predict when he was writing his novel. The most surprising part of Huxley's essay is the central one, from chapter III to Chapter VI, in which he expresses his visions of a future society that is extraordinarily similar to the one we already have today and whose full establishment is waiting just around the corner.

Brave New World Revisited is available on the internet for free. Here are the meaningful titles of the twelve chapters:

Foreword
I Over-Population
II Quantity, Quality, Morality
III Over-Organization
IV Propaganda in a Democratic Society
V Propaganda Under a Dictatorship
VI The Arts of Selling
VII Brainwashing
VIII Chemical Persuasion
IX Subconscious Persuasion
X Hypnopaedia
XI Education for Freedom
XII What Can Be Done?

Chapter two

Never ending story:

the would-be conviction of the alleged natural born corrupter

the frantic Italian *teatrino della politica*

Prime Minister Renzi as vicarious Berlusconi:

a natural born corrupt society

Dear reader who has read up to this point,
in the light of what I have carried on so far I'm asking you now to reconsider the quote from *Brave New World Revisited* I used in the opening section of this paper:

> *The best of constitutions and preventive laws will be powerless against the steadily increasing pressures of over-population and of the over-organization imposed by growing numbers and advancing technology. The constitutions will not be abrogated and the good laws will remain on the statute book; but these liberal forms will merely serve to mask and adorn a profoundly illiberal substance. Given unchecked over-population and over-organization, we may expect to see in the democratic countries a reversal of the process which transformed England into a democracy, while retaining all the outward forms of a monarchy. Under the relentless thrust of accelerating overpopulation and increasing over-organization, and by means of ever more effective methods of mind-manipulation, the democracies will change their nature; the quaint old forms -- elections, parliaments, Supreme Courts and all the rest -- will remain. The underlying substance will be a new kind of non-violent totalitarianism. All the traditional names, all the hallowed slogans will remain exactly what they were in the good old days. Democracy and freedom will be the theme of every broadcast and editorial -- but democracy and freedom in a strictly Pickwickian sense. Meanwhile the ruling oligarchy and its highly trained elite of*

soldiers, policemen, thought-manufacturers and mind-manipulators will quietly run the show as they see fit.

I suppose you are now in a position that makes it easy for you to agree with the prophetic quality of this quote, so I invite you to consider whether our Italian reality has overcome fiction, if it is already worse than Huxley's prediction. The writer says that *the constitutions will not be abrogated and the good laws will remain on the statute book; but these liberal forms will merely serve to mask and adorn a profoundly illiberal substance even if the quaint old forms -- elections, parliaments, Supreme Courts and all the rest -- will remain.* Actually the triumvirate King Giorgio, *PD/PDL* and the present Enrico Letta government are planning to change the Constitution, the ultimate stronghold against the final collapse of democracy. Since King Giorgio's re-election in May 2013, and the subsequent 'great coalition' government – the 'inciucio' – the King imposed, the altering of our Charter has been a must of the President. A bipartisan parliamentary commission of 'saggi' – 'wise men' – was established for the purpose, its members old time politicians and 'experts' representing the corrupt ancient regime. It is not a 'maintenance' operation but a radical rewriting of the Charter that the Constitution itself allows with a complicated procedure; 69 articles are to be revisited so that the parliamentary commission would have constituent powers which imply a possible distortion of the whole constitutional architecture. The reduction in number of MPs and the change of the 'perfect bipolar system' of the *Camera* [our House of Commons] and the Senate, necessary 'maintenance' operations, have become an excuse to alter our Charter. These modifications point to the creation of an 'absolute Prime Minister' who would hold almost all power, and we know only too well what this has meant in Italian history. Last but not least, there is the attempt to change the key article 138 which deals with the procedures to follow in order to change the Constitution. The coalition government has the required two third majority to change the article in question without a popular referendum to confirm the change. But today's Parliament is biased by our seven-year-old 'bullshit' electoral law, the *Porcellum*, which does not represent the voters' will and that allows the parties' leaders to impose their candidates for both the Houses to the voters. The *Porcellum*, a law that should be changed immediately, remains in charge while the Chart is going to be unduly changed: it is the reversal of logic that menaces democracy we have seen so many times and it is another example that the prediction *the good laws will remain on the statute book* is a bit too optimistic. If the change in article 138 succeeds, it will be a very dangerous precedent that will allow any future majority to change it again for its own sake. So maybe *the constitutions will not be abrogated* in our country but it may be distorted indeed. On October 12, 2013, a huge demonstration against the change was held in Rome. It followed a petition proposed by *Il Fatto Quotidiano* that was signed by almost 500.000 people. The best mind of the 'moral minority' were there and the 'would-have-been' President Stefano Rodotà – that our country does not deserve anyway – was the most critical voice towards the establishment saying that what is happening is a *dangerous shortcut without consent. To 'stay around' the Constitution today means to avoid a risk for democracy.*

Some months have gone by now, *demolition man* Renzi has become Prime Minister with the purpose of changing the country completely and, consequently, the proposed modification of the Constitution I have just described has been interrupted after the fall of the Letta government. Anyway the dance around the Constitution has remained the same. The Renzi government, we already know from part two, is based on the so-called *Patto del Nazareno*, the secret Berlusconi – Renzi agreement of which we can only see the tip of the iceberg. Of public domain is the deal on the new electoral law and the transformation of the Senate into a non-directly-elected institution. The proposal is vague and, as tradition imposes, it changes every day, according to the way the wind blows. All we know is that the new Senate should be a chamber representing the regions whose members will inevitably be appointed by political power. The proposed new electoral law as well, nicknamed *Italicum*, is a *patarracchio* – a mess – that keeps changing. One thing seems to be sure anyway: there will be a clear winner of the elections. The price to pay to having a winner is a shortage of democracy since there is going to be a *premio di maggioranza* – *prize for the majority* – which will boost the winner's representation and cut the minority parties', leaving some of them out of Parliament. Berlusconi, notwithstanding his conviction, keeps erupting ideas and proposals to the nation, or, to be more precise, to *the Caste*. So we hear again the twenty-year-old refrain about the need of a Presidential Republic and of the reformation of justice, B.'s monomaniac commitment. When I heard Renzi declare, on his nomination speech in February 2014, that the reform of Justice was a priority of his agenda to be done in June I felt shivers down my spine. In June nothing really happened about justice but the Patto del Nazareno was confirmed in another Renzi-Berlusconi meeting. Soon afterwards, twelve generic propositions about the reform of justice were presented to the press; the government said that July-August is the period for society's suggestions and that in September the administration is going to decide. This procedure looks like a façade of democracy and the suspicion that the reform of justice is an important part of the Nazareno deal is obvious and very disturbing: we have seen enough of the justice-according-to-il-Cavaliere to stand it any longer.

On August 28, 2014, the Renzi cabinet approved a timid justice reform. It was part of a series of measures to revamp Italy called *Unblock Italy decree*, meant to promote investments and lift the economy out of the new recession summer had brought, notwithstanding the premier's optimism which accompanied his announced 'revolution'. Renzi showed up on TV in the shape of Mr. Slide once again (see next pages), showing the world full coloured images with simple phrases to illustrate the government's actions, a step forward from B.'s *ventennio*'s posters, whose lesson, as far as propaganda is concerned, the premier has learnt well. Up to now, September 2014, Renzi has promised every possible radical change in every possible field of public life, right here right now, but unfortunately nothing important has been done so far. Announcements seem to be Renzi's ultimate media strategy, notwithstanding what's behind the words. "I want to get out of the Truman Show" the Premier said on February 24, but after some months he seems to be still deep in it. To follow Renzi's announcements is a full-time job: slogans, catchwords, slides, tweets, hashtags, posts and so on. Renzi is following Berlusconi's strategy to 'personify' politics in just one face and just one mouth, always open. Actually, his '100 days' revolution has already shifted to '1000 days'. Our PM should revise A. Lincoln famous motto *you can fool all the people some of the time, and some of the people all of the time, but you cannot fool all the people all the time*.

Renzi's justice reform measures focus on civil justice – he promised to halve the backlog of civil cases – because it is a more neutral area, less haunted by the *Patto del Nazareno*. For it there was a *decreto legge* (an act issued by the government that is the same as a temporary law that must be turned into an ordinary one by Parliament in 60 days), while the DDL for the criminal justice's measures has only been announced (*DDL, Disegno di Legge*, is a rough text of an act that will possibly become a law). One of the first things Renzi said is 'chi sbaglia paga' – 'one must pay for his own mistakes', referring to the introduction of judges' civil responsibility (judges liable for negligence and malfeasance). Then he said 'nessun bavaglio nè limiti nella capacità investigativa' – 'neither gag nor limits to investigative capacity', referring to the use of phone tapping, but announcing restrictions to their publications. These two topics were two obsessions of Berlusconi's, as I have pointed out many times so far. Renzi also promised the reintroduction of the crimes of *falso in bilancio* (false financial statements, false accounting) and *autoriciclaggio* (self money laundering), both abolished by B., and the suspension of the statute of limitations, B.'s best friend, after the first trial. It is a compromise solution, obviously, not to offend il Cavaliere. Besides, there's no hurry for these criminal justice issues, as the missing DDL witnesses. The *National Association of Magistrates* stated that it gives the 'impression of a punitive reform', that *the message given out is that justice does not operate well because the magistrates make mistakes, and it opens the way to specious actions against the judges … a reform that follow an old logic.*

In late June an agreement on the structure of the future Senate was also reached by the *PD*, *Forza Italia* and the racist *Lega Nord*. Reuters sums it up:

> *Italian Prime Minister Matteo Renzi's centre-left Democratic Party (PD) has reached an accord with centre-right parties over proposals to curtail the powers of the Senate, one of the key planks in a wider constitutional reform package. The changes … are intended to create the conditions for more stable government. They would concentrate power in the lower house and make it easier for a party to win a reliable parliamentary majority. Under the current system of "perfect bicameralism," the Senate has virtually equal powers with the lower house but is elected through regional votes rather than a single national ballot. That increases the chances the two houses will end up with different majorities. Under the accord, the Senate would become a regional chamber which would lose its*

> *power to pass legislation and to vote "no confidence" and bring down a government. It would still have the power to request amendments and vote on constitutional issues. Responding to pressure for a cut in the cost of the overall political system, the number of senators would be cut from 315 to 100. Instead of being directly elected, they would mainly be mayors and local government representatives with a small number nominated by the president. The accord will require a two-thirds majority in parliament to change the constitution, which it should get if the agreement with the opposition holds up. It is expected to be brought up for debate in parliament next month.*

From the Renzi government's proposals one thing is for sure in any case: the Constitution is still in danger and the changes Berlusconi has proposed in his *ventennio* are now Renzi's choice. And the best mind of the 'moral minority', derisively referred to as *professoroni* by the premier, issued another appeal in March 2014 titled *Verso la Svolta Autoritaria – Towards the Authoritarian Turning*:

> *Powerless, we are watching the plan to overturn our Constitution, by a Parliament explicitly delegitimized by sentence no.1-2014 of the Constitutional Court [which declared the Porcellum illegitimate], in order to create an authoritarian system that gives the Prime Minister master powers. With the prospect of monocameralismo – one single House – and the centralizing simplification of the administrative order, Matteo Renzi and Silvio Berlusconi's Italy is changing its face (...) The responsibility of the Democratic Party is huge because it is allowing the implementation of Berlusconi's former plan, a plan persistently opposed in the past in words and now quietly accepted. (…) This project must be immediately stopped, and it must be done with the same determination with which it was stopped when Berlusconi inspired it.[9]*

---

9 *Stiamo assistendo impotenti al progetto di stravolgere la nostra Costituzione da parte di un Parlamento esplicitamente delegittimato dalla sentenza della Corte costituzionale n.1 del 2014, per creare un sistema autoritario che dà al Presidente del Consiglio poteri padronali. Con la prospettiva di un monocameralismo e la semplificazione accentratrice dell'ordine amministrativo, l'Italia di Matteo Renzi e di Silvio Berlusconi cambia faccia (...) La*

The same *professoroni* took part in a rally organized by the association *Libertà e Giustizia* on June 2, Festa della Repubblica day, a few days after the *PD* and Renzi had won the May 2014 European elections, to demonstrate against Renzi-Berlusconi's authoritative project again. *Libertà e Giustizia*, whose honorary president is renowned constitutionalist Gustavo Zagrebelsky, is a non-profit association of intellectuals and simple citizens that care for democracy, for the *Res Publica* and for the Constitution, an organization that means to be 'the missing link among the best ferments of society and the official space of politics'. The meeting was in my hometown, in the central piazza 'XX settembre' which has become the 'Greenwich Village' area of Modena city center. Like other three thousand caring citizens I resisted the temptation to go to the seaside and challenged the blistering afternoon sun to attend the rally. And I made the right choice, since the words I heard were music to my ears, the impression of belonging to a community of peers and sharing values stepping in once again. Magistrate Gian Carlo Caselli, Florence University history teacher Paul Ginsborg, journalist Marco Travaglio, professor Stefano Rodotà and other representatives of what we call the *società civile* were there as an intellectual dam against *demolition man*. Rodotà words again: *The fundamental law of the State is once again in the crosshairs of a government and just this week the process for the first of the reforms that should redesign the architecture of the Republic, the Senate's, resumes: from tomorrow we will have before us the risk of leaving representative democracy and of altering the constitutional balance.* [10]

The first part of the process of the reform of the Senate was approved at the Senate itself on August 9, 2014. As for any amendment to the Constitution, this reform needs, luckily, a

---

responsabilità del Pd è enorme poiché sta consentendo l'attuazione del piano che era di Berlusconi, un piano persistentemente osteggiato in passato a parole e ora in sordina accolto (...) Bisogna fermare subito questo progetto, e farlo con la stessa determinazione con la quale si riuscì a fermarlo quando Berlusconi lo ispirava.

10 "*La legge fondamentale dello Stato è di nuovo nel mirino di un governo e proprio questa settimana riprende l'iter per la prima delle riforme che dovrebbe ridisegnare l'architettura della Repubblica: quella del Senato. Da domani abbiamo di fronte a noi il rischio di uscire dalla democrazia rappresentativa e di turbare gli equilibri costituzionali*".

complicated process that entails two readings in each house of the Parliament, and a two-third majority in the second of these passages. On that day, the show the Senate put on was sad: it ended up with hugs and kisses between *PD* and *PDL*, among the left and the right wings senators, a *vasa vasa*[11] show that visually personified the 'inciucio' between former false enemies, united in common intentions and interests, erasing the only place where a conflict of interests should be normal. Young very inexperienced 'minister for the reforms' M. E. Boschi kissing B.'s political right arm Verdini, a businessman under trial for criminal association, bankruptcy and fraud, is the iconic image of the event. The words of *PDL* spokesman P. Romani sum it all up with a simple phrase: "the reforms carry two names: Renzi and Berlusconi", a palace plot built from secret agreements on justice and, possibly, the new president of the Republic. The speakers of the reform were *PD* senator Anna Finocchiaro, a former magistrate, and Northern-League senator Roberto Calderoli, a dentist who, all of a sudden, has turned into an expert in Constitution. Calderoli is notorious for his racist ideas about immigration, different religions, different races and gays; he backed up the former League secretary Bossi when he said 'il tricolore lo uso per pulirmi il culo' – 'I use the *tricolore* (the Italian flag) to wipe my ass', since the *Northern League* has as its primary aim the creation of an independent Northern Italian State called *Padania*. In the European Parliament the party joined Le Pen's *Front National* group. Last but not least, Calderoli is the creator of the *Porcellum*. With these qualifications he was appointed vice-president of the Senate after the 2013 political elections and was the perfect leading character to carry on the changing of the Constitution. Finocchiaro – Calderoli *vasa vasa* was another very sad picture of that day.

Italian constitutionalist Gustavo Zagrebelsky sent minister Boschi a text with his alternative proposals for the Senate reform in May 2014, but the minister ignored it, evidently considering the suggestions of one of the most famed intellectuals in the country less valuable than Calderoli's ideas. Zagrebelsky, who had already expressed fears that demoting one chamber of the Parliament might pave the way to an authoritarian system, in an interview to *Il Fatto*

---

11 *Vasa vasa – bacia bacia, kiss kiss* - is a Sicilian expression referring to the local habit, much used by mafiosi, to kiss each other when people meet.

Quotidiano on August 28, 2014, discusses the links between J.P. Morgan's *Memorandum 2013* and Renzi's agenda. J. P. Morgan, the American multinational banking and financial services holding company, was one of the protagonists of the disastrous projects of the 'creative finance' that brought to the 'subprime' crisis in 2008 that, in turn, gave birth to the economic crisis we are still living nowadays; the company was taken to court by the American government as one of those responsible for the crisis. In the *Memorandum*, in the section *The Euro area adjustment: about halfway there*, we read:

> *At the start of the crisis, it was generally assumed that the national legacy problems were economic in nature. But, as the crisis has evolved, it has become apparent that there are deep seated political problems in the periphery, which, in our view, need to change if EMU is going to function properly in the long run.*
>
> *The political systems in the periphery were established in the aftermath of dictatorship, and were defined by that experience. Constitutions tend to show a strong socialist influence, reflecting the political strength that left wing parties gained after the defeat of fascism. Political systems around the periphery typically display several of the following features: weak executives; weak central states relative to regions; constitutional protection of labor rights; consensus building systems which foster political clientalism; and the right to protest if unwelcome changes are made to the political status quo. The shortcomings of this political legacy have been revealed by the crisis. Countries around the periphery have only been partially successful in producing fiscal and economic reform agendas, with governments constrained by constitutions (Portugal), powerful regions (Spain), and the rise of populist parties (Italy and Greece).*

Professor Zagrebelsky says that the fact that a finance giant talks about politics, institutions and Constitutions as if these had to be subdued to the interests of economy does not create a scandal nowadays. He goes on saying that this is not only an Italian phenomenon, this subjection is an international matter, a new kind of destiny for the countries which have to face the financial blackmail of the 'failure of the State'. *The 'financialization' of economy on a world scale is something new* says the professor. *The fact that its dominance on politics is proclaimed and pretended so clearly is something new: I mean, that such a revelation takes place without shock, reactions, anxiety.* When the journalist says that J. P. Morgan's document has become Renzi, Napolitano and Berlusconi's agenda, Zagrebelsky replies: *There are more general transformations that go beyond the single person's will, willy-nilly, conscious or unconscious, of good or bad intentions. There is a metamorphosis in the system.* In other words, taken for granted that the multinational corporations have been ruling the world since the birth of globalization in the 1990s (N. Klein's 1999 *No Logo*, the bible of the anti-global movement, is a book that proves this topic unequivocally), on a local scale Renzi's planned constitutional changes and economic reforms are part of this game, the local face of 'neo-con' thought, which has become the only existing ideology in the world, disguised as neo-socialist instances.

In conclusion, joining together the various planned reforms, both ordinary and constitutional, the overall picture is very disturbing to a mind which is willing to look 'over the cuckoo's nest'. In theory a party with a 20% relative majority could get a 55% majority in the elected House, thanks to the new electoral law. The Prime Minister and the government might have a favorable new non-elected Senate (which will have parliamentary immunity as well), they might indirectly influence the election of the President of the Republic, of the Constitutional Court and of the 'Consiglio Superiore della Magistratura'. On the other hand, the opposition would surely shrink because of the high minimum threshold, Berlusconi's laws on TV networks and conflict of interests that made information less independent are not going to be abolished and the number of signatures for laws proposed by the people will rise. It sounds like a sort of dictatorship of the majority, another forthcoming event in the erosion of democracy show.

It's October 2, 2013, one pm, and I'm off. I rush to my car heading to the East coast (the Riviera Romagnola, on the other side of the Riviera Ligure where I first heard the news of B.'s guilty verdict three months ago). I'm joining a group of old secondary schoolmates of mine for one of those reunions which we organize once in a while: this time the place is a seaside town called Riccione where we are hosted by a friend in his beautiful sea-view apartment. I'm looking forward to a swim&tan late summer's afternoon and an outdoor fish dinner, dressed with drinks and nostalgia, before autumn comes. As I drive, I turn on the radio. Today there's going to be a showdown in Parliament: a few days ago B., still a senator and still heading his party and politics in general as if nothing had happened, ordered his ministers to resign because the *PD* senators had decided to vote in favour of his expulsion. King Giorgio, whose main aim is to keep the 'inciucio' working, ordered a parliamentary vote of confidence. B. has been tough in the past few days and his decision is taken, no second thoughts. It means the fall of the government, probably new 'porcellum' election and a campaign that B. could direct as leader and victim of an International Communist Mega-Plot, hoping that the dull 'immoral majority' would vote for him once again. *Onrevole* Renato Brunetta - a neurotic-looking MP that seems to step out from one of Fellini's movies, an old time politician from the Craxi era and today *PDL* spokesman - is announcing to the press that the decision to vote against the government has been taken *unanimously*, his voice dividing the syllable of the word to underline its meaning like a primary school teacher. Some minutes later I hear senator Sandro Bondi, the prototype of the vicious filthy secretary of the boss in a *strictly Pickwickian* sense, another member of the unbelievable circle of vulgar people that surrounds B., I hear senator Bondi say the nastiest things a politician can cry out against the government he has backed up to now. I turn off the radio and stop for a sandwich and a cup of coffee; half an hour later I'm driving again, the warm wind of the coast starting to blow. B. enters the Senate as I turn on the radio again and, unexpectedly, asks permission to talk. His speech lasts 2.41 minutes: he says that even if the decision has been taken 'con un certo travaglio' – 'with a certain travail', please note the 'Freudian slip-of-the-tongue' – he has decided to vote in favour of the government in the interest of the country (!!!). It's a *coup de théâtre* that makes me jump at the wheel in amazement and laugh out loud a second later, bewildered by that unprecedented vaudeville show. What happened between his serfs' speeches and his own is that a paparazzo took a picture of a *PDL* minister holding a list of traitors: some ministers, some senators and MPs were about to betray B. for the first time, an event he could not even dream of, because they started to love their privileged positions and were not willing to let them go to help the decaying leader. The rebels are now called 'doves' and they are basically former DC members; the loyalist are called 'hawks' and they belong to the right wing. B. has been forced to vote in favour not to remain isolated with his hawks in the Senate, ready to eat his carcass when the time comes. So the government has the same majority as before, and there has been much ado about nothing. Politically speaking, instead, the government of *PD* Prime Minister Enrico Letta, a previous Christian Democrat himself like many other Dem Party MPs and ministers, has a possible new majority almost entirely composed of previous DC members, the same 'prima repubblica' ambiguous politicians who have followed power wherever it goes (another exemplification of *trasformismo*). In conclusion, it means turning the clock back to the Andreotti Age. The doves are led by vice PM Angelino Alfano, B.'s previous 'dolphin', and the two of them, Letta and Alfano, are now a couple on their honeymoon and the very symbol of the 'inciucio'. Today the Prime Minister is very proud of his new potential majority and refuses to see that the doves are all small size B.s, ready to betray him for the next winning newcomer (as it would soon happen with the election of Matteo Renzi in February 2014). Considering B.'s unexpected new support to the government, it is one more time clear that the Democratic Party is not ready to live without B. since he is a counterweight to keep the identity-less *PD* in artificial balance.

It's now late in the afternoon and my host and I are watching the sunset from his flat's balcony. Maybe inspired by the day's foolish events, he starts telling me that it was Mussolini who made Riccione renowned. Next to his apartment there is a museum, a white villa by the beach now an exhibition centre. It is called Villa Mussolini because il Duce bought it for his wife Rachele Guidi, known as Donna Rachele, in 1934. At weekends Mussolini used to arrive off the coast of Riccione by hydroplane from Rome and refuse the official welcome by the local authorities: he would jump into the sea, swim ashore to show the physical strength of the Italic race inherited by the Ancient Romans and would enter Donna Rachele's house. A few blocks away, in a room of the Grand Hotel, his 'official' lover Claretta Petacci - whom he met in 1932 and that was thirty years younger than him - or some other lover of the period was waiting for him. It is also well known that the duce used to have his many lovers brought directly to his Roman studio in the afternoons of the working days. Back then nobody bothered him about it, his afternoon *bunga-bunga* did not need secrecy and Donna Rachele and Claretta accepted the betrayal as natural. The times have changed but the habits have remained the same and it is quite unfair that poor ole B. has to fight everyday to keep this all Italian fake macho practice alive for the envy of his voters.

The following day I'm driving home in the late afternoon. The sky is cloudy and it looks like rain. Not so in the small island of Lampedusa, south of the Sicilian coast, one of the southernmost stretches of land in Europe where summer never ends. It's the radio again that informs me of the tragic events of the day, taking me back to the real country and making me forget all about yesterday's political *sceneggiata* and its detachment from the real world. Lampedusa is a gateway to Europe for African people that risk their lives to cross the Mediterranean in search of hope, of survival from wars, famine and dictatorships. No matter the price, they are willing to risk it all for a chance in the future. Desperation and hunger carry them forward: they would perish anyway in their homeland. It's a contemporary version of the 'middle-passage' that brought African slaves to America, the 'land of milk and honey'. Today a boat carrying hundreds of illegal migrants from Libya sank off one of the island's beaches where rich tourists were spending their holidays, sun tanning and swimming in the same waters in which the migrants were drowning. It's another snapshot of Italy's *Inferno*, a wonderful surface that conceals the suffering and desperation of a society rotten to the core. The emergency response of the Italian Coast Guard rescued 155 survivors. The death toll after searching the boat was 366 but further bodies are still missing, lost in Mediterranean Sea, the largest cemetery in the world. This is just one episode of a tragic story that has been going on for decades, and we have got so used to it that only when a tragedy of today's dimension takes place we notice it and pity and pray and listen to the politicians talking in vain. When these people arrive on Italian soil they are sent to prison-like *centri di accoglienza* – *welcome centres* –, then accused of illegal immigration and trialled, then sent back home. The ones who manage to escape become illegal *extracomunitari* either enslaved by the mafia or destined to the labour black market, to do the jobs the Italians don't want to do anymore, and they are often discriminated like in the American Deep South of the 50s. The immigrants who survived told the authorities they had to pay 3,500 euros to the local bosses in Africa, then they were sent to 'concentration camps' established in the no-man's-land desert zone near the Libyan border. There, all women, also the ones with children, were raped and beaten. Afterwards, they were taken to the coast and had to pay 1,500 additional euros to cross over to Lampedusa. One of their masters was later recognized by the migrants, there was an attempt to lynch him and he was finally arrested. What B.'s government has produced on the topic is a law called 'Bossi-Fini' which introduced the crime of illegal immigration and expulsion in a blind attempt to stop the 'invasion of the body snatchers'. Fini was the acclaimed leader of the post-fascist *Alleanza Nazionale* party and Bossi the historical leader of the racist party *The Northern League*. One of its members has recently published a picture of the Secretary for Integration, the coloured Ms Kyenge, with a chimpanzee head in his *Facebook* profile. Angelino Alfano was in Lampedusa the day after, Enrico Letta and European Commission's President José M. Barroso were there a few days later, amid the inhabitants' boos, proclaiming to the world media that they would take immediate action: so incisive their acts were that a new shipwreck, that occurred 120 kilometres from Lampedusa on October 11, caused 34 new casualties. Actually a few weeks later the Letta government would establish a task force in the Italian waters, called *Mare Nostrum*, to take care of the problem: compared to B.'s right wing governments, as extremist and anti-welfare as the American 'tea-party', the Letta all-DC government is showing a pale attention to social care, even if the privileged are not touched by its acts at all. It's indeed a fake democracy a society that is not able, or is not willing, to deal with the real social problems and to pursue social justice, a political caste only self-centred, interested in its own survival, in the maintenance of its benefits, engaged in byzantine palace games completely detached from everyday life.

In 2014 the number of illegal immigrants who tried to reach Sicily from Libya increased dramatically and that stretch of water became the invisible cemetery of this contemporary holocaust. *Mare Nostrum* saved a lot of lives, but it was not enough, since the Middle-East and North-African war zones kept pushing those desperate men away from their homeland. All that democratic, Christian, 'welfare' EU was able to do was to plan to substitute *Mare Nostrum* with a EU directed operation called *Frontex Plus*, an enterprise with very limited funds and means.

As far as *liberal forms masking an illiberal substance and the ruling oligarchy and its highly trained elite of soldiers, policemen, thought-manufacturers and mind-manipulators quietly running the show as they see fit* is concerned, what has happened to B. since his August 1 guilty verdict? The anticorruption law he himself voted, the 'legge Severino', says that after the final verdict a senator loses his position *immediately*; moreover, in October the appeal court recalculated the length of B.'s banning from public offices the Court of Cassation had ordered on August 1: B. has now been banned for two years (a verdict definitively confirmed by the highest court in March 2014). We logically think that it's time for him to step down from Senate and that a four-year sentence is to be put into practice at once: the offender must go to jail, or, if the judges agree according to the criminal's attitude and behaviour, he is granted house arrest or is sent to a community for re-education. More than legal dispute, this is common sense. Just like in a normal society an anticorruption law is not only enforced by law, it is implied in public life and offices. So what has happened to B. so far?

For four months all the byzantine legal strategies and palace games have been carried on to let B. maintain his seat as senator, or at least delay his stepping down, by B.'s lawyers, party members, senators and MPs, with the informal complicity of the *PD*, the government and the President. B. has threatened the existence of the government, he still considers himself as the *PDL* leader and the nation's boss, a victim of the Red Scare. All the most hilarious acts of the 'teatrino della politica' – 'the cheap theatre show of politics' – have been used. A series of disputes in the Commission that has to admit the legitimacy of the guilty verdict, the parliamentary agenda that would never fix the date of the vote for B.'s resignation, the discussion if the vote has to be public or secret, the attempt to send the Legge Severino to the Constitutional Court to check if it is applicable in retrospect, the menace to appeal the European Court, and so on and so forth, a series of meaningless pointless acts on which Parliament has spent all its energies and time. In this period the ghost of King

Giorgio's pardon has always been there, because the President has been trying to find an impracticable balance between the survival of the coalition government – his main goal – and the respect of the law. At a certain point, in October, the King sent a note to Parliament invoking a general pardon or an amnesty for humanitarian reasons because of the problem of jail overpopulation. The question exists but, of course, B. would benefit from the act, once again the problems of a single person vs. the ones of the whole of society that keep biasing Italian politics.

Winter has come all of a sudden, as usual. Outside my window the air is chilly and dry and I can see the snow covered mountains glittering in the sun. The call of the wild is the same as it was on August 1, with its deep blue sea inviting you for a refreshing dive. But here I am again, sitting on my sofa and watching Ray News 24 one more time. The Senate is in session, B.'s stepping down is what's on today's agenda, a day I have doubted to see until yesterday. B. has set his circus in motion at its highest speed these last days, a ridiculous final desperate attempt to keep his senatorial position against all odds and reason. It's been a continuous 'reality show' broadcast live, a TV drama with a new episode every day. One and a half months after his Neapolitan 'sceneggiata' on October 2, he has re-founded his original party *Forza Italia* with his hawks, withdrawing his support to the government. The doves, instead, have formed another parliamentary group that backs up the coalition Letta government called *Nuovo Centro-Destra – New Centre-Right*. In his permanent television invasion he has declared that his decadence is a real golpe, an attempt for democracy, the end of the Republic. He has also said, to the fake adoring crowd facing him, that the President should grant him pardon without him asking because he is innocent, pure and has a dignity (a dignity!!) to defend. He has addressed the *PD* and *M5S* senators to reconsider their vote because their conscience will haunt them till the end of time, to do it at least for their children. Finally, like in a soup opera climax, the day before his decadence he showed new documents he had received from the USA which contained last minute evidence and a list of brand new witnesses that would prove his innocence unequivocally, television being the only 'institution' to show trial evidence according to il Cavaliere [actually, I could not find out whether B. presented the magistrates such an obvious 'bufala' (bullshit), but two and a half years later nothing has happened]. So here I am, waiting, and still unsure that it's really happening, while il Cavaliere has gathered his fans outside his Roman residence for a last public speech before the Senate's vote.

The big showdown is a flop, actually. A mourning silence hangs inside the Senate while the speaker reads the results of the voting, except for the obstinate procedural objections made by the Cavaliere's inner circle. At 5.42 pm Berlusconi *decade da senatore* (is a senator no more), three months after the guilty verdict, which in Italy means immediately (his alternative penalty is due to start on April 12). B. is not present in the Senate and in the next few days he disappears, either sheltered in one of his mansions with his new 'magazine cover family' – the calippo eater 'girlfriend' and their dog Dudù –, the papers say, or on some beauty farm for further facial lifting. Occasionally he is heard or seen in his media, declaring his strong opposition to the Letta government he has helped to create, of course not because the *PD* voted in favour of his decadence but 'for Italy's sake'. B. continues to lead *Forza Italia* and plans to campaign for the European elections in May 2014, the first convicted and non-eligible political leader in the West ever. And he is planning to be the new centre-right PM candidate in the political elections to come, asking 51% of the votes to radically reform the country he has been destroying so far. After all, his claims are not a lunatic's vision, in a country like ours… For example, Minister of Justice Anna Maria Cancellieri, despite the scandal she has recently been involved in, is preparing a bill to extend the three year grace granted to almost every criminal today, so that B. could find himself a free man in six months time (even if, with the incumbent new court verdicts, his chances seem slim). A State that has no means to send a criminal to jail because the criminal himself is powerful and rich, actually more powerful than the State itself, is the final and most obvious example that the *liberal forms will merely serve to mask and adorn a profoundly illiberal substance. We are indeed witnessing a reversal of the process which transformed England into a democracy, while retaining all the outward forms of a monarchy.*

In the days that followed his decadence, Italy was a family without its patriarch, an association without its godfather and maybe on the brink of taking the road to normality. But one month later, when the country was slowly getting used to living without B., all of a sudden he was offered a helping hand to come back to centre stage, and with the spotlight on him. Who helped B.? Not much effort is needed to guess: faithful to the 'inciucio' tradition, on January 19, 2014, the newly born *PD* superstar, the mayor of Florence Matteo Renzi, who had become the party's secretary in December 2013 after his stunning victory at the party's primaries, met Berlusconi officially at the *PD* headquarter to make a deal with him about a new electoral law, named *Italicum* but soon nicknamed *Silvium*. As I said earlier in this chapter, the agreement (the 'Patto del Nazareno') included the proposal to amend part of the Constitution, transforming the Senate into a non-elected regional chamber and rewriting the 'Titolo V' that deals with regional powers. As we know, many intellectuals denounced it as a threat to the Constitution and to democracy. For sure it showed again that B., to a certain extent, was vicariously acting through his 'blue-eyed son' Renzi since the deal carried on the basic ideas of constitutional changes Berlusconi proposed in his *ventennio*. Il Cavaliere, who had left the Senate from the back door, re-entered the political scene through the (*PD*) front door and sat under the giant portrait of Che Guevara to decide once again about the destiny of Italy. Renzi, who would become Prime Minister in February 2014 and would lead his party to the greatest victory ever in the European elections of May 2014, is supposed to be a revolutionary leader, not because he likes 'el Che' – to whom he prefers Fiat/Chrysler CEO Marchionne – but because he wants a generational revolution. He is 39 and was former called 'il rottamatore' – the scrap dealer, or *demolition man* according to the British press definition: in his early political days he said that everyone had to be politically vaporized at a certain age, regardless of his capacity, since youth meant wisdom. His mantra is action, to do the things that Italy needs at once instead of talking about it for ages, which is positive of course. Politically speaking, Renzi is a 'liberal conservative', a moderate who carries on the *PD*'s inexorable movement towards the political centre, DC's realm in the First Republic. Berlusconi likes him and wishes he could have a young leader like him for *Forza Italia* while, on the other side, Renzi seems to make an exception in his 'scrapping', as if recognizing the alleged immortality of Italy's godfather. The Renzi-Berlusconi liaison carries on the tradition of the *PD*'s attitude towards il Cavaliere in his times of trouble, as we have pointed out here and there in this paper, another example of *il Gattopardo*'s motto that *everything must change so that nothing really changes*. Moreover, revolutionary Renzi is the first centre-left leader to formally accept il Cavaliere as political interlocutor notwithstanding his new status of convict. *Finché c'è il PD c'è speranza – since when the PD is there, there's hope*, paraphrasing the proverb *finché c'è vita c'è speranza, since when there is life, there's hope* – B. is supposed to have said after meeting Renzi.

Have you ever seen a convicted politician, sentenced for massive tax fraud, forced to lose his senatorial seat, banned from public offices, defendant in a trial for corrupting an opposition senator, who officially encounters the President of the Republic as party leader in the Constitutional meetings to form a new government?

My rhetorical question became reality on February 15, 2014, when B. met President Napolitano on the eve of the new Renzi government which took office on February 22. On that day, previous *il rottamatore/demolition man* Matteo Renzi replaced his own party's PM, Enrico Letta, and became the youngest Italian PM ever. The new coalition government had basically the same majority as before, based on the promise of an ambitious programme of 'revolutionary' moderate reforms that Berlusconi, as just stated, does not dislike to say the least. Renzi's attitude, promises and political climb are similar to Obama's ones in 2008; the new PM is a young man of great energy and charisma and has given rise to high hopes. But what can a 'revolutionary' leader do in a political frame made of people he wanted to 'demolish'? *Demolition man* may be 'revolutionary' but his methods are the old-fashioned Italian ones: he tweeted *Enricostaisereno* [Enrico (Letta) be serene] and *never PM without elections* and a few days later he became Prime Minister. B. said Renzi looks like himself when he was young and so suspicions that actually B. is Renzi's puppeteer run wild, even if *Forza Italia* is opposition again and the new government is backed by the former *PDL*'s 'doves' that formed the 'Nuovo Centro Destra' led by former B.'s *delfino* – heir apparent – Angelino Alfano, Home Secretary in Renzi's government. A government, we suppose today, that is here to stay up to the 2018 political elections. One of the first acts of the Renzi government was the announcement of the declassification of secret files about Italy's terrorism in the lead years. Prof. Rodotà publicly said that the 'Nazareno deal' should be the first to be 'declassified' because it is now supposed to be a much bigger agreement than the part we know, creating a rising concern that B. is still secretly running the show even if his poor results at the European elections pictured his inevitable political decline: Italy's grandmaster, even if politically agonizing, is like a romance dragon with seven lives.

When Silvio Berlusconi stepped out of a shiny black limousine on Friday morning, May 9, 2014, to begin serving his sentence for tax fraud at a hospice for Alzheimer's patients outside Milan and then some days later, on the Friday night before the European elections, I saw him campaigning on state television answering the questions the editor-in-chief of *Libero*, one B.'s newspapers, was asking him, the phrase 'no jail could hold him' flashed to my mind. It was an irreversible last piece of evidence that the State is not able to apply its laws to powerful citizens, let alone omnipotent il Cavaliere.

As the Guardian reported the *77-year-old leader of the Italian right was convicted last year and given a four-year sentence. Three years were taken off because of the continuing effects of an amnesty passed by a centre-left government in 2006, and under legislation approved when Berlusconi was in office, convicted criminals over the age of 70 cannot be sent to prison. He will work at the hospice once a week (…) Paolo Pigni, head of the Catholic-run Fondazione Sacra Famiglia, near Milan, said the former Italian Prime Minister would work in the part of the centre dedicated to caring for people with dementia and Alzheimer's disease (…) The media magnate – who has been ordered to work at the centre for disabled and elderly people one day a week for at least four hours – will help out with a morning programme including motor activities, reading, writing and games.*

Berlusconi's pro-forma sentence at a hospice for old and disabled people is really a *Divine Comedy*'s *contrappasso*: from *bunga-bunga* nights with young girls to morning service to help old people in need is exactly what Dante would have thought for this kind of sinners in his *Inferno*. Actually, Berlusconi has been free as a normal law-abiding citizen since his August 2013 conviction, the day in which I felt the moral duty to write this book. His fake penalty, which has granted him the 'agibilità politica' he kept asking for, was given him against any plausible reason by the 'Bolshevik' magistracy, B.'s ultimate enemy, which has proved to be itself influenced by il Cavaliere's mighty power. Social services are granted to convicts who accept their faults, repent and respect the judges, exactly the opposite B. has done in his life and after his guilty verdict. Every time I turned my TV on in May he was there, invading his own media and the public ones as before, campaigning and promising and telling us the he is the answer to social problems, as if he had lived on the moon in the last twenty years. His name is still on the party logo; I suppose it is the first time a non eligible *pregiudicato*'s surname appears in a party symbol because that name means many more votes. It's a metaphor of *Forza Italia*, of the country in general and another example of erosion of democracy.

The European elections showed one thing for sure: the economic crisis weighing on the citizens' shoulders since 2008 has created an area of discontent and mistrust towards the European national governments often forced to apply the unpopular measures imposed by the austerity policy of the EU. It is a vast area of voters, from 20% to 30%, which have given rise to populist Eurosceptic protest movements of different types, either demagogical against-it-all parties or, more dangerously, to neo-fascist extreme-right racist xenophobic parties which have slimmed the traditional progressive or conservative parties to such an extent that in some cases they have become their nations' top parties. With the exception of Greece, in which the left wing Syriza has channelled protest in an updated traditional left wing policy, the rage of the suffering people has been directed into a sterile pointless protest that gives them no hope. It is the fall of traditional political thought, a dramatic sign of the times, in a way a European follow-up to what has happened in Italy for the last twenty years, a country, as we know well by now, in which too many poor people thought that a corrupt multimillionaire charlatan would govern taking care of their problems instead of his own. It is also a further step towards the realization of Huxley's dystopian predictions. As *the Guardian* reports the day after the elections, in Greece *in a historic day for the left, the anti-austerity Syriza won the ballot by a margin of nearly four points [getting 27% of consent] over the conservative New Democracy party led by Prime Minister Antonis Samaras. Instead, with about 9.37% of the vote, it was the far-right Golden Dawn's showing that is likely to shake the Greek political establishment most.* In France *the far-right FN had done better than even it had probably expected or hoped, polling a historic 25% of votes in theEuropean electionsand becoming France's top party on the European stage.* In the U.K. *the Eurosceptic party's victory [the Ukip led by Nigel Farage] marked the first time in modern history that neither Labournor the Conservatives have won a British national election. In a stunning warning to the established political parties, Ukip was on course to win as much as 28% of the national poll.* In Italy *figures from the interior ministry put former comedian Beppe Grillo's M5S on 21.2%*

(…)

In an astonishingly strong showing that not even the most optimistic of PD figures had expected, Renzi's pro-European party – which last year performed disappointingly at the general election under a previous leader – was on 40.8% on Monday morning with most votes counted … M5S on 21.2% [is considered] a disappointing performance for a movement that had vowed to be Italy's largest party at the European elections. The Forza Italia (FI) party of former Prime Minister Silvio Berlusconi, meanwhile, took just 16.8% – the lowest ever vote share for the tax fraud-convicted media magnate. His one-time heir apparent, Angelino Alfano, who split from him last year to form the New Centre Right (NCD) and who is the key coalition partner in Renzi's government, only just managed, with 4.4%, to get over the threshold for representation in the European parliament. The rightwing, Eurosceptic Northern League won 6.2%. Italians were voting to elect 73 MEPs, the same number as Britain.

In Italy we have a strange way to read electoral results: over 4.600.000 people voted for a party whose leader is a convict banned from public life and its co-founder is in a state prison with Totò Riina, and we keep saying it was a debacle. *M5S* got over 21% and is credited of a defeat, but actually for a protest movement born a few years ago, that entered Parliament last year, it is in reality a success. Of course it was Matteo Renzi who led the Pd to this unprecedented success: his pervasive energy and his promises for a real change got to the people's belly, an energy similar not only to that of Obama in 2008, but also to Berlusconi's in 1994. It's the new messiah Italy is always waiting for: he has made the promises, now the country is waiting for the facts. In the days after his taking office he appeared on TV showing a series of slides with the reforms his government is bound to make and their timing, an early-Berlusconi media performance that gave him the nickname of Mr. Slide. Most of the social, political, moral reforms he promised are the urgent things to do in Italy, from the point of view of a moderate political leader. Politically, they can be discussed both from the left and from the right, but they are a starting point.

Alas, I have to say now, after some months in charge as Prime Minister, Matteo Renzi's slides have become the cover of an empty book. As I report earlier in this chapter, up to now, September 2014,

Renzi has promised every possible radical change in every possible field of public life, but unfortunately nothing important has been done so far. His '100 days' revolution has already shifted to '1,000 days' since realpolitik has stepped in leaving inexperienced Renzi and his mediocre ministers trapped into the dark reality of Italy. Time will tell, of course: 1,000 days, three years, means the end of his mandate, and this a more reasonable time to make reforms for good. But, as far as I can see, the chances for a real change are slim because Renzi is slowly revealing himself as the usual almost Christian Democrat politician, a soft version of the 'neo-con' philosophy, as I have defined him a few pages ago. Up to now he has actually granted an extra 80 euros per month to workers whose salaries are below 1,500 euros a month (the so called *bonus Irpef*), but the important reforms are still to be started. Not necessarily this is negative fact, since we have seen that the reforms made in Berlusconi's *ventennio* and the ones started in the early months of the Renzi government have actually been counter-reforms, as if every time we touch the status quo, a much needed affair, things get worse, paradoxically. Of Renzi's promised reforms to change the face of Italy once and for all, we have already discussed immigration, the *Unblock Italy* decree, the first legs of the reforms of the Senate and of the *Italicum*, approved by the Lower House thanks to the Berlusconi-Renzi agreement but then forgotten because of the contrasts among the parties.

Still missing are the majority of the promised first steps towards the solutions of the troubles the government indicated: the Bourbon state bureaucracy, the debts of the Public Administration, the prison system, public housing, Italy's enormous Public Debt, Europe's strict austerity, the negative figures of the GDP that has helped the development of recession, the privileges of political *Caste*, the help to families, the cut to military expenses (to the F35 war planes mainly), the spending review, the reassessment of RAI and its relationship with politics, and so on. As far as employment is concerned, in October 2014 Renzi won the most important parliamentary confidence vote of his eight-month-old government on labour reform proposals that he hopes will boost his EU credentials (the so-called 'jobs act'). *The government's proposals are still very broad-brushed, however, and it remains to be seen how far Renzi's proposed reforms will go... Senators voted on a so-called "delegating law" [DDL] which authorizes the government to work out the details of the reform over the coming months (the*

Guardian). It is as usual a low-profile compromise solution, another act in reality postponed to better days with a very conservative flavour attached. The Senate session for the approval was another lipstick comedy show as the ones I report later in this chapter. The reform of education has just been presented with a lot of emphasis and propaganda, as usual. All the ministers went to the school they attended on the first day of the new school year. This is my cup of tea and, after the dark age of Berlusconism which cut cut cut money for education and considered teachers as enemies, I expected a more challenging reform from the top priority Renzi gives, in words, to the school system. Nothing really new and brilliant is visible behind the surface and so the long run of the proposed reform is once again welcome.

In the beginning of the Renzi age there was the unkept promise to solve the problem of the conflicts of interests, to fight corruption, tax evasion and the mafia. Indeed the question remains the same: since he came on duty without election, how can energy propelled Renzi carry on his plans when his majority is the same ancient corrupt regime he wants to get rid of? Just to give an example, he must satisfy the former Berlusconi's political right arm Alfano and his new right party of old FI and DC leaders, most of them in deep trouble with justice. At this point, other overwhelming questions come naturally: is Renzi there because Berlusconi wanted to? Are the fearsome changes in the Constitution we have discussed and, in general, the realization the reforms wanted by B. the real beef of the 'patto del Nazareno'? Is the convicted Cavaliere still so strong to impose his will and to blackmail? Is, in the end, today's 'revolutionary' government a continuation of Berlusconi's bloodline? Comparing the 2009 and 2014 elections, who did the mafia vote for this time? There are indeed many clues pointing in the direction of political continuity: where has the promised law against the conflict of interests gone? And the promise to cancel the immoral laws *ad personam*? And the contrast to tax evasion, to corruption? A real fight against the mafia? These last issues are the only spending review that makes any sense in our country. Corruption, tax evasion and mafia business amount to 400 billion euros a year approximately: fighting them for real would mean forcing criminals and dishonest citizens to pay the price of the economic crisis, instead of the normal ones, taxpaying and honest, who have paid so far. Some days before the printing of this book,

October 2014, I patiently listened to Renzi illustrating the two Houses of Parliament his 'Millegiorni' plan that can be followed at the official governmental site 'passodopopasso – mille giorni per cambiare l'Italia' – 'step by step – 1,000 days to change Italy'. Not a single word was uttered on the topics I have just mentioned, while the catchphrases on the reforms to come we have got used to by now were repeated again, together with a light accusation to the press and to magistrates in a soft Cavaliere style. In the very following days Renzi proposed to abolish the most important article of the Italian Statute of Workers, article no.18, that forbids employers to fire their workers without a right motive. The abolition would pave the way to a First Industrial Revolution kind of master-worker relationship, an act of contemporary servitude that B. has always tried to approve. Renzi is not listening to the Unions' protests but in Detroit he has just met Fiat/Chrysler CEO Marchionne, the personification of the dismantling of the rights of the working people, as if they were the best of friends.

As far as justice and corruption are concerned, why did the *PD* propose as European candidates characters who are being investigated or are under trial, notwithstanding Renzi's verbal intransigence against corruption? It is the old Berlusconian tune that says that they are innocent until proved guilty. But this is not true in politics: politicians under investigation must resign for public moral's sake, and, if they are later found innocent, that is a price to pay to honest politics, a little fee compared to the privileges public office grants.

This is exactly what happened to the former President of Germany Christian Wulff: on February 17, 2012, Wulff resigned as President of Germany, facing the prospect of prosecution for allegations of corruption relating to his prior service as Prime Minister of Lower Saxony. According to Italian standards, the accusations were trivial: there were questions concerning the purchase of a house, for which Wulff accepted a loan from an entrepreneur with whom he was friend (Scajola and Galan *docet*). Then he tried to influence the media coverage before the breaking of the scandal (I can still hear B.'s laughter). Additional investigations were launched into Wulff's political dealings with various entrepreneurs with whom he and his family spent their private vacations (Italian politicians' favourite pastime). Since it was not clear who had paid for these holidays, Wulff was subsequently accused of favoritism and unethical behaviour. In February 2014 the former President was acquitted of all corruption charges but he did not go back to the political scene, and no one was surprised. For us, cold efficient, and moral, Germany is still very far away: could you think of Berlusconi acting like the president of Bayern Munich, former football star Uli Hoeness, who in March 2014 was sentenced to three and a half years in jail for tax fraud (it cost the state more than €28.5m), but did not appeal the verdict and went to prison. In Italy, this is still science-fiction.

In conclusion, I want to underline for the very last time the fact that in a country like Italy whatever has to be done needs a deal with the corrupt ones who still hold power in their hands. Let me just quote at random some of the facts about our public life we have discovered in the last days. Even if the macroscopic examples of *malaffare* that follow refer to a very short period, we can take them as paradigmatic of our reality *tout court*.

To begin from the top, two ministers of the Letta government have been involved in scandals. The Minister of Justice Anna Maria Cancellieri, called 'the nanny of Italy', was wiretapped while trying to help a rich and powerful family in the real estate building business, the Ligrestis, most of whom are in jail for corruption. The minister said it was just a humanitarian help to people in need who happened to have her mobile number and so she refused to step down. Now I expect every prisoner in Italy is given her number so he can call the minister directly as soon as he has a problem, instead of reporting it to the prison's authorities. The other case is the one concerning the Minister of the Agrarian Policies Nunzia De Girolamo, a young lady who was a former Berlusconi fan and *PDL* MP, now a 'lamb' of the *Nuovo Centro Destra*. It has been discovered that she allegedly leads a mafia style organization which imposed 'its people' in top positions and awarded contracts to 'its firms' in the National Helth Service branch of Benevento, a town near Naples, the minister's hometown. Inspired by her idol, she said it was just a plot against her by unknown forces, but in the end she was forced to resign. Despite Renzi's theory of the *rottamazione*, young and old politicians still act the same way. Besides, on. De Girolamo is also married to a *PD* MP, the 'inciucio protocol' at family level.

Going local, 546 regional councillors are under investigation in 16 (out of 20) Italian regions for electoral refunding: they just took the public money and used it for their personal expenses, trying to imitate the Great Gatsby lifestyle one century afterwards. The 'top' region is Sicily, not a difficult guess, with its 97 councillors. 60,000,000 euros is the amount of money the magistrates are now checking. This Italian attitude has its nationwide hero, the former Lazio councillor and *PDL* member Franco Fiorito, the tall fat guy who seems to have come out of a minor gangster movie and that was known all over the capital for his Ancient Rome style parties and its naïve show-off of wealth. In 2013 he was sentenced to 3 years and 4 months in jail by the lower court. In the public mind, he is the perfect partner of Francesco Schettino, the commander-in-chief of the Costa Concordia liner who abandoned the sinking ship full of passengers after he had made it hit a rock near the Isola del Giglio in January 2012. The accident led to 32 casualties; the first leg of Schettino trial started in December 2012 [The captain was given a 16 year sentence in the first trial in February 2015].

Some councillors of the centre-left mayor's cabinet (including the vice-mayor) have been arrested and other are being investigated in L'Aquila, the town not far from Rome destroyed by the 2009 earthquake. Berlusconi used the catastrophe for political speculations and even moved the July 2009 G8 summit from Sardinia to L'Aquila. He promised the world he would soon rebuild the town with unknown efficiency for the Italian standard: today the town is still in ruins. We all heard the wiretapped conversation between two real estate entrepreneurs, a few hours after the quake, who were laughing and joking on how lucky they had been, the 900 casualties a motive of happiness for the business to come, sure as they were to get the assignment for the reconstruction from the national *Protezione Civile – Civil Defense* – which was later proved to have very corrupt top managers. Now the arrested councillors were wiretapped saying the same things, using the expression 'che culo il terremoto!' – 'what an ass the earthquake!', a vulgar idiom meaning 'what a stroke of good fortune …'. The *PD* mayor Massimo Cialente stepped down after a few days, but then he thought twice about his decision, following the Italian typical protocol. The old bribing system seems quite old-fashioned today: when bribe money is not enough, these criminals hope for a natural catastrophe: the higher the casualties, the better. Che culo!

In February 2014 one of B.'s political allies, Raffaele Lombardo, President of Sicily from 2008 to 2012, was sentenced to six years, eight months in jail for 'concorso esterno in associazione mafiosa' ('external complicity in mafia association') in the first trial. He matches former Sicilian President and B.'s ally Salvatote Totò Cuffaro, in charge from 2001 to 2008, currently serving a 7 years jail sentence for aiding the mafia ('favoreggiamento aggravato' – 'aggravated aiding and abetting'). The Cuffaro administration was 'famous' for the peculiar operating system of the Sicilian public Health Service which gave most of the public money to mafia-governed private hospitals and clinics [Cuffaro was sentenced in January 2011 by the Court of Cassation but left prison in December 2015, after almost five years in jail].

In these days the government has started a spending review in order to try to build up a new public image of 'clean politics': the assessment started examining the annual expenses of palazzo Chigi, home of the government. It has been found out that last year 20,000 euros were spent for mineral water, 2,000 euros for hand soap, 6,000 euros for paper boxes, 2,000 euros to rent bed sheets (what do sheets have to do with the government's offices? Was it done under *bunga-bunga* influence?), 25,000 euros to wash the curtains, 4,000 euros for coffee capsules and, last but not least, 14,000 euros for Rome's American Football team, an institution clearly linked to the government's affairs. This last item is borrowed from a consolidated procedure attached to the 'Legge di Stabilità', the 'stability law' issued every year which approves the annual budget of the State: many MPs manage to insert in the law a paragraph in favour of their community of the most extravagant kind, which has nothing to do with the social institutions the stability law finances for the survival of the state itself.

To end this review of last days' news, in *Servizio Pubblico* Marco Travaglio reported that, according to his researches, the *Guardia di Finanza* has discovered an enormous amount of money of tax evasion that the State has a legal right to claim; unfortunately, the State is not able to legally force the evaders to give the money back.

The worst thing is that we all know what's going on, but we don't care, and so nothing really happens except endless talks, a fact I suppose my foreigner reader is hardly able to comprehend. It is the final evidence that Berlusconism has penetrated every alveolus of public life, and that Huxley was absolutely right: just read the quotation that opens the following 'what can be done' section!

As I hinted in the introduction, while I was reviewing this work, on February 3, 2014 the European Commission issued its first *Anti-Corruption Report* (a European Commission proposal to publish a bi-annual report to monitor and assess the efforts of Member States of the European Union in tackling corruption). In reading it I was both relieved and angry at the same time. On the one hand they confirmed all I have said so far with their authoritative voice, reassuring myself I'm not a visionary lunatic, but on the other hand they kind of overlapped my writing and my effort. First of all the report states that Italy alone is responsible for half the amount of corruption in the whole of the UE (28 countries): *The Italian Court of Audit pointed out that the total direct costs of corruption amount to EUR 60 billion each year (equivalent to approximately 4% of GDP)* while it is EUR 120 billion altogether. This fact alone should have made the front page headlines but the majority of the media preferred the ongoing never-ending daily episode of the 'teatrino della politica'. As the commission wrote about our media, a sad issue we know well, *while the capacity of printed media to report corruption is quite high, independence and ownership, mainly of electronic media, have faced considerable challenges over time, notably due to a long-standing quasi-monopoly ... Italy has a low score in the 2013 Freedom of the Press index of Freedom House, which places it in the category of countries where the press is assessed as 'partially free'.* The report confirms that Italian people are used to all this and don't care anymore: according to the commission, 97% of Italians agree that corruption is widespread in their home country and 88% of Italian citizens believe that bribery and the use of connections is often the easiest way to obtain certain public services. *Also mistrust in public institutions appears to be widespread (...) The public offices and sectors most distrusted are: political parties; politicians at national, regional and local levels; officials awarding public tenders and officials issuing building permits. As for business, 92% of Italian business respondents to the 2013 Eurobarometer Business Survey on Corruption believe that favouritism and corruption hamper business competition in Italy.* The section *Issues in Focus* opens with a chapter titled *High-level corruption and links with organized crime* in which all the dangerous liaisons among politics, mafia and business I have discussed with reference to il Cavaliere are pointed out and also become didactic: *the case of Italy is among the most illustrative for showing how closely organised crime and corruption are related*. The example chosen is that of former *PDL* MP Nicola Cosentino and his links with the Camorra[12]. In 2013 Cosentino became famous as he moved straight from Parliament to prison and in 2014 for having the keys of the *Reggia di Caserta* to jog there undisturbed by the vulgar masses. The *Royal Palace of Caserta*, a town near Naples, is another Italian artistic treasure of the XVIII century. It is a royal residence constructed for the Bourbon kings of Naples, one of the largest buildings in Europe; today it is a UNESCO World Heritage Site. Unluckily, in April 2014 Cosentino was arrested again with the accusation of being the boss of a camorra racket dealing with petrol distribution, and had to return the keys [in September 2015 the trial began].

The second chapter, titled *Financing of Political Parties*, describes what I have just written in the previous paragraphs. The report praises the anti-corruption 'legge Severino' issued in 2012 but underlines the fact that it is not in the least enough. The new law does not change the perception of a normative picture of almost unpunishability. The report then describes all the causes of the

---

12 *A series of corruption cases in recent years has also led to resignations of party leaders and senior members. In many of these cases the allegations concerned misuse of party funds. More than 30 MPs of the former Parliament have been or are being investigated for corruption-related offences or illegal party financing. Some of these are still undergoing investigation or court proceedings, and some have been convicted in the first instance. For some, the cases were dismissed as they became time-barred or the offences were decriminalised. For some, the statute of limitations intervened before the cases were adjudicated in court through a final decision. One case to be mentioned concerns an MP [Cosentino]investigated for links with the Camorra – the Casalesi criminal group – related to the financing of his electoral campaign in exchange for exerting political influence at national level, notably in the area of recycling toxic waste. A pre-trial arrest of the MP in question was twice denied in the Italian Parliament (i.e. refusal to lift immunity). During the parliamentary electoral campaign of early 2013, a petition circulated and gathered over 150,000 signatures from citizens and 878 from electoral candidates who committed to making the new anti-corruption law more effective.* (EU Anti-Corruption Report 2013 - Italy)

present situation my patient reader knows well: the statute of limitations, B.'s best friend, is granted a whole chapter in which the Mills-Berlusconi case is used as example. It is followed by a precise description of the other *ad personam* laws il Cavaliere has left as his endgame gift to our country (Lodo Alfano, ex-Cirielli, legitimate impediment, decriminalisation of false accounting and so on.[13]). Then the other notorious aspects linked to corruption are reported, from the lack of transparency in party financing and in public contracts to the issues of money laundering and of 'voto di scambio'. *We must be happy that Europe raps over our knuckles because of the mafia – politics relationships; on the contrary, we keep denying also those between Andreotti and Cosa Nostra* writes former Palermo Public Prosecutor Giancarlo Caselli in an article titled *Mafia e Politica, qui si continua a negare tutto* written as editorial on the UE report. Actually, in April 2014 the Democratic Party and Forzia Italia, to confirm the Berlusconi-Renzi's background agreement, voted in favour of a new law against 'voto di scambio politico-mafioso' (vote in exchange of favours between *mafiosi* and politicians) which is a step forward, if compared with the previous one that was completely inefficient. However, *Forza Italia* imposed a lowering of the penalty period for that crime, so that in reality no politician will seriously run the risk of going to jail for such a popular offense.

---

13 *Establishing a legal framework that would ensure effective processing and finalisation of court proceedings in complex cases was hampered on various occasions. On a number of occasions, Parliament passed or attempted to pass ad personam laws favouring politicians who were also defendants in criminal proceedings, including for corruption offences. One example is the draft law on 'short prescription term' (prescrizione breve) [ex-Ciriellí] which would have increased the risk of dismissing cases involving defendants with no prior convictions. Another one was the law allowing for the suspension of criminal proceedings until the end of the term of office for offences committed prior to or while in office by a certain category of high-level officials [lodo Alfano]. The law was later found to be unconstitutional. Another law adopted in 2010 gave the members of the Council of Ministers the possibility to invoke a 'legitimate impediment' for not showing up at court hearings in a criminal proceeding. These provisions were declared unconstitutional. Decriminalisation of certain offences, such as certain forms of false accounting in 2002, could also be mentioned in this context.* (EU Anti-Corruption Report 2013 - Italy)

In the same period, Stefano Livadiotti, a journalist of the weekly magazine *l'Espresso*, has published a book about tax evasion in Italy in the last thirty years titled *Ladri. Gli evasori e i politici che li proteggono (Thieves. Tax evaders and the politicians who protect them)* published by Bompiani. It is a detailed survey based on figures and objective scientific data which tells us the way the centre-left governments tried to fight it while B.'s governments systematically dismantled this attempt. The author asks himself if it is just the unhealthy idea of considering taxes as absolute evil to guide the hand of Berlusconi. Unfortunately, the explanation that emerges from the book is bleaker: sociologists and political analysts ensure that, after the fall of ideologies, the party of tax evaders has become crucial to win the elections in Italy.

Finally, as my reader knows from chapter one of part two, 2014 is the period of the maxi scandals of the Milan 2015 Expo, of the Venice *Mose* and of *Mafia Capitale*, three big neo-Tangentoli cases that confirmed the EU Commission report.

In the same days the Italian Parliament showed its most tragic-hilarious face in a feud we would expect in a silent movie era's lipstick comedy or in a hooligans' street fight. It was a riot caused by the Lower Chamber's President's decision to 'guillotine' parliamentary discussion on a bill in order to put an end to *M5S*'s stonewall. The *M5S* MPs reacted in a way that reminded me of the behaviour of the fascist party in the 1920s. The riot had a live soundtrack too: the *M5S* MPs chanted 'fascists' to the other groups, in response the left wing MPs sang the partisans' hymn *Bella Ciao* while the right wing MPs vocalized the national anthem *Fratelli d'Italia*; in the middle of it all different sexist vulgar remarks were addressed to female MPs by their male counterparts. It was an unprecedented scene in the West we had seen only in developing Asian/South American countries. Hereafter you can see the riots in the *Euronews* report and *Scelta Civica* MP Stefano Dambruoso's aggression to *M5S* MP Loredana Lupo. Paradoxically, Dambruoso is the Chamber's police superintendent (*https://www.youtube.com/watch?v=fRrPFQcn4mM;https://www.youtube.com/watch?v=o9rhln42l0Y&feature=youtu.be*).

[The *Foreword to the 2016 edition* is an update to the *Frantic Italian teatrino della politica*. In deals with the period in which the fall of *Il Cavaliere* merged with the rise of *Demolition Man*]

Chapter three

Corruption, violence, beauty in Italian football:

a mirror of society

Coppa Italia - *Three Napoli supporters wounded by pistol shots: one risks his life, the shooter beaten to a bloody pulp. A firefighter wounded by a flare. Fiorentina – Napoli kick-off delayed 45 minutes by the chief of the police after an unnerving negotiation with Napoli ultras. The 'Olimpico' final was supposed to be a celebration, instead it was a picture of the sad condition of our football –* La Gazzetta Soportiva front page headline, May 4, 2014

As I am watching the tranquil countryside rolling by from the window of the high-speed train that is carrying me back home from Rome, the thought flashes to my mind. Italian football is the mirror of our society: it means organized crime connections, both at top management level or at mafia and camorra rank; it means corruption, in match fixing, slush funds creation and drug use; it means another weapon of mass consent in the hand of the demagogical political candidate. But it also means beauty and aestheticism. It's May 4, 2014, the day after camorra-linked 'Gerry the swine' and his gang of Naples ultras have shown Italy and the whole of Europe, live on TV, who the boss is in the country. Last night at Stadio Olimpico Prime Minister Matteo Renzi and all the Italian top authorities were there, sitting in their VIP seats and taking no action, just watching the hooligans in the *curva* dictating Napoli captain Hamsik their conditions in order to let the match begin and to maintain public order. The game in question was Coppa Italia final Napoli vs Fiorentina, which was about to become a battle inside and outside the Stadio Olimpico. And I happened to be there.

Outside my window the country is green up to the top of the hills on which most of the medieval villages of central Italy were built. They come and go quickly, constantly changing the skyline; above them the clouds are rolling away, leaving the sky bright and azure, bringing in the long hot Mediterranean summer. The striking beauty of the landscape is the ideal background for emotions recollected in tranquillity: the violent scenes I witnessed yesterday and the picturesque sight outside my window are another example of the dichotomy superficial beauty / hidden Inferno that characterizes our nation, a leitmotiv of this essay of mine. It all started in the afternoon after I left my favourite *trattoria* in Trastevere and decided to take a stroll and enjoy my lazy Roman Saturday afternoon. I crossed the river Tiber, walked through the Isola Tiberina, stopped to enjoy the view I had seen in the final sequence of *The Great Beauty* and kept walking until I reached Largo Argentina. There I sat down among the ancient Roman ruins with my headset on and my smart phone transmitting *Serie B* live. My favourite team, Modena FC from my hometown, struggling for a play-off position, were playing Siena away. The score was 1 – 3 with still ten minutes to go and there I was, amid the ancient ruins, waiting for the final whistle that seemed never to come. There's no need to admit that I am not immune to the football craze which is spread all over the country. We all know that down here, in the Deep South of Europe, the modern holy trinity is *la mamma, il Papa, la squadra di calcio.* We also know that some – if not most – of our football is fake, so why do we keep watching it, as if under a spell? Sure enough there has always been aestheticism in our football, which is at present being blown away because of the development of the athletic part of the game and of its global standardization, an evolution which holds inside an involution process similar to the erosion of the hallmarks of the country – from creativeness to moral values – done by commercial television in this second *ventennio*. In *The Dark Heart of Italy* Tobias Jones saw it clearly:

> *Comparing Italian and British football (not necessarily at the top level, but down the divisions) is like comparing snooker with darts. One is cerebral, stylish, slipping the ball across the smooth green felt; the other a bit overweight, slightly raucous, throwing the occasional arrow in the right direction. The more you watch Italian football, the more you realise why Italy, having been introduced to the sport by the British in 1893, has won three World Cups [actually four]: Italians are simply very good at the game. They play the most beautiful, cultured and skilful football imaginable. Talk to any Italian about the strengths of the Italian game, and they will always mention the two vital ingredients lacking in Britain:* fantasia e furbizia -- *fantasy and cunning. Fantasy is*

the ability to do something entirely unpredictable with the ball. The British, I'm endlessly told, will always try to pass through a defence, or run past it, but they never actually outwit it. That's what Italian fantasists do: they produce a nanosecond of surprise that springs open a defence. It can be a back-heel, a dummy, a pretence of being off-balance. It's the one side of football that can't be taught. It has to be instinctive, suddenly inspired, which is why the fantasisti are so admired: they are touched by an indefinable genius.

Unluckily, in the last decade, *fantasisti* like Roberto Baggio have slowly disappeared from our pitches, blown away by the roboplayers science has produced, while in England the arrival of foreign coaches has added class to the traditional masculine British style. Anyway, all over the world of football, the never ending flow of sheiks' money has spoiled the game, creating hyper-rich teams of top players which form a caste of their own.

Even if the traditional beauty of our football is vanishing and at the same time we know that some of it is false, why do we keep watching it? I redirect the reader to the part of this essay in which I discuss reality control, *doublethink* and brainwashing, in our society controlled by media propaganda, which have made the Berlusconi phenomenon possible. Probably the blindness of many Berlusconi voters is the same as the Juventus *tifoso*'s who still believes that the *scudetti* won thanks to doping, match fixing and referees' corruption in the Moggi era were real.

In Italy political power has always been intimately linked to football, and there's nothing new about one determining the other write Jones in a chapter called *Penalties and Impunity*, written when corruption in football was just a suspicion. I would add to the statement that our football is also intimately linked to big (and often corrupt) business and the mafia, and that the three entities are so closely tied that sometimes they merge making it difficult to say which is which. If politics is insanely linked to the two of them (like the 1992 Mani Pulite investigation, today's Milan Expo 2015 *tangentopoli* and Berlusconi's alleged agreement with the mafia in the period of the 'State-mafia negotiation' exemplify at a microscopic level), why should football not be?

It is a fact that the mafia, the *camorra* and the *'ndrangheta*, which rule in the South, have deeply penetrated local football, the lower the division the more the fact is evident. It is one of the best ways to reinforce social consent and it is also a good way to launder the dirty money of their illegal businesses. At top level, the use and abuse of football made by Berlusconi throughout his political saga is a well-known fact. AC Milan, of which he has been president since 1986, is another bullet of his Weapon of Mass Deception I have identified mainly with il Cavaliere's possession and control of most of the media in Italy. My foreign reader knows well B.'s usage of the football jargon in his political career: his party's name itself, *Forza Italia*, was named after a chant from the terraces, his MPs were the *azzurri*, his political engagement was a *discesa in campo*, the party's anthem is like a football hymn and throughout his career he has always used the most commonplace football metaphorical expressions. According to his alleged natural born corrupter's style, assumingly Berlusconi used his team as a source of tax evasion and slush funds creation so that *Milan's trophy cupboard contains skeletons as well as trophies*. The most famous example is the Lentini case. In 1992 Milan paid Torino football club the then extraordinary sum of 18.5 billion lire for the player Gianluigi Lentini. The president of Torino alleged that 6.5 billion lire of that amount was a black payment made to a Swiss bank account to avoid taxes, B.'s standard suspected procedure as businessman and politician we have seen so far. Since the player had his proposed salary cut from four billion to one and a half billion lire a year, the Torino president also suspected that Berlusconi topped it up in cash from his slush funds, which, presumably, he has never been short of throughout his career. Besides, it was claimed that in the affair Milan got shares in Torino, a rival club, a further example of the conflicts of interests this essay is filled with. The court case, named after Clean Hands, became known as Dirty Feet. The Dirty Feet case is another edifying case of conflict of interests: as we know, when Berlusconi became Prime Minister a few years later, he cancelled the offence of false accounting; consequently, as usual, due to the new laws, the statute of limitations killed the proceeding and therefore the case was closed with an acquittal on July 4, 2002.

The absolute power that il Cavaliere has had in the political field in his *ventennio* has been challenged in football by The Old Lady of

Italian football, Turin's Juventus, owned by the Agnelli family, the proprietors of the FIAT corporation, always referred to as the owners of Italy before the age of Berlusconi, whom they see as a disturbing parvenu. Even if they considered themselves as real gentlemen, they did not hesitate to use all the illegal methods to win again when, in the nineties, B. challenged their supremacy both in power and on the pitch. Since B. had bought Milan in 1986, the *rossoneri* had won an astonishing number of trophies. In 1994, the year of B.'s discesa in campo, Juventus decided to hire the Neapolitan administrator Luciano Moggi, nicknamed Lucky Luciano by Marco Travaglio[14], who would became the absolute gray eminence of Italian football, establishing a mafia-style *cupola* that would fake results in favour of Juventus, until the cupola was discovered in 2006 and *calciopoli* and *scandalo doping*, as for *calcioscommesse*, entered the Italian and the international dictionaries.

Its background is described by the 2004 article titled *The drug scandal that blackens the name of Juve's team of the Nineties – Club doctor sentenced to jail as doping controversy intensifies* published in *The Independent*:

> *In 1994 Italy's most successful club, Juventus, had not won the league title for eight years. The club's proprietors, Giovanni and Umberto Agnelli, owners of the Fiat motoring empire, were extremely concerned. They dreamt of a new golden era, but knew they had to overhaul the club's senior management if it was to become reality. In making changes they were ruthless. In came the former Fiat executive Antonio Giraudo as managing director; Luciano Moggi, then with Roma, and an acknowledged master of the transfer market, was hired as sporting director; the club's former striker Roberto Bettega was made vice-president. The triumvirate promptly appointed Marcello Lippi, then with Napoli, as the club's new head coach. The revolution extended to a shake-up of backroom staff with Riccardo Agricola, a neuro-pathologist who has been part of the medical team since 1985, promoted to club doctor.*
>
> *The changes worked spectacularly. There was also an influx of new playing talent, and inspired by the likes of Zinedine Zidane*

---

14 Ala Sinistra, Mezzala Destra (pseudonyms for Marco Travaglio), *Lucky Luciano. Intrighi maneggi scandali del padrone del calcio Luciano Moggi*, Kaos edizioni, 2006.

and Alessandro Del Piero, Juventus embarked on a period of success impressive even by their own high standards. The Old Lady, as the club is affectionately known, won Serie A titles in 1995, 1997 and 1998, and reached the Champions' League final in three successive years, winning it in 1996. They also won the European Super Cup, the Coppa Italia and two Italian Super Cups.

It was a remarkable era, but now the brilliance of that team and their dominance has been seriously questioned, and there are many in Italy who are asking whether it was all too good to be true.

We all remember fragile players like Alex Del Piero building up their bodies as if they were body-builders in no time, the obvious effect of the EPO they were supposedly given to enhance their performances. The story of the illegal drug use made by Juventus is brilliantly told in the novel *Quarto Tempo* by doctor Claudio Gavioli who has been club doctor for professional football teams for the last twenty years. The court case that followed ended up exactly like all the trials against il Cavaliere we have followed so far: in the end, against all logic, Juve got away clean, a further example, if needed, that in this country powerful people are never touched by the law. Penalties, alas, exist on the pitch only:

Last Friday in Turin's Palazzo di Giustizia, Judge Giuseppe Casalbore sentenced Agricola to 22 months in jail for supplying Juventus players with performance-enhancing drugs, including the banned blood-boosting hormone erythropoietin (EPO), between 1994 and 1998. Agricola was also barred from practising medicine for 22 months and fined €2,000 (£1,390) (…) Eugenio Muller, a pharmacologist, reported that the club had systematically supplied its players with prescription-only drugs, with no therapeutic justification but with the aim of boosting energy levels or speeding recovery after injury.

(…)

The high profile of the club guaranteed media interest in the trial from the outset and that interest sharpened considerably when stars like Zidane and Del Piero gave evidence last year. But there was a fair degree of cynicism about whether the trial would achieve anything. Many view the legal system as one of interminable trials and appeals which fizzle out after years and where no one pays, especially not the big guys. So the sentencing of an official at Italy's biggest club – even though the sentence, for a first offence, will be suspended – shocked the Italian football world in a way that none of its previous scandals had done. Giacomo Aiello, the former head of the anti-doping team at the IOC, described the verdict as "historic".

In 2007 the Supreme Court declared doc. Agricola and Giraudo guilty of doping and sportive fraud but the statute of limitations, Berlusconi's court cases killer we have seen at work throughout his *ventennio*, extinguished the penalty.

Luciano Moggi was for the Agnelli family what Marcello Dell'Utri has been for Berlusconi in politics. The difference is that Dell'Utri, in these very days definitively sentenced to seven years in prison for mafia collusion, was the middle-man between il Cavaliere and the mafia while Moggi himself was the boss of the cupola he built up to fix matches, according to the judges. After years of rumours and lack of transparency, it all became clear in 2006 when the publication of several wiretappings showed that Moggi manipulated referees, referee organizations, team managers and players, a network of relationships whose ultimate goal was to make Juve win matches. He determined, in pure mafia style, the careers of referees and players as well, since his son Alessandro had the most powerful agency of football agents and managers called *GEA World*. He also influenced the results of other teams, which had to become affiliate to have his protection, as in the 2005-06 Serie A championship Fiorentina and Lazio did to remain in serie A. Moggi assumingly fixed some matches in their favour, the sacrificial lamb was Bologna FC, which went down to *Serie B* in their places. Even politicians contacted him when they needed a favour for their hometown team. After the 2006 season, he announced that he would resign from his position and would retire from the world of football altogether, but only after having sung the old Berlusconian tune of a forces-of-evil's plot against him. Moggi was sentenced to perpetual ban for any position inside the FGCI (Italian Football Association) in 2011. As far as criminal justice is concerned, the *Calciopoli* trial is still under way: in 2013 Moggi was sentenced to two years and four months in prison by the Appeal

Court. If he is condemned in the final leg of the trial, the 2006 pardon will see to his not stepping past the threshold of the prison [The Court of Cassation cancelled the penalty in March 2015 – the criminal act had already been affected by the statute of limitations – but the court motivations reaffirm the existence of the sportive and criminal fraud pictured previously]. As for the *GEA World* trial, once again the statute of limitations set him free. As far as Juventus is concerned, they were stripped of 2005 and 2006 *Serie A* titles, were out of 2006–07 UEFA Champions League, had three home games behind closed doors and were relegated to *Serie B* with a nine points deduction. The overall idea is the same once again: no penalties outside the pitch for the big guys. *Non paga nessuno* is the expression we use for the never ending line of VIPs who get away from justice unpunished.

The physical presence of organized crime in football and the feeling that no one pays were made explicit by the latest episodes of *Calcioscommesse* which have emerged since 2011. *Calcioscommesse*, match fixing linked to illegal betting, is a regular host to Italian football since the eighties when, for example, the would-be World Champion and Nazionale striker Paolo Rossi was banned for some time. These latest episodes were accidentally discovered by the Naples magistrates investigating the camorra. They discovered that the *camorristi*, linked to international criminal organizations, both in Eastern Europe and in the Far East, offered selected players huge amounts of money to fix the matches they had to play, so earning enormous sum of money from illegal betting, both 'live' and on line. From Serie A to minor leagues, players have regularly been arrested but, in the end, the feeling that they are not properly punished is very widespread. Some are banned for a certain period, some teams are fined and have points deduction but, after the three legs of the trial, the initial penalty goes down to almost nothing and the criminal justice is too slow to take trials to conclusion in a reasonable time. One example is Lazio captain Stefano Mauri, a midfielder who began his career in my hometown team: he was jailed, sportive justice asked for a six year ban but today, after six months, he is back on the pitch, still captain of the team and still protected by the club which has never let him down.

When the final whistle that put an end to Siena-Modena at last arrived I felt relieved, got up and started walking towards the bus stop. I just wanted to go home and relax before starting my way to the Stadio Olimpico, a modern odyssey I was forced to face since I had to meet a group of teenage players, among whom was my son, I was in care of inside the stadium. As the bus left, the open air museum which makes up the city of Rome started passing me by but its beauty suddenly merged with a feeling of anxiety: I knew that another glimpse of Inferno was probably waiting for me behind the corner. At 7 p.m. I was at the Stazione Termini with my adult mates, waiting to start the journey to the Stadio Olimpico, the only one in the world, I guess, which is not serviced by an underground or an overground train. You can only get there by car or bus and everybody knows that the city comes to a complete stop every Sunday before and after Serie A matches. We got out of the underground close to Vatican City; as we were walking in the opposite direction to get the bus that should have taken us straight to the stadium, I turned around hoping Papa Francesco was saying a prayer for us. The bus was not that crowded: next to me lower middle-class families of Napoli supporters were talking in a loud voice with their strong local accent, gesticulating and quarrelling among themselves, a *commedia all'italiana* sketch we have seen so many times on film that, on the occasion, provided a pleasant entertainment during our trip. But a few minutes later the police stopped the bus and diverted it. A bit further down the road, by the river, traffic was in complete chaos: along the Tiber a row of cars, almost stuck to a halt, were roaring, the drivers blowing their horns, trying to pass one another on the right and on the left, screaming at an imaginary interlocutor or addressing an invented crowd or talking on their mobiles. The real journey to the Olimpico had begun. It took us an hour to get to the stadium bus stop and in that time span the comedy inside the vehicle slowly degenerated into a row: a Roman citizen was screaming on the phone with his lawyer; when I told him we were not very interested in the conversation, he started to shout louder telling the exhausted passengers that the Neapolitans were yelling more noisily than himself. The quarrel began with a crossfire of parolacce that lasted until we finally got out, the comedy about to turn into tragedy, a miniature of what was happening out in the streets North of the stadium. I descended the bus with the vision of a lady, who lived nearby and that was trying hard to get back home, repeating *se la giocassero a casa loro 'sta maledetta partita (why don't they play this goddamned match in their hometown?)* over and over again.

Across the river stood the Stadio Olimpico, as white as the marble statues that surround it, framed by the dark green hills of the luxury residential area of Monte Mario at sunset. We could see our entrance just across the footbridge, a short walk away. We showed the street fight attired police our tickets, but there was no way to get in: the bridge was closed so we had to walk all the way down to the next bridge to the South, cross the river and walk back to the stadium, a twenty minute stroll as warm-up before the match. Our seats were in the *tribuna* Tevere which had been assigned to the Naples supporters. The *tifosi* from Florence had been given the opposite *tribuna* Monte Mario and they had to walk like we did but in the opposite direction, crossing over at the next bridge to the North to avoid physical contact. The two similar routes were patrolled by policemen dressed in black that looked like the dark brothers of the statues around the stadium. The risk that a group of people wearing azure jerseys met a group in violet was too high, it would have meant urban guerrilla and ordinary hooligans' foolishness. I wondered about the amount of public money we spend just because two factions of supporters cannot meet without giving birth to a violent feud and I remembered me and my son sitting among Real Madrid and Valencia supporters in a *curva* at the Mestalla stadium watching the *Copa del Rey* final some years ago. It was a normal fact even for the hot blooded Spaniards, but for me it was quite a shocking but revealing experience.

When we finally entered the stadium it was kick-off time but no players were to be seen on the pitch. An unreal silence was hanging over the sold out Olimpico like a heavy cloak. Policemen and stewards were all around the running track. Nothing was happening, like in a still picture, but in the air there was the feeling that something unpleasant was about to occur anytime. It went on like this for some minutes. The opposite *curve* were full of silent people in violet and azure. Some kids around me started to cry and soon they left with their parents. As I said, I had to meet a group of young kids, among whom was my son, but they were nowhere to be seen. Not a word came from the speakers until a squadron of policemen moved from the changing rooms to the Naples *curva* escorting the team captain Hamsik who, we would later realize, was going to talk to

Gennaro la carogna (Gerry the swine), the nice guy wearing the *Speziale Libero* black T-shirt whose picture would be on every front page of the international press the morning after. The ultras boss silenced his *curva* with a sign and jumped over the barrier to talk to the player. It was in that moment that I understood, like in an epiphany, who was deciding what would happen next. Hamsik, we were later informed, gave 'the swine' the latest news on the wounded comrades of his, the hooligans who had spent the time before the match fighting against the police and Daniel De Santis, a famed ultra-violent fascist Roma ultra. Once updated, 'the swine' decided that the match would be played, communicated his decision to the captain that, in turn, reported it to the police officials that brought the news to the authorities in charge. Before our arrival at the stadium, the ultras had decided that the game did not have to be played because there had been rumours that a Neapolitan *tifoso* had been killed, and their decision had been met. To remind the State representatives who led the game, a hail of flares and firecrackers were launched from the *curva* to the policemen and the stewards, to ensure that they kept their distance. Some policemen were wounded and terror ran all over the stadium, sped up by the explosions and the smoke. As usual, I wondered how on earth these weapons can enter stadia all over Italy when normal citizens are searched at the entrance. The answer is not difficult: it can only be done with the clubs' consent. Half an hour later the players entered the pitch, boos from the Naples *curva* were addressed to the national anthem sung live, then the match began. The Naples ultras were like stiff soldiers waiting for orders either to allow the match to be played or to invade the playing field, attack the spectators, exit the stadium and sack the streets of Rome like the Visigoths did when they conquered the Urbe. Luckily, the match was a forceful sedative and slowly menace gave way to attention to what was happening on the pitch, the ultras trying hard, often in vain, to be silent in protest as the match unfolded before their eyes.

Who is Gerry la Carogna and why was he wearing that T-shirt? What had happened before the match that would start the fire of violence and menace inside the stadium? How can the street fight hooligans and the *curva* ultras behave like this without any fear of punishment? On May 5, in the article *Juve's scudetto hat-trick overshadowed by Coppa Italia final violence*, The Guardian reports events as follow:

Perched atop the barrier at the front of the Napoli enclosure was a man with short dark hair and a wealth of tattoos. Gennaro De Tommaso – nicknamed Genny (Genny the swine) – has been known to authorities for some time as a leading figure among Napoli's ultras. Multiple Italian newspapers identified him as the son of Ciro De Tommaso, a man with alleged connections to the Camorra crime syndicate. On Sunday Gennaro De Tommaso wore a black shirt with the slogan "Free Speziale" on the front. The presumed reference was to Antonio Speziale, a Catania ultra who was jailed for eight years in 2007 for killing the policeman Filippo Raciti in the wake of a Sicilian derby.

Roberto Saviano's tweet the day after the match is the best comment on the situation: *Do we notice only now that inside the Neapolitan organized supporters (and not only) the camorra and criminality are in command?* Saviano's statement is also an indirect answer to Rome's police chief Massimo Mazza's declaration the following day. "There was no negotiation with the Napoli ultras. Nobody ever thought of not playing the match – not the football federation, not the forces of order, not the clubs. Napoli only asked us if we had no objections to the captain explaining to the fans what the situation was, also because there were some reports going around that a fan was dead". The affirmation did not fool anyone: *the damage was already done. Rightly or wrongly, the lasting image of Saturday's game was that of an angry ultra – one who has already served one five-year stadium ban for previous misdemeanours – putting his demands to a team captain,* The Guardian article comments. Even the politicians' declarations, the day after, mentioned stronger penalties on occasions like these that, in the 'no-one-pays' country, nobody can believe:

On Sunday both the Italian Football Federation president, Giancarlo Abete, and the minister for the interior, Angelo Alfano, spoke about the need to clamp down even harder on bad behaviour, each raising the prospect of lifetime stadium bans. Given that Saturday's shooting took place out in the street, it might be time to acknowledge that a broader view is required.

Going back to Saturday afternoon before the match, while we were deep into our odyssey to get to the stadium, in the North part of town the ordinary scenes of foolishness we have got used to were taking place, urban hooligans' guerrilla the British have long got rid of but that keeps haunting us, like a natural element existing by dogma. Here again is *The Guardian* report:

> *There were roughly two and a half hours left until kick-off in Saturday's Coppa Italia final when shots rang out on the Viale di Tor di Quinto, a major thoroughfare that sweeps by the Tiber in the north of Rome. Small groups of Napoli supporters had been gathering there as they prepared to walk down to the Stadio Olimpico for the match against Fiorentina.*
>
> *The circumstances around the shooting were, initially, unclear. What was known was that three men [Napoli ultras] had been wounded and one of those was fighting for his life. Ciro Esposito, a 27-year-old from Scampia, a northern suburb of Naples, had been struck in the chest by a bullet that passed through his lung and lodged in his spinal column.*
>
> *An ambulance eventually took him to the Villa San Pietro hospital, (…) then moved to the nearby Policlinico Gemelli for surgery. On Sunday the press was informed that an initial operation had gone smoothly but that his condition remained critical.*
>
> *(…)*
>
> *Up until that point, accurate information had been hard to come by. As time ticked down towards kick-off on Saturday evening, a rumour went around that Esposito had died. Napoli supporters at the Stadio Olimpico started pulling down their banners and demanding that the match be abandoned.*
>
> *(…)*
>
> *Police believe they have identified the shooter. Daniele De Santis, a known Roma ultra (he was among the group who scaled the barriers to speak to Totti at the abandoned Rome derby in 2004) was arrested on Sunday on an attempted murder charge. At a press conference on Sunday, a police statement was read out alleging that he had acted alone; initially throwing fireworks at passing Napoli fans on the Viale di Tor di Quinto, then turning his gun on them after they chased him down in response. The incident was portrayed as a one-off, unrelated to organised hooliganism or the skirmishes that took place between rival*

supporters closer to the stadium. Not everyone, though, will find those strands so easy to separate out. At its very simplest, this was still just another story about violence between football fans.

On Sunday, May 4, Repubblica gives the shocking details of the sheer reasonless violence:

> Twenty of them [Napoli Ultras], perhaps after coming into contact with some policemen, bumped into a nearby kiosk run by a well-known Roma ultras, Daniele De Santis (...) De Santis, visibly upset, was seen hastening towards some groups of Napoli ultras: "We saw this huge guy, very fat and bald, – witnesses say – he was drunk, he staggered but screamed like a madman 'I'll kill you all, I'll kill you all.' The strange thing is that he was alone, heading against a group of Napoli fans." With him he had a small arsenal of paper bombs and smoke bombs (...) On the ground, not far from where six shells would be found, three men were rescued, one wounded in a hand, one in an arm, the other dying. The witnesses continue: "After a while we saw De Santis running back. He kept cursing against the Neapolitans, and they chased him, screaming, they must have been twenty. They reached him, caught him and beat him. They left when they saw he was on the ground and did not move anymore." At that point, from a building nearby, a film production company, the Ciak, a man came out and tried to help the wounded, bringing him inside. "After a few minutes, however, we heard some noise." Other Napoli fans were coming back to do justice, this time in a group of fifty: their anger had developed enormously because of the first tragic news of Esposito's bad health conditions. They broke open the gates and entered. "They tried to kill him in every way, they kicked him, punched him, beat him. They twisted his ankles and broke his legs. Then one picked up a yellow heavy trolley ... and hit him in the head." When De Santis again gave no signs of life, the group abandoned the Ciak, but not before admonishing the owner, the man who had provided first aid: "If my brother dies – said one of the attackers, with an evident Neapolitan accent – I'll come back here and kill you too."

Like the other two wounded supporters, Ciro Esposito was under arrest. He is from Scampia, Naples' the Bronx, a poor degraded borough which is the camorra headquarters, one of those areas in which the State is either felt as absent or as a Bourbon foreign oppressor. I met a group of students from Scampia in Edinburgh last April, when I heard the 'overwhelming question' which gave birth to writing of this book for the last time. They were attending a school of English in a kind of 'social care' programme. On their first day they had to be in the classroom at nine a.m.; at 10 only three out of twenty were there, two teenage girls and a boy weirdly dressed and bizarre looking. The headmaster asked me if we came from the same country and the two courageous teachers in charge of the group told me, as soon as we met, that they had to go to jail to make most of the student's fathers sign the permits to take them abroad. Scampia is a pitiless picture of social disease and consequently the hooligans' attitude is plain to understand. Nevertheless, generally speaking, the fact that incidents like the one we are talking about keep happening at a regular pace is also due to what we have already said: *in Italy there are no penalties other than on the football pitch. Crime is never followed by punishment because, at least for the powers-that-be, there's guaranteed impunity.* Jones's statement was true when the book was written and is more than true now, ten years later, as Berlusconi's *ventennio* and, hopefully, this book have shown.

> *All of which made me think that the real problem wasn't about penalties, about whether the referees lean slightly towards the Old Lady of Italian football or the Prime Minister's team when they blow their whistles and point to the spot. The debate is really about another type of penalty, or the lack of it. It's the fact that, as Italy's moral minority always complains, non paga nessuno, which basically means that no one in Italy is ever, ever punished for anything: 'nobody pays'. Ever since I had arrived I had heard one half of the country, that law-abiding half, complain bitterly and incessantly about the furbi who appear to bend and break the law at will, without ever facing the consequences. In Italy there are no penalties other than on the football pitch. Crime is never followed by punishment because, at least for the powers-that-be, there's guaranteed impunity. You can get away with anything. As long as you play the game, you'll be played onside. Take Nandrolone, field*

illegal players, fiddle the accounts, put up fascist banners [I add, as an update, have a cupola to buy referees, dope players, fix matches for betting]: non paga nessuno

Against all odds, the match was enchanting: the rhythm was fast, the technicality superb, the initial Napoli's *doppietta* – brace – was balanced by Fiorentina's goal in the second part of the first half, guaranteeing a thrilling second half. During the break we had the feeling that the fog of distress which cloaked the stadium was slowly vanishing. The intense second half, in which Fiorentina attacked coming close on several occasions to an equaliser while Napoli acted fast in the traditional Italian *contropiede*, contributed to the lifting of the fog that became a light mist at the end of the match. Napoli scored another goal in the very final minutes and won 3-1 in the end. The result was a sign of good omen for public order. At the end of the game, the Neapolitan *tifosi* invaded the pitch to celebrate, breaking the last rule that was left to be broken, and in so doing giving time to the Fiorentina supporters to leave the stadium unharmed. I left some minutes before the match after seeing that the kids I was in charge of were in safe hands. I wanted to avoid the chaos, the possible riots outside the stadium and another night odyssey to get back home. I left with friends who had parked their car some blocks further North along the river, in the newly restored entertainment area of via Flaminia. The clouds had disappeared and a bright moon was shining over Monte Mario as we walked along the river, in the opposite direction of the crowd. The long walk helped us to leave tension behind. Via Flaminia was filled with night life: outdoor and indoor restaurants, bars and pubs were full of a vibrant Saturday night fever, a thousand miles away from the events at the Stadio Olimpico. We sat at a pizzeria and ordered a true Neapolitan pizza *margherita* and a pint of beer, the best prescription for further relaxation. One hour later, in the wee wee hours, the bright lights of the city shone through the car window as we were riding towards the Stazione Tiburtina on the Salaria highway on my way back home. The stadium lights had been turned off and the Olimpico had disappeared into an obscurity that seemed to have wiped away the foolish events of the evening.

More than an hour has gone by since I left the Capital. As the train keeps rolling, the quiet green hills of the Tuscan *chiantishire* announce our imminent arrival in Florence, the Renaissance quintessential city, a cradle of urban beauty and good manners which bred the Fiorentina supporters who behaved so well last night.

Yesterday's tragic events reinforce the idea that football is the mirror of our society. The negotiation between Gerry the swine and the authorities is a small scale 'trattativa Stato-mafia', the by now established 1992-94 negotiation between legal and criminal powers that ended up with the mafia-Berlusconi alleged deal that, if true, helped il Cavaliere to win his first political elections (we have extensively dealt with the matter in the previous pages, see chapter 2, part 2, *Deal with the devil?*). These negotiations spring from the idea that the mafia, the camorra and the like exist as an ineluctable fact, like acknowledged institutions, a shocking attitude we have accepted as normal. The State authorities that today say that *there was no negotiation with the Napoli ultras* behave like the top officials, the former cabinet ministers and the politicians who were the assumed protagonists of the trattativa but never admitted it. At present some of them sit at the defendants' bar next to the mafiosi bosses in the Palermo trial. Today *the Italian Football Federation president, Giancarlo Abete, and the minister for the interior, Angelo Alfano, spoke about the need to clamp down even harder on bad behaviour, each raising the prospect of lifetime stadium bans*. It sounds pretty much like the promises the politicians have made since the Prima Repubblica, when Prime Minister Giulio Andreotti used to announce its governments' engagement in fighting the mafia while he was secretly meeting and kissing its boss Salvatore Riina.

I turn towards the window and see the hills of Tuscany now giving way to the Apennines, its highest peaks already capped in white and shining in the afternoon sun. The train goes in and out long tunnels and in no time gets to Bologna, my hometown's cousin city, and I feel home. Bologna FC has just descended to Serie B but no attacks against the players and the club, 'routine' reactions under these circumstances, have been made, no violent reaction has emerged. A few minutes' train ride takes me back to Modena, and I feel ready for a normal working week and a normal weekend. Next Saturday afternoon my son and I will cycle to the Stadio Braglia to encourage the *canarini* (the *canaries*, as Modena FC players are nicknamed because of the yellow jersey) in their climb to Serie A amid the other ten thousand spectators, quietly sitting in the terraces and supporting their team. Afterwards I will enjoy a 'white night' stroll through the open museums and the many outdoor events, enjoying the warm night air. It is hard to believe, but areas of civility, at least in some sectors of public life, can still be found in post Berlusconi Italy.

The disastrous performance of the Italian team at the 2014 World Cup in Brazil, the same as in South Africa 2010, is a picture of the decadence of our contemporary football. The last *fantasista* left in the squad, Andrea Pirlo, announced he had played his last games with the *Azzurri* on the occasion (even if he he would decide to play again for the national team some months later). Now it is Mario Balotelli who sets the standards of the players of today. He is an overvalued mediocre striker and a spoilt character, lunatic, egotistical and detached by the team, untouchable because whoever criticizes him is accused of racism.

During the World Cup, Ciro Esposito died in hospital on June 25, 2014. His funeral took place in his native borough of Scampia, in the same degraded setting which is used in the Sky TV series *Gomorra*. Alas, this was not fiction, and the rhetoric comments which followed his departure were as unbearable as his death. Ciro's mother then became the endorser of non-violent football and came to Modena to award the *Canarini* as the Italian team with the most correct supporters in August 2014, before the Modena-Chievo match for the *Coppa Ghirlandina*. On that occasion the barrier and the net which separated the spectators from the pitch were removed, British football style, a fact that could never be imagined in most of Italian stadia. The 2013–14 Fair Play Cup was given to Modena F.C. before the opening match of the 2014–15 championship on September 1.

To solve the problems of Italian football, in August 2014 Carlo Tavecchio, 71, was elected president of the Italian Football Federation notwithstanding the international outrage he caused with his racist comment about African players: "Here [in Italy] let's say there's [fictional player] Opti Poba, who has come here, who previously was eating bananas and now is a first-team player for Lazio. In England he has to show his CV and his pedigree." UEFA opened a disciplinary investigation because of these comments and soon after Tavecchio was banned for six months. Tavecchio is to sport what Berlusconi – or better, Berlusconism – is to politics, and that's the main reason why he was elected. As Furio Colombo writes in *Il Fatto Quotidiano* on August 9, 2014, *Tavecchio was like that already, when he made his evidently irresistible career in amateur soccer. So we have to assume he was all right that way, or, better still, he was liked that way ... Look at Tavecchio, listen to Tavecchio and you'll wonder whether we – many of us – are in the wrong country. How is it possible to prefer, for any task, a man with such a high degree of vulgarity and, moreover, a man who is to used to show (with success, evidently) that vulgarity in public?*

The first act of his presidency was the appointment of Antonio Conte, former Juventus player in the years of the scandals and the last coach of the Old Lady, as manager of the fallen *Azzurri*, becoming the first coach of a National Team with a sentence of sportive corruption and consequent banning in his pedigree. Italian style is always recognizable! Conte was found guilty of failure to report attempted match fixing when he was the manager of Siena in 2010-11, was banned from football for ten months, then reduced to four on appeal, by the Sportive Federal Court of Sportive Justice (in July 2015 Conte would be indicted for *frode sportiva* - sports fraud - by the State Magistracy). Conte reacted Berlusconi's way, accusing the sports judges of not being impartial and considering himself the victim of injustice, and all the attached Berlusconian cliché (Conte and Juventus were accused and sent to sportive trial because of these remarks and both of them took a plea bargain of 25,000 euros each to put an end to the court case). I remember Conte sitting in the grandstand surrounded by policemen during the Champion's League match Chelsea – Juventus in the period of his ban, looking like an unwelcome guest. Last but not least, Conte is the first trainer to receive a double salary, one paid by the Federation (about 1.6m euros a year) and the other by the sponsoring multinational Puma (almost 2m euros a year), which funds many players as well. It is another example of the intrusion of multinational business in public affairs: who will decide the *Azzurri*'s next line-up, Conte or Puma?

[In 2015 new match fixing scandals emerged in the minor football series and another tax evasion case hit also various serie A teams and top managers. But, as far as football corruption is concerned, Italy seems to be an average country, if we consider what happened inside FIFA with the arrest of its top officials and the launch of World Cups inquiry in May, an investigation that put an abrupt end to the obscure Blatter age and caused the fall of M. Platini as well. All the world is – really - a (football) stage!]

Chapter four

Conclusion: what can be done?

So, what can be done?

Actually, this is the overwhelming question I ask myself now, the same one Huxley asked himself back 1958. The answer, alas, seems to be same. In the final part of his essay, the novelist wrote:

> *In the United States and America ... an actual majority of young people in their teens, the voters of tomorrow, have no faith in democratic institutions, see no objection to the censorship of unpopular ideas, do not believe that government of the people by the people is possible and would be perfectly content, if they can continue to live in the style to which the boom has accustomed them, to be ruled, from above, by an oligarchy of assorted experts. That so many of the well-fed young television-watchers in the world's most powerful democracy should be so completely indifferent to the idea of self-government, so blankly uninterested in freedom of thought and the right to dissent, is distressing, but not too surprising. (....) If the bread is supplied regularly and copiously three times a day, many of them will be perfectly content to live by bread alone -- or at least by bread and circuses alone. "In the end," says the Grand Inquisitor in Dostoevsky's parable, "in the end they will lay their freedom at our feet and say to us, 'make us your slaves, but feed us.'*
>
> *(...) for when things go badly, and the rations are reduced, the grounded dodos will clamor again for their wings -- only to renounce them, yet once more, when times grow better and the dodo-farmers become more lenient and generous. The young people who now think so poorly of democracy may grow up to become fighters for freedom. The cry of "Give me television and hamburgers, but don't bother me with the responsibilities of liberty," may give place, under altered circumstances, to the cry of "Give me liberty or give me death." (...) The older dictators fell because they could never supply their subjects with enough bread, enough circuses, enough miracles and mysteries. Nor did they possess a really effective system of*

mind-manipulation (...) Under a scientific dictator education will really work -- with the result that most men and women will grow up to love their servitude and will never dream of revolution. There seems to be no good reason why a thoroughly scientific dictatorship should ever be overthrown.

Back then, for the young generation, burgers and television were already a State drug like *soma*, but in the following decades there was some light of hope. Soon the 60s came and brought along Martin Luther King and the Civil Rights Movement, Malcolm X and the Black Panthers, a juvenile rebelliousness inherited by the Beat Generation that gave birth to the Folk Revival, the Hippies and the Woodstock generation: *the young people who thought so poorly of democracy grew up to become fighters for freedom.* In Europe the 1968 'French May' sparkled the fire of the '68' rebellion that swept throughout Italy in the following years. I remember watching it from my 'middle school' classroom window looking down in the street below where the demonstrations used to go on. Then in 70s came the 'lead years' of terrorism followed by the yuppie 80s of hyper-conservative 'Iron Lady' M. Thatcher and of R. Regan, a Hollywood-B-movie-star president that established Huxley's model of a media-friendly candidate in the hands of Big Business. The *fighters for freedom* seemed to have vanished for good but at the turn of the millennium they reappeared in the shape of the *Anti-Global Movement,* spreading from Seattle to the whole world, the first disobedience movement to go global thanks to the new communication technologies. The movement spread to the end of the first decade, the period of the Al Qaeda terror and of G.W. Bush's pre-emptive wars which brought erosion of liberties inside the Western democracies, moving them in the direction of illiberal societies. The most dramatic event of the period took place in Genova in July 2001 during the anti-global demonstrations at the G8 summit. In those few days the B. government literally suspended our *Stato di Diritto* – Constitutional State – and all of a sudden we found ourselves deep into Fascism and *Stato di Polizia* – Police State. Peaceful protesters from all over the world were wildly beaten and wounded for no reason by the police under the direction of the Home Secretary G. Fini, leader of the extreme right party *Alleanza Nazionale*. The first decade was also the period of the huge anti-war movements that flooded the street of

American and European capitals and, recently, a new light of hope has been represented by the various 'occupy' and 'indignados' movements. Nevertheless today we are again in the situation described by Huxley, as I have pointed out throughout my essay: *young people in their teens, the voters of tomorrow ... would be perfectly content, if they can continue to live in the style to which the boom has accustomed them, to be ruled, from above, by an oligarchy of assorted experts.* TV and food are still part of the *soma* process: *Mediaset* television is much more efficient in brainwashing than Huxley could have imagined; people are not well-fed, they are overfed by the junk-food (real and metaphorical) that we, the cradle of the Mediterranean healthy cuisine, paradoxically import from the US. Besides, today's teenagers have a more dangerous enemy to deal with: the internet, smart phones, virtual reality machines in general. Notwithstanding the potential instances of democracy the net might bring, like and more than TV, the constant misuse of social networks and of the connecting tools at large, has created a generation of addicts who spend all their time adoring their mobiles and living in a never ending virtual reality that distances them from the real world and its social issues while injecting massive doses of consumerism's blank ethics. The following is a little example from yesterday's headlines, a shocking case which involve teenagers which is a mix of Italian shortcuts, loss of values, fascinations for blank consumerism and imitation of *bunga-bunga*. It's B.'s way that, as we say, *fa scuola – is pervasive*:

> *Two 14 and 15 year old girls sold their bodies to be able to have 'cose griffate' – branded objects – and cocaine: it is another part of the truth on underage prostitution discovered in Rome.*

> *Authorities reported of complete sexual intercourses with men well aware the young prostitutes were underage. They got 200-300 euros, depending on the client's requests, and had more than one encounters in a 24 hour period. "We are pretending girls. We want cars, clothes, 'cose griffate'". Prostitution was the right way to get much money easily. The mother of one of the girls denounced the fact to the police in the end while the other mother is in jail. The magistrates accuse her to induce her daughter to prostitution* (extracts from *Roma, due baby-prostitute ..., Il Giornale*, Nov. 7, 2013).

In this age of *pensiero unico* – single, one-direction thought –, of one unique social model, as our 'inciucio' governments witness, hope is almost gone. The 2010 'Arab Spring' was the last example of social consciousness and upheaval, the realization of Huxley's predictions which was made possible by the internet (this is an example of its dual possibilities): *bread was no more supplied regularly and copiously three times a day so the grounded dodos clamored again for their wings and became fighters for freedom. The cry of "Give me television and hamburgers, but don't bother me with the responsibilities of liberty," gave place to the cry of "Give me liberty or give me death." The older [Arab] dictators fell because they could never supply their subjects with enough bread, enough circuses, enough miracles and mysteries.* Unluckily, the Arab Spring has almost come to a failure: the last example is the 2013 Egyptian military golpe that looks like restoration very much. In the rich West nothing of the kind is taking place, *well-fed* young internet-addict *television-watchers* are sleeping the big sleep and the angry crowd throwing coins at Bettino Craxi in the times of Mani Pulite is history.

How strong today's *soma* must be to let us continue to accept the 'Rome buffoon' (as the *Financial Times* called B.) and its underlying iceberg of rotten politics and corrupt society! We all remember B. shamelessly stooping in front of Colonel Gheddafi and kissing his hands several times while proclaiming his friendship, only to bomb Libya a few days later when the international political wind changed direction. The distrust has only produced a 'populist' movement like *Movimento 5 Stelle* lead by comedian Beppe Grillo, whose dictatorial leadership makes him similar to B., his hated enemy, in a certain way. As we know, the movement has reached an astonishing one third of the electorate and may look similar to Marine Le Pen's *Front National* or the Greek party *Golden Dawn* in its demagogical approach, if not in the fascist ideology: it is a Berlusconian way to take advantage of the low-cultured people's basic gut instincts. To tell the truth, since its existence *M5S* has also carried on social instances which have always been close to the left wing political area, due in part to the fact that the *Progressisti* – the centre-left – are sleeping the Big Sleep too, deranged into the Democratic Party's ectoplasm or fractioned in a pointless series of minor parties. For some political analysts, *M5S*'s alliance with the British *UKIP* party after the 2014 EU elections has revealed a lot about the nature of the movement.

The following quotation is from Edward Snowden's *Guardian* interview on June 9, 2013 in Hong Kong. The young NSA technician seems to have learnt his lesson well from his work experience and Huxley's predictions, that Snowden probably does not know, are his prophecies:

> *The greatest fear that I have regarding the outcome for America of these disclosures is that nothing will change. People will see in the media all of these disclosures. They'll know the lengths that the government is going to grant themselves powers unilaterally to create greater control over American society and global society. But they won't be willing to take the risks necessary to stand up and fight to change things to force their representatives to actually take a stand in their interests. And the months ahead, the years ahead it's only going to get worse ... a new leader will be elected, they'll find the switch, say that 'because of the crisis, because of the dangers we face in the world, some new and unpredicted threat, we need more authority, we need more power.' And there will be nothing the people can do at that point to oppose it. And it will be turnkey tyranny.*

The final words belong to Huxley by right:

> *The victim of mind-manipulation does not know that he is a victim. To him, the walls of his prison are invisible, and he believes himself to be free. That he is not free is apparent only to other people. His servitude is strictly objective. ... a psychological captive, compelled to think, feel and act as the representatives of the national State, or of some private interest within the nation, want him to think, feel and act ... Paradoxically, the right to vote ... is a great privilege. In practice, as recent history has repeatedly shown, the right to vote, by itself, is no guarantee of liberty ... there should be legislation to prevent political candidates not merely from spending more than a certain amount of money on their election campaigns, but also to prevent them from resorting to the kind of anti-rational propaganda that makes nonsense of the whole democratic process.*

We, the self-appointed 'moral minority', the honest who care for the community, sense that living in this Italy, that we nickname *il bel paese (the beautiful country)*, is a nightmare; we feel we're stuck and mangled in Lucifer's mouth like Cassius, Brutus and Judas Iscariot and it won't be easy to get out *a riveder le stelle (to behold the stars again)*. The paradoxical contrast between surface and interior, came to my mind once again in an early January morning watching the shining Dolomite mountain village of San Vigilio, where I was spending the Christmas holidays, from the top of a nearby mountain. From the terrace of a mountain *rifugio* – wooden cabin – I could see the steep alpine ski slopes running down to the valley. Down there the little village was gleaming in the brilliant wintry sunshine at the bottom of the canyon-shaped valley. The resort is surrounded by an evergreen pine forest that was all dressed in white for the snowfall of the previous days; above it the Monument-Valley-like rocky Dolomite tops frame the vale to meet the bright azure sky which seemed to provide a natural ceiling to the picture. On the other side of the valley a winding road ascends to a mountain pass. Next to it, cross-country ski trails cross the forest and lead to the frozen lake near the pass. In the horizon the Marmolada glacier seemed to mingle with the sky. Again, *a poet could but be gay in such jocund company!* But then again, dear English-speaking reader, take a tip from one who has tried: next time you'll visit Italy be sure to enjoy its excellent surface, its natural beauty, its climate, its monuments, its art, its creativity, its fashion, its cuisine, the natural friendship of the people – that anyway will pinch you as soon as they can. But, please, don't dig this surface, the radioactive waste illegally buried by the mafia in the field of Campania, where tomatoes grow and mozzarella is produced, might come to the surface and poison your Grand Tour: Italy is an illusion, a girlfriend in a coma, a beautiful dream from which you, while you still can, don't have to wake up before going back home to old cold civil United Kingdom or to young mannerless America or to some other distant shores.

From the age of uniformity, from the age of solitude, from the age of Big Brother, from the age of doublethink – greetings, once again.

Italy – country profile

The following miscellanea of information is taken both from *Encyclopaedia Britannica* and *Wikipedia* (quotations are in italics) at the entry 'Italy'. Both sources give correct information but I have taken the liberty to edit Wiki's sometimes broken English and add some updating information.

State organization and government
Italy has been a unitary parliamentary republic since 2 June 1946, when the monarchy was abolished by a constitutional referendum. The President of Italy (Presidente della Repubblica), currently Giorgio Napolitano since 2006, is Italy's head of state. The President is elected for a single seven years mandate by the Parliament of Italy in joint session. Italy has a written democratic constitution, resulting from the work of a Constituent Assembly formed by the representatives of all the anti-fascist forces that contributed to the defeat of Nazi and Fascist forces during the Civil War. ... Parliament is perfectly bicameral: the two houses, the Chamber of Deputies (that meets in Palazzo Montecitorio) and the Senate of the Republic (that meets in Palazzo Madama), have the same powers. The Prime Minister, officially President of the Council of Ministers (Presidente del Consiglio dei Ministri), is Italy's head of government. The Prime Minister and the cabinet are appointed by the President of the Republic, but must pass a vote of confidence in Parliament to become in office.

Political Parties in Berlusconi's ventennio
From the end of World War II until the 1990s, Italy had a multiparty system with two dominant parties, the Christian Democratic Party (Partito della Democrazia Cristiana; DC) *and* the Italian Communist Party (Partito Comunista Italiano; PCI), *and a number of small yet influential parties. The smaller parties ranged from the neofascist* Italian Social Movement (Movimento Sociale Italiano; MSI) *on the right to the* Italian Socialist Party (Partito Socialista Italiano; PSI) *on the left; a number of small secular parties occupied the centre. The DC, in various alliances with smaller parties of the centre and left, was the dominant governing party, and the principal opposition parties were the PCI and the MSI. The postwar party system described above was radically altered by the fall of communism in the Soviet bloc in 1991, by a wave of judicial prosecutions of corrupt officials that involved most*

Italian political parties [named Clean Hands], and finally by the electoral reforms of the 1990s. The DC, driven by scandal, was replaced by a much smaller organization, the Italian Popular Party (Partito Popolare Italiano; PPI), *which played a diminished role after elections in 1994. By that time three new parties had arisen to dominate the political right and centre-right:* Forza Italia (FI; loosely translatable as "Go Italy"), *an alliance created in 1994 by the media tycoon Silvio Berlusconi and dedicated to the principles of the market economy;* The Northern League (Lega Nord; LN), *formed in 1991, a federalist and fiscal-reform movement with large support in the northern regions; and the* National Alliance (Alleanza Nazionale; AN), *which succeeded the MSI in 1994 but whose political platform renounced its fascist past. Meanwhile, the PCI remained an important electoral force under a new name, the* Democratic Party of the Left (Partito Democratico della Sinistra; PDS), *later shortened to the* Democrats of the Left (Democratici di Sinistra; DS). *Thus, the Italian political spectrum, which had previously been dominated by parties of the centre, became polarized between parties of the right and left. The political centre was left to be divided by various short-lived multiparty alliances — for example, at the turn of the 21st century, the centre-right* House of Freedoms *and the centre-left* Olive Tree. *In 2007 a new centre-left party, known simply as the* Democratic Party (Partito Democratico; PD), *emerged when the DS merged with the centrist* Daisy (Margherita) *party. Soon afterward the FI joined with the AN to create the new centre-right* People of Freedom (Popolo della Libertà; PdL) *party. AN leader Gianfranco Fini withdrew from the alliance in 2010 to form the rival centre-right* Future and Freedom for Italy (Futuro e libertà per l'Italia; FLI) *party.*

Today the political centre has merged in Mario Monti's party *Civic Choice (Scelta Civica)* created in 2012. The racist *Northern League* has almost disappeared trapped in corruption and trials, a typical Italian paradox since their birth in the 90s was based on the slogan *Roma Ladrona* (loosely *Rome Big Thief*), meaning that the party was born to fight against political corruption. The 2013 election saw the astonishing ascent of the *Five Star Movement (Movimento Cinque Stelle, M5S)* lead by former comedian Beppe Grillo.

M5S is a political party in Italy launched by Beppe Grillo and Gianroberto Casaleggio, a web strategist, in 2009. The M5S is considered populist, anti-corruption, environmentalist and Eurosceptic. ... This party also advocates direct democracy, E-democracy, free access to the Internet, the principles of "zero-cost politics", nonviolence and de-growth.... Party members stress that the M5S is not a party but a "movement" and it may not be included in the traditional left right paradigm.

In 2013 there was the birth of the *New Centre-Right (Nuovo Centrodestra, NCD)*. Its leader is Angelino Alfano, who had been Silvio Berlusconi's protégé and national secretary of *The People of Freedom (PdL)* from 2011 to 2013. The party was formed by splinters from the PdL on November 15, 2013. Its founders were strong supporters of Enrico Letta's government and refused to join the new *Forza Italia (FI)*, founded upon the dissolution of the PdL. All five PdL ministers, three under-secretaries, 30 senators and 27 deputies MPs immediately joined *NCD*. Most were former Christian Democrats and, consequently, many of them have had (and are having) ongoing trials or are being investigated for corruption and mafia links. In February 2014, after the fall of Letta's government, *NCD* joined a new coalition government led by Matteo Renzi, who had been elected secretary of the *Democratic Party (PD)* in December 2013. In the new government *NCD* retained three ministers.

Elections and governments in Berlusconi's ventennio

In 1992–1994, the political system was shaken by a series of corruption scandals known collectively as Tangentopoli *[or as* Clean Hands*]. These events led to the disappearance of the traditional governmental parties. Consequently the* Democratic Party of the Left *and the post-fascists* National Alliance *gained strength. Following the 1994 general election media tycoon Silvio Berlusconi became Prime Minister at the head of a coalition composed mainly of three parties: its brand new party called* Forza Italia *(joined by many members of the former mainstream parties), the* National Alliance *and the* Northern League *[The first Berlusconi government lasted only a few months].*

Between 1996 and 2008, Italian political parties were organized into two big coalitions, the centre-right Pole for Freedoms *(which was renamed* House of Freedoms *after the re-entry of the* Northern League *in 2000) and* The Olive Tree *(part of the new, broader coalition* The Union *in 2005) on the centre-left. The centre-left governed from 1996 to 2001 and again between 2006 and 2008, while the* House of Freedoms *was in power between 2001 and 2006.*

In 2008 The Union *government came to an end and the newly founded* Democratic Party *decided to break the alliance with the* Communist Re-foundation Party... *On the centre-right,* Forza Italia *and* National Alliance merged to form the People of Freedom, *which continued the alliance with the Northern League and secured a big majority in both Chambers at the 2008 general election.*

In November 2011 the Berlusconi government was forced to resign *(after his resignation, the booing and jeering continued as he left in his convoy, with the public shouting words such as "buffoon", "dictator" and "mafioso")* and president Napolitano imposed the first coalition government. Centre-right and centre-left coalitions gave their confidence to the so-called technocrats' government lead by prof. Mario Monti, rector of the Bocconi University in Milan. In December 2012 the centre-right coalition withdrew its confidence.

In the February 2013 general election, the political scenario was much more fragmented with four big groupings: the centre-left led by the Democratic Party, *the traditional centre-right alliance between* The People of Freedom *and* Lega Nord, *Beppe Grillo's* Five Star Movement *and the new centrist coalition, Mario Monti's* Civic Choice.

The first three groupings had approximately a bit less than 30% votes each while *Civic Choice* scored a dull 10%. Since the country was stuck in political quicksand, President Napolitano accepted to be reelected (an event which had never happened before) and he imposed the first political 'grand coalition' government lead by the DP Prime Minister Enrico Letta (April 2013). In November 2013 *The People of Freedom* split up in two parts. After his expulsion from the Senate, Berlusconi looked back, in anger, and formed the 'new' *Forza Italia* party withdrawing confidence to the government. His previous 'dolphin', Angelino Alfano, vice-PM and Home Secretary, created a new parliamentary group called *New Centre-Right* supporting the Letta Cabinet. On February 22, 2014 previous *il rottamatore/demolition man* Matteo Renzi, after winning the primaries of the *PD* in December 2013, replaced his own party's PM Letta and became the youngest Italian PM ever. It is a coalition government with the same majority as before based on the promise of an ambitious programme of 'revolutionary' moderate reforms that Berlusconi does not dislike.

The 2014 European elections handed Italy's Prime Minister, Matteo Renzi, a resounding victory as the centre-left leader's *Democratic party (PD)* won more than 40% of the vote and trounced the anti-establishment *Five Star Movement (M5S)*. Figures from the interior ministry put former comedian Beppe Grillo's *M5S* on 21.2% – a disappointing performance for a movement that had vowed to be

Italy's largest party at the European elections. The *Forza Italia (FI)* party of former Prime Minister Silvio Berlusconi, meanwhile, took just 16.8% – the lowest ever vote share for the tax fraud-convicted media magnate. His one-time heir apparent Angelino Alfano and his *New Centre Right (NCD)* only just managed, with 4.4%, to get over the threshold for representation in the European parliament. The right-wing, eurosceptic *Northern League* won 6.2%. The left wing party *L'Altra Europa con Tsipras (The Other Europe with Tsipras)*, born for the occasion, won 4% of the vote. The Italians were voting to elect 73 MEPs, the same number as Britain.

The Judiciary

As Berlusconi has had troubles with the law since the beginning of his public life, the Judiciary is one of the main 'characters' of my essay. The Italian system is divided into three separate independent parts: the Legislative branch, the Executive branch and the Judicial branch. Also the structure of the Italian Judiciary is divided into three tiers. Consequently, each criminal case may have up to three degrees of judgment and the first two proceedings are actually independent trials: the first trial is held by the *Court of First Instance* (lower court), the second by the *Appellate Courts* (appeal court) and the third and final trial by the *Court of Cassation*. Together with the notorious inefficiency of the Judicial branch, these three steps make trials last for many years before getting to a final definitive verdict and are often threatened by the statute of limitations (one of Berlusconi's main 'friends', besides his notorious laws *ad personam*).

published by: SelfPublishingVincente.it

Printed in Great Britain
by Amazon